The Best
of
From Our Own
Correspondent

4

BBC

The Best
of
From Our Own
Correspondent
4

Edited by
Geoff Spink

Foreword by
Brian Redhead

I.B. Tauris & Co Ltd
Publishers
London · New York

Published in 1993 by
I.B.Tauris & Co Ltd
45 Bloomsbury Square
London WC1A 2HY

175 Fifth Avenue
New York NY 10010

In the United States of America
and Canada distributed by
St Martin's Press
175 Fifth Avenue
New York
NY 10010

The text of this book is drawn from original
material broadcast by the BBC News and
Current Affairs and the BBC World Service
Directorates.

'BBC' and the BBC logotype are trade marks
of the British Broadcasting Corporation
and are used under licence.

A full CIP record for this book is available
from the British Library

A full CIP record for this book is available
from the Library of Congress

ISBN 1-85043-783-1

Typeset by The Midlands Book Typesetting Company,
Loughborough, Leics
Printed and bound in Great Britain
by WBC Ltd, Bridgend, Mid Glamorgan

CONTENTS

CONTENTS

CONTENTS

FOREWORD

JOURNALISM SHOULD BE seen, and heard, as the first attempt at writing history. It is the eye-witness's account of what happened, and why. Journalists are there as paid members of the public to tell the rest of us what we missed.

And there is no more satisfying job. None of us know what we really think about anything until we are compelled to put it in writing or to say it out loud, and that is what journalists do. If they are true to their calling, they record, they report and they explain.

Every day journalists who are accomplished at their craft learn something new—about politics, behaviour, crime, sport. Whatever people get up to, for good or ill, is the journalists' legitimate concern. They learn about power and its abuse, about preferment and its pretensions, about the idealism and about the fecklessness of the human race. They are literally in the middle of events, and the scope is enormous.

They can be specialists or generalists. They can travel the world or concentrate on one arena. They can question world statesmen or share the thoughts of the dispossessed. They can have their say, or simply report the sayings of others. And they need never have a dull day.

This volume is a testament to that truth. The five dozen BBC correspondents who have contributed to this anthology file daily reports for news bulletins, answer the immediate questions of programme presenters, and constantly pursue the events in their territory. And then, once or twice a week, when asked, they compose and proclaim their thoughts on recent events.

But these are not second thoughts, nor are they summaries. They are radio essays, as personal as letters to a close friend, vivid and illuminating. They recall incidents, recount events, explain issues and, above all, they engage our attention.

They make the world a more interesting place.

Brian Redhead

ACKNOWLEDGEMENTS

THE EDITOR WOULD like to express thanks to the following for their help in the preparation of this volume. Firstly, to Vanessa Whiteside, who spent innumerable hours helping to compile the manuscript. Also to Lucy Wade, the long-suffering Production Assistant on *From Our Own Correspondent*. Several other colleagues at the BBC also deserve a mention: Tracy O'Keefe, Eileen Phillips, Brian Walker, Chris Wyld, along with that great body of unsung heroes without whose professionalism and dedication no programme—let alone book—would ever appear. I refer, of course, to the traffic managers, studio managers, the staff of the News Information service and countless others. Also to Emma Sinclair-Webb at I.B.Tauris who took on a mammoth project at very short notice. Finally, to all the correspondents around the world who have contributed to this book and who regularly send in despatches for the programme—often at short notice, under extreme pressure and in dangerous situations—my undying gratitude.

WESTERN EUROPE

HOPES BETRAYED

WILLIAM HORSLEY   BONN   3 SEPTEMBER 1992

In Germany, violence in the east of the country—formerly the German Democratic Republic—once again raised questions over the country's political stability; gangs of extreme right-wing youths, shouting racist slogans, attacked a refugee centre in the Baltic port of Rostock in August 1992, and were urged on by crowds of local people. In spite of these images—redolent of darker times in Germany's past—there were grounds for optimism about the future of the region.

'IT USED TO be the Jews; now it's the weakest in the society and the foreigners. This is intolerable.'

The words of Wolfgang Thierse, who looks like an Old Testament prophet but is, in fact, one of the few national politicians who can speak constructively for the people of the former East Germany. It reflects the fact that the complacency of Germany's political élite was shattered in a single night of violence.

Ten days ago in Rostock a mob, wielding clubs and petrol bombs and shouting 'Germany for the Germans', stormed the high-rise block, from which some two hundred Romany refugees had been evacuated, and set the lower floors alight. More than a hundred Vietnamese guest workers and their families were still inside another part of the 11-storey block. So were the area's race relations officer and a German television team. The TV crew recorded the rising panic among those trapped, as it became clear that all telephone calls to the local police and fire services either went unanswered or, worse, were met by evasions at the other end of the line. Outside, a footbridge over a main road to another drab residential area was crowded with local people, many of them cheering on the attackers.

Last weekend a trickle of people from the Lichtenhagen estate were using the same bridge; but they weren't cheering. After a week in which their streets had been turned into a battleground, they were battening down the hatches for another invasion. Convoys of buses brought in a several-thousand-strong army of young people from the left-wing or anarchist scene in Berlin and other cities. Some wore black leather, with masks or hoods adding to the studied impression of violent chic. Placards showed fists smashing into swastikas. These people see themselves as the Hell's Angels of rough justice against the neo-Nazi scourge.

Thousands of concerned citizens, in bourgeois slacks and shirts, were also there. For the many Rostockers among them, it was the first experience in their lives of joining a demonstration of their own free will. They clutched their children to their sides and shone with pride and excitement, despite the unhappy events which had moved them to come there. The march had moved barely two hundred yards before some of the black-leather anarchists from Berlin got into a verbal exchange with one of the locals standing outside a block of flats. In seconds, a dozen athletic youngsters had peeled off from the procession and began throwing drink cans and stones up at the windows, as the spectators inside hurriedly pulled their heads in. 'Nazis out!' came a roar from down below. For a few moments it looked as though things might get out of hand; but then a counter-chant was got up from a group of marchers at the back: '*Keine Gewalt!*'—no violence. The procession continued, with one or two smashed windows the only evidence of the fracas.

The procession around the vast housing estate last weekend was, at least in part, meant to be a chance for politically highly charged Germans from Berlin and other western cities to teach a lesson—not only to the shadowy underclass of right-wing gangsters who had stormed the refugee hostel—but also to the burghers of Lichtenhagen. The local people I spoke to were not really angry about the mass intrusion, but they defended themselves, saying that outsiders didn't understand the pent-up frustration that they had to live with every day. Two years after they threw off their communist chains, many were without jobs and without real hope. Many of their former bosses were still lording it over them, as well as the new bosses from the West in their smart suits and shiny cars. Meanwhile the local government had ordered that hundreds of Gypsies, part of the huge westward exodus from Romania and other countries going on overland into Germany, should live indefinitely on their housing estate. Why had those in charge forced the Gypsies to camp in tents on the grass outside, until the other residents were sick of the crowding and the mess on their doorstep? The question, just like the 'phone calls to the fire brigade a few days before, was unanswered.

From Rostock, with its superb white sand beaches and now silent shipyards, I drove miles south through eastern Germany. The half-finished motorways; the spanking new 'phone kiosks standing in the rest areas, where the wires are sticking out waiting to be connected to telephones; the hundred-mile stretch of road without a single petrol station; all are evidence of the halfway house that the region has now become—suspended between the promise of development and the fear of a collapse into lawlessness. Beyond Berlin, towards the Polish border, and into eastern Brandenburg, an area of abandoned lignite mines, rising joblessness and more youth gangs. Here, they are organized by local gang members, with pretensions to revive Nazi ideas of giving the Germans the *Lebensraum* of which, the argument goes, they have always been cheated.

On to another refuge hostel, this time in Cottbus. Here, 120,000 inhabitants have seen the former Soviet army barracks in a southern suburb turned into a large refugee camp; the refugees have been assaulted, for several nights in a row, by hundreds of local youngsters infected by the virus of violence. Unlike the one in Rostock, the Cottbus community has formed neighbourhood watch committees who regularly 'phone the police when they see groups of skinheads preparing petrol bombs and getting rowdy. When I was there, the local theatre was crowded with concerned citizens, debating how best to stand up to the threat being posed to their lives and hopes from within. The banner on one wall summed up what the meeting was all about: the large letters PROUD TO BE GERMAN had been amended to read instead PROUD TO BE HUMAN. And the message from the floor, from a dozen impassioned speakers, was that they are trying, after a lifetime of thought control, to lay the building-blocks for a democracy that works—with or without the complacent national politicians. They haven't bothered to go to Cottbus, or to Rostock, to see what is going on in the land of hopes betrayed.

DECISIONS, DECISIONS

STEPHEN JESSEL   PARIS   19 SEPTEMBER 1992

*The people of France went to the polls in September 1992
to decide whether or not they should ratify the Maastricht
Treaty. The referendum marked the end of a hectic week
for European Community politicians: a week that began with
uncertainty on the money markets, which saw the pound and
the lira withdraw from the Exchange Rate Mechanism and
which ended with a souring of relations between London and
Bonn. In France itself, comparisons were being drawn between
this and a previous referendum.*

SNEEM HAS BEEN much on my mind these last few weeks; Sneem and
its telephone numbers: Sneem 3, Sneem 4, Sneem 5, Sneem 6. For a
week, almost quarter of a century ago, they suddenly and briefly became
urgently important. Even reporters deserve a little luck from time to
time; in the spring of 1969, the newspaper which at that time was
kind enough to employ me thoughtfully sent me to the west of Ireland.
The hotel in which I and the rest of a large herd of journalists stayed
was exemplary, though it had, I think, only one outside line, Sneem
3. The 'phone box in the nearby hamlet was Sneem 6, and the post
office was Sneem 4. There were few 'phones in Sneem in those days;
doubtless now there are hundreds, all with six-figure numbers. Apart
from the communication problems, life was an idyll. In the morning,
teams of beaming waiters would tow in Irish breakfasts, each with more
cholesterol than is now consumed in the entire Los Angeles area in a year.
Sometimes the head waiter would appear at one's elbow and confide that
a boat was going out in search of prawns, and would sir be interested in

some for dinner? Sir thought sir probably would be. The only disruptive element was the occasional crash, as the Irish police evicted yet another *Paris Match* photographer, found trying to reach the grounds of another, much smaller hotel nearby. It was situated on a spit of land jutting into a bay. I think the number of that hotel was Sneem 5. There were only two guests: Mr and Mrs Charles de Gaulle.

It was here that they had come immediately after the General had resigned as president, following the rejection by the French people, in a referendum, of proposals for constitutional changes. He had been in power for more than ten years; the nation wanted a change, and when his proposals were repudiated the General stepped down. Eighteen months later, he was dead.

Of course the parallel doesn't really hold up: de Gaulle made it clear that if the answer in his referendum was no, he would go; President Mitterrand started by saying that he would stay on whatever the outcome of this weekend's vote, though of late he has begun to equivocate. If you are looking for parallels, it could be noted that in 1964 de Gaulle was operated on for a prostate condition, and the next year he won a handsome electoral victory. But this referendum is full of echoes and resonances. Take the date, September 20th. That is the 200th anniversary—to the day—of the battle of Valmy, in which the troops of the infant republic confronted, and defeated, the Germans—or, to be more precise, the Prussians. I am not accusing the Duke of Brunswick, the Prussian commander, of losing deliberately, but it was never quite clear why, at his death, precious stones from the French crown were found among his effects. Maybe it was an early form of European Monetary Union. Valmy was, in a sense, the founding act of the French republic; that same day, the National Convention opened in Paris, and the next day it abolished the monarchy; the monarch himself was abolished later. Or take the date of President Mitterrand's one and only television appearance in support of the Treaty: September 3rd. It may be coincidence that that date is the anniversary of the start of the Second World War, or it may not. Or take the three principal right-wing opponents of the Treaty, whose triple act has won them the soubriquet of 'The Three Musketeers'; their great friend was d'Artagnan, who died at Maastricht. I have no confidence in predicting how France is going to vote this weekend, but I am pretty sure that the margin won't be seventy to thirty for a 'yes', as the polls had suggested at the time that the referendum was called; and this referendum was not constitutionally necessary. The two houses of parliament had ratified Maastricht by a margin of around nine to one.

So was Mr Mitterrand being too clever, seeking not only to display France's European credentials but also to wrong-foot a divided opposition? Possibly; but at least the French will have been consulted. One lesson from this whole episode is that governments have got too far ahead of the governed on the European issue. Those who are going to vote 'no' in France—the farmers, the middle-aged, the working class, the small shopkeepers—have not been persuaded that the promises for the future outweigh the fears of today: fears about Germany, about unemployment, about the ending of French history. It is interesting that the strongest support for Maastricht comes from the young, who might be expected to have general European sympathies by virtue of a common, European youth culture; but even more, from those aged sixty-five and over; the one category that had first-hand experience of what the old tribalism and nationalisms of Europe actually led to. If France says no—which, though far from impossible, on balance is probably unlikely—it is better that Maastricht dies now, and quickly, rather than act as a focus for the rage and frustration of millions of Europeans, inside and outside France, swept down a path that they do not wish to tread.

And what of Mr Mitterrand? Until a few days ago the question was whether he would go if the answer were no, whether he would wait until the opposition wins the general election in March, or whether he would see out the remaining two and a half years of his presidency. A reason for voting 'no' was to put pressure on Mr Mitterrand. News that he has cancer, even a common and easily treated cancer, suggests that he will go sooner rather than later. Paradoxically, such would be the disorder after a 'no'—markets in chaos, the whole political class repudiated—that he might feel that he had to stay as a stabilizing factor. In the event of a 'yes', what better moment to go, especially given his health problems? Should that be the case, I have the address (though not the 'phone number) of an excellent small hotel in the west of Ireland.

WE DO IT OUR WAY

GRAHAM LEACH   HATFIELD   24 SEPTEMBER 1992

The crisis over sterling and its erratic movements, along with those of other European currencies, called the future of the EMS into doubt in the autumn of 1992. The continuing uncertainty over the future of the Maastricht accord, too, meant further moves towards European integration were unlikely. It was arguably the most unsettling time for the European Community since Margaret Thatcher's campaign to win a budget rebate for Britain in the early 1980s.

COVERING EUROPEAN COMMUNITY meetings, over the past three and a half years, has taken me to a number of inviting places where, along with the rest of the EC press corps, I have been royally received by the host governments. I remember the splendid lunch of mouthwatering salmon which the Irish served up in a huge marquee in the grounds of Dublin Castle; then the Guinness bar which suddenly appeared in the press room in Galway at the end of another EC meeting, an occasion memorable for one of Charlie Haughey's press officers dancing an Irish jig. I recall sunbathing in the grounds of a luxurious château in the south of France overlooking the Mediterranean at Antibes, waiting for gruelling talks to end, involving the then Chancellor, Nigel Lawson, who was battling with his partners over Europe's future currency; *plus ça change*. The Spanish took us around the Alhambra in Granada, and we toured Venice with the Italians. Our first meeting under the British presidency took the EC travelling media to a press centre at the exotic location of the University of Hertfordshire. It is a measure of how long I have been abroad that it came as quite a surprise to discover that Hertfordshire actually had a university.

The journalists and the communications facilities were housed in the refectory. We queued up for our Sunday lunch in the adjacent kitchen. Greek, French and Italian colleagues were asked, by formidable ladies in blue aprons: 'Do you want one roast spud or two?' Then we were invited to ladle our own gravy from a free-standing vat. Of course I am being rather facetious; the food was perfectly acceptable and the overall press arrangements worked smoothly. But in the twistings of your correspondent's contorted mind, that Sunday lunch—roast beef, Yorkshire pudding, roast potatoes and greens—seemed to assume the status of a British political declaration: it was as if to say, 'That's how we do things in this country: down to earth, nothing fancy, none of your airy-fairy Euro-cuisine here.' The catering somehow symbolized Britain's role in Europe: the offshore island, talented in introducing down-to-earth common sense in EC negotiations when they stray too far into the fantasy land of the most ardent Euro-federalists. I suppose it is partly to do with Britain's historically wider experience on the world stage. On the other hand, I do not think we have ever fully grasped how the memories of the war, particularly of occupation and of social and economic breakdown, drive continental Europe towards deeper integration. The corset of European unity may not fit all countries all of the time, but the occasional pressure points are worth withstanding, it is reasoned, if overall the body can be held together. But the corset is now splitting at the seams, following the currency crisis and uncertainty over Maastricht in the wake of the French referendum.

To switch metaphors for a moment, the French Foreign Minister, Roland Dumas, has spoken of an earthquake beckoning, with no telling which way the houses will collapse. John Major speaks of a fault-line in the Exchange Rate Mechanism. In fact there are two cracks appearing across the EC, one political, the other economic, which could result in the crust splitting into several geographic plates. Men like Chancellor Kohl and President Mitterrand are alarmed by what they are hearing from John Major. A half-sentence remark from him the other day, which was barely reported by the media, focused on the benefits of those parts of the Maastricht accord which were outside the Treaty of Rome; in other words, those sections which provide for greater inter-state co-operation, without the European Commission and other EC institutions getting involved. Such comments convinced the supporters of greater Community-based integration that Mr Major would try to hide behind the skirts of the Danish rejection, in order to delay British ratification and thereby scupper European union. On the economic level, the currency crisis has resulted in several countries finding themselves outside or on the margins of the ERM, but with Britain determined, it seems, to stay outside for any length of time. Even the weakest countries want to clamber back into some kind of currency grid as soon as possible, fearing that they will be left behind in a second lane. The decisions facing the British government in the coming weeks and months are no less momentous than in 1955 when we chose to stay outside the original Common Market. For there seems little doubt that if Maastricht fails, or is debilitated, a hard core of countries, led by Germany, will move forward on their own.

Because of Britain's EC presidency, I have been over to the UK a couple of times recently. On one visit I came off the motorway at Spaghetti Junction to meander through the Black Country. It was an appalling shock to a visiting exile: mile after mile of derelict warehouses, shoddy public housing; an industrial wasteland relieved only by the occasional redevelopment. Was this the pain endured over the past two years by holding the pound at DM2.95, or was it the result of Britain's much longer industrial decline? Better economic minds than mine will have a view. But what I saw that day seemed to explain why Britain has been forced to give up the race to stay in the premier league. The evidence I saw with my own eyes was more convincing as a reason than anything that the Bundesbank might have been up to.

BRINDISI AND THE
INDIA MAIL

DAVID WILLEY   BRINDISI   24 SEPTEMBER 1992

The blocking of international rail and road traffic through the former Yugoslavia in 1992 led to a massive increase in the number of passengers travelling by sea to Greece and Turkey through the southern Italian port of Brindisi. The port used to be one of the British Empire's main transit points; it was the land terminal of the India Mail *service.*

IMAGINE THE SCENE, one day towards the end of the last century, on the quayside in Brindisi, one of the Mediterranean's safest natural harbours. The *India Mail*, the famous express train, puffs into Brindisi after a forty-two-hour journey across Europe from Cannon Street Station in London, via Calais, the Mont Cenis tunnel, Turin, Bologna and Bari. Out pour the passengers: soldiers, civil servants, Indian princes with their retinues, merchants' wives and children. On board go the mailbags, carrying all official and private correspondence between the mother country and the subcontinent. Here the *India Mail*, run in conjunction by the P&O Navigation Company and the newly built South Italian Railway, connects with the *Bombay Packet*—a steamer that plies between Brindisi and Bombay, via the Suez Canal, taking only four days. The total journey time between London and Bombay—120 years ago—was just 147 hours.

In his futuristic novel *Around the World in 80 Days* Jules Verne had his hero, Phileas Fogg, setting off via Brindisi on the *India Mail*—a train even more famous, in its day, than the *Orient Express*. The period was the 1870s. Three great triumphs of Victorian engineering had helped to reduce the journey time between London and Bombay to less than a week: the development of Europe's railway system; the cutting of the first railway tunnel through the French and Italian Alps; and the digging of the Suez Canal linking the Mediterranean and the Red Sea.

The arrival of the *India Mail* service in distant Bombay was also something of an event. The steamship used to be greeted with a four-cannon salute when it entered the harbour. Negotiations, for the new trans-European express rail and steamer service to India, went on for several years between Britain and the government of a newly united Italy. The French were annoyed that Marseilles was not chosen as the port of embarkation for this lucrative express traffic between Britain and Bombay. But technical considerations proved decisive. By travelling at speed, on land, as far as Brindisi, the *India Mail* chopped an extra fifty hours off the total journey time to Bombay.

The outbreak of war between France and Prussia in 1870 caused the service to be diverted across Germany to Italy via the Brenner Pass. But from 1872 until the outbreak of the First World War, every week the *India Mail* used to transit through Brindisi. A luxurious new hotel was built by the British on the quayside and it is still there today: a bit run-down, but with some fine turn-of-the-century decoration surviving. When the Bombay steamer docked, a gangplank was thrown across, straight into the first-floor balcony of the hotel, to enable first-class passengers to disembark direct (rather like in a modern airport) and refresh themselves in dignified surroundings.

Photographs, railway posters and other memorabilia concerning the *India Mail* have been collected in Brindisi by a local antique dealer who dreams of one day reviving the *India Mail* and running a service for wealthy tourists from London to Bombay along the route of the old express—like the successful *Orient Express*, which now runs again between London and Venice.

Apart from the old International Hotel, there are no other easily visible relics of the *India Mail* service, apart from a coal bunker built to fuel the *Bombay Packet*. Brindisi today is a transit point for hundreds of thousands of holiday-makers on their way to Greece. The main street from the railway station to the harbour is full of straggling backpackers; the only recent technical innovation is a monster hydrofoil that cuts the journey time, across the Straits of Otranto to Greece, to a mere three hours; it is not to be recommended in choppy seas.

The disruption of communications by war in the former Yugoslavia means that the citizens of Brindisi have got used to seeing hordes of new travellers, to and from Eastern Europe, using their port. Last year the town was almost swamped by more than 10,000 hungry and impoverished Albanians who suddenly arrived in search of food and jobs. The memory of that crisis is still alive in Brindisi, where jobs are scarce and the crime rate is high. You really feel that you have arrived at the end of the line in Europe in this somnolent Mediterranean port with its echoes, not only of nineteenth-century engineering enterprise, but also of a much more remote transit traffic between the twin poles of the ancient world: Greece and Rome. Here, the poet Virgil died on his return from Greece in 19 BC. Mark Antony and the Emperor Augustus were reconciled in the town. From Brindisi, the Crusaders set out to conquer the Holy Land. This was, quite literally, the end of the road from Rome and northern Europe. The famous Appian Way terminated here. It is marked by two ruined columns towering over the quayside where the *India Mail* now docks no more. Only backpackers queue to embark on the ferryboat for Athens to gaze upon the Acropolis.

WAR OF WORDS

LEO ENRIGHT   DUBLIN   12 NOVEMBER 1992

The Irish government collapsed in November 1992, amid recriminations; the country then faced a general election, after the junior partners in the coalition, the Progressive Democrats, claimed that their leader, Des O'Malley, had been accused of perjury.

THE POWER OF language. Seldom has it been illustrated so forcefully as in the political turmoil here in Ireland in recent days. Can you recall when last a government fell because of a single word? When four letters plunged a prime minister towards a political nemesis? When something less than a fourteenth-century adjective with a Latin root might have saved a country from a general election? The psephology will take over next week, but etymology has brought things this far. Only a master wordsmith could truly explain how words and their meanings can have had such a central role in the political drama of recent days. Words spoken, unspoken and mis-spoken all played their part, as the three-year-old coalition government lurched towards its own destruction.

The most important word in the script of this drama was never uttered—at least not by the player who was ultimately booed off the stage for it. The word was 'perjury', the player was Albert Reynolds, and the scene was a crowded courtroom in the course of a judicial inquiry into Ireland's beef industry. The Prime Minister was confronted with allegations that he had been incompetent in his handling of beef export insurance. The charge was made by his own cabinet colleague, Des O'Malley. Mr Reynolds replied, carefully, that Mr O'Malley was reckless, irresponsible and dishonest. Later, helpfully, he added that he believed that his Industry Minister had given information to the tribunal under oath which Mr O'Malley knew to be false. Well, my dictionary says to perjure oneself is to give false evidence under oath. Mr O'Malley's Progressive Democrats found the same definition and issued an ultimatum: that is a noun, by the way, meaning 'a final statement of terms, rejection of which by the opposite party will involve a rupture'. Mr Reynolds then replied that the Progressive Democrats were acting 'childishly'. That adverb provoked further exchanges, as Mr Reynolds insisted that the whole matter was being exploited by his coalition partners. A spokesman for the Democrats replied that Mr Reynolds was being 'naïvely disingenuous'. The experts tell me that this is a hypercorrection, suggesting that the speaker didn't understand the meaning of either word! That same Democrat spokesman moved quickly to more precise language. The coalition would be saved, he said, *only* if Mr Reynolds made an 'abject apology'. The fate of the government was sealed, perhaps, when the Prime Minister's advisers told him that this fourteenth-century adjective would require him to make an 'utterly wretched, hopeless, forlorn and submissive expression of regret or contrition'.

Mr Reynolds declined, preserving the dignity of his office. But a new word—a most undignified word—then hit the political fan. Mr Reynolds angrily responded to opposition attacks by describing them as . . . well, it's a four-letter noun; where listed by dictionaries, it is described as a taboo word, and it probably comes from the medieval Dutch: *crappen*—which means 'to break off'. When he used that word, Mr Reynolds' personal standing in the polls 'broke off' and went into free fall. A 20 per cent drop in popularity means he went into this election more unpopular than just about any Irish prime minister in modern times. In Parliament an opposition speaker chortled that, like Richard Nixon's notorious Committee for the Re-election of the President, or CREEP, Mr Reynolds might now consider a Committee for the Re-election of Albert as Premier. Amid the taunts and the public protests and the plunging polls, Mr Reynolds offered an abject apology for any offence caused by his use of such a naughty word.

Meanwhile another word spoken out of turn landed the other coalition leader in very serious trouble indeed. Des O'Malley claimed that a special investigation was under way to settle the argument between him and his premier. Within hours *he* was apologizing to the President of the Irish

High Court. There was to be an investigation, but it was *not* a special investigation; the distinction was judged to be an important one.

So that was one week in the semantics of Irish politics, and of the language they call Hiberno-English. For the English spoken here in Ireland is different, and the attention to detail is not as bizarre as it might seem. Language, we are told, is the armoury of the dispossessed. In Ireland certainly, the poetry, the romantic legends and the myths all represented aspirations beyond the harsh realities of their day. The careful use and abuse of language has been central to Irish politics. The rebel leader, Eamonn de Valera, for instance, entered the Irish Parliament, the *Dail*, after he (a republican) had signed an oath of allegiance to the king. De Valera defined that oath, back in 1927, as being 'of no binding significance in conscience or in law. In short, merely an empty political formula.' Nevertheless he took the precaution of placing the Bible in a far corner of the room while the oath was signed. In his scholarly new biography of Edmund Burke, Conor Cruise O'Brien lays out the lexical complexities that allowed that Irish Protestant MP to make the case for home rule without offending the Commons. Conor Cruise O'Brien himself contributed to the lexicon with the coinage of the most famous new word of modern Irish politics: GUBU. As his arch-enemy, Charles Haughey, sought to explain the succession of disasters that befell his government in the summer of 1982 and, most spectacularly, the discovery of a murderer in the home of his unsuspecting Attorney General, Haughey described the events as 'grotesque, unprecedented, bizarre and unbelievable': GUBU.

Words alone do not define the history of Irish political language; the punctuation matters too. At the Imperial Conference of 1926, for instance, Irish delegates insisted that the punctuation was all-important. They refused to sign a document describing the King of England Scotland Wales Ireland and so on, because there were no commas to divide the entities of the empire. It was the well-known principle of co-ordinating conjunction: if there are no commas, everything is subordinate to the main. By insisting on commas, the negotiators established the separateness of each country, and so (according to the Irish history of that time) Irish grammatical correctness won concessions for the peoples of a whole empire.

Grammatical correctness has not always won the day though. In 1916, the barrister, Serjeant Sullivan, had the task of defending the

Irish insurrectionist, Sir Roger Casement, against charges of treason. The law relied upon dated back to 1351, and the reign of Edward III, against levying war against the king, or being an adherent to the king's enemies. Sixty pages of the historic court transcript are devoted to arguments about that principle of co-ordinating conjunction. Where were the commas, and what did they mean? The three judges found no commas where it mattered; and Roger Casement was hanged.

CELTIC MYTHS

LEO ENRIGHT   DUBLIN   24 DECEMBER 1992

On Christmas Eve 1992, there was something of a first for listeners to From Our Own Correspondent. *Normally, contributors broadcast from studios, or hotel bedrooms, or breathlessly down the 'phone from battlefields, or even by satellite. Leo Enright, in Dublin, went to Europe's oldest cathedral—as he called it—built roughly at the time when Noah and his family were flooded out, to record a seasonal report on Celtic myths and their influence upon Christian thought.*

I AM STANDING in the burial chamber at the heart of the great megalithic tomb at Newgrange in Brú na Bóinne, Ireland's Valley of the Kings. This place is older than Stonehenge; older than the great Egyptian pyramid at Giza, perhaps by as much as 1,000 years. Above me is the oldest constructed roof in Europe; and I am in what may well be the oldest astronomical observatory on the planet.

This is an extraordinary place. And this week, as in every Christmas week, there is an eerie reminder here that Christians were not the first to celebrate this season as a holy one. The great designer who built this tomb has ensured that, after more than 5,000 years, the sun, the earth and this place still come together to celebrate the winter solstice. This place is so constructed that, even at the end of the twentieth century, in the days around mid-winter the first rays of morning sunlight come down the long, narrow passageway leading from the entrance and strike the tomb wall behind me. A quarter of a million tonnes of stone have been arranged around this chamber into a megalithic cathedral by a long-lost civilization.

As the sun rises over the River Boyne below, only the frequent clouds can obscure a seasonal event that was first witnessed here almost 2,000 years before the Celts came to Britain, and here to Ireland. And so we know virtually nothing about the men and women who built Newgrange; even what we know about the much more recent Celts is second-hand, at best. And what we do know comes from the folklore and tradition that have been handed down, often changed through several religious transformations.

In fact, not just Christmas but many of the great festivals of the Christian church in Ireland are more than echoes of the past; they continue it. The success of Christianity owed much, in its early days, to the ability of the first Christian proselytizers to take what they found here among the natives and to adapt it to the new ideology. There are remarkable traces of this even today: so-called pagan gods and rituals that have become a part of the modern Ireland. The country's devotion to female saints, for instance, is not a surprise to most observers. In the Celtic world, goddesses had immense importance and one of the greatest of them was called Bright. She wasn't the goddess of love—there wasn't one—but of wisdom and of poetry. Most scholars agree that it is just too much of a coincidence that the most important woman saint in Ireland today is called Bright. The beautiful church of St Bride in Fleet Street in London is dedicated to this much-loved Irish saint, who may be a good deal older than people think. Equally, the cult of Saint Anne has identified holy wells throughout Ireland associated with her name. One such holy well was found by archaeologists to have traces of devotion dating back 2,000 years. There is a Celtic goddess of supreme importance called Anu. In all, there may be 5,000 holy wells throughout Ireland, many of them visited especially by pilgrims on Lady Day, 15 August. This coincides exactly with the Celtic harvest feast of *Lúnasa*. And those so-called coincidences go on and on. Hallowe'en, the Eve of All Hallows, also has huge religious importance here. It coincides with the Celtic feast of *Samhain*—the festival of the dead. All the major Christian feasts, in fact, now coincide with important dates in the Celtic calendar.

There is one striking coincidence which is no more than that—a coincidence—but which has intrigued some scholars here. The passage graves that dot the Irish landscape are common throughout Europe, but nowhere else do they so regularly take the form they have here. They take the shape of a cross. Can that most Christian of symbols have, in some way, been prefigured in the Stone Age?

Ireland's great Celtic tradition has been passed down through a filtering system. The new Celtic Christians sought to preserve their past by incorporating it within the traditions of the new religion. Suddenly, great Irish heroes became blood relatives of Noah and of Abraham and of Moses. In one wonderful adaptation, Noah's granddaughter Cessair led an expedition to Ireland after she was refused a place on the Ark.

As I stand here in a Stone Age cathedral that may have been built before Noah's Ark, I am struck by one central fact: that it has survived. Of course it was built to survive the ravages of time; but it has also survived the ravages of man. God may know how many religions have passed this way. But every one of them has treated this place with reverence. It is a rare monument to a religious tolerance that has lasted 5,000 years.

IN SEARCH OF
BLACK DIAMOND

STEPHEN JESSEL   CAHORS   28 JANUARY 1993

At the beginning of 1993, much concern was being expressed in southern France concerning the dwindling supplies of one of the gourmet's most sought-after delicacies—the black truffle of Périgord. Stephen Jessel—something of a gastronome himself—went to see what all the fuss was about.

IT WAS A small pig, not especially friendly, and—rather insultingly, I thought—its owner had not bothered to give it a name. But it knew its job all right. Snuffling through a field studded with oak trees, it found what its owner was looking for: it shoved its snout into the earth and burrowed until it had unearthed the buried treasure. The treasure being *tuber melanosporum*, the black truffle of Périgord (though they are not much found around there any more), not to be confused with any other kind of truffle and known, with a degree of hyperbole, as the 'black diamond'. It is found growing at the ends of the roots of oak and nut trees, anything up to six inches underground. With its wrinkled skin it is deeply unimpressive to look at; encrusted with earth, its size varies, typically, from that of a large walnut to that of a smallish potato. Wash away the soil and remove a fraction of the skin with a sharp knife. If the inside is black, marbled with white veins, you have hit gold; or, if not quite gold, a product quoted at a price of £280 a pound by a shop in London earlier this month.

Even in the Tuesday afternoon market, in the main street of the little village of Lalbenque near Cahors, where locals gather—minus pigs but with baskets of truffles—to transact business with professional buyers, the price a few days ago was more than £70 a pound. Dealing was brisk: the truffles were sold by weight (earth and all), and the deals were concluded in private with the rapid exchange of sheaves of high-denomination notes. The Tuesday afternoon market is remarkable for the shyness of some of the locals in front of outsiders who might, I suppose, just possibly be connected with the tax authorities.

It is clearly a rather special fungus if people will pay that kind of money for it, and if ingenious crooks will take the trouble to gather inferior sorts of fungus—including one variety of white summer truffle—and dye them black, passing them off as the real thing. Queen Anne is reputed to have given her cooks a special allowance to buy them. No one who expects to earn a living with words is allowed to use the adjective 'indescribable', but I have to say that it is not easy to explain the taste and smell of *tuber melanosporum*. It has an overwhelming aroma: go into the room in Cahors where the Pebeyre family—four generations of it in the truffle business—supervises the sorting, cleaning, grading and despatch of truffles, and the smell is so intense that it produces a headache. A refrigerator still reeks more than a week after a sealed plastic bag of them has been left there overnight. To the extent that there is such a thing as a mushroomy smell, it is not that; nor is it exactly earthy. The word most often used is musky, an almost animal scent, a distant cousin of a hot, wet horse crossed with a compost heap. And people pay money for that? They do indeed: to marry wafery slices with pasta, or with a salad of potatoes; to insert between the skin and the flesh of a chicken; to transform a pâté; above all, to chop into scrambled eggs or omelettes—anything delicate or bland that will swallow the flavour and be transformed.

First, however, catch your truffle; and that is becoming harder and harder to do. The authentic black truffle is found only in south-west and south-east France, in parts of Spain and Italy. At the beginning of the century the generous earth of France alone would yield 1,000 tons; in some recent years the figure has been a fiftieth of that. The weather is partly to blame: the truffle likes a stormy summer with plenty of rain; a succession of dry summers has cut production. The depopulation of the countryside means that fewer people have the time or will to walk their pigs across the winter landscape from November to March; in any case, pigs, which will eat the truffles themselves, given half a chance, and which have to replaced each year as they get too big, are these days giving way to dogs. Some researchers think that there may be some natural disease which is attacking the fungus. The march of motorways, housing developments and other by-products of the late twentieth century have diminished the oak plantations where most truffles are gathered. It takes years for an oak to produce truffles—if indeed it ever does—and fewer and fewer young people are prepared to invest the time and money in planting trees for so distant and problematical a return.

Resourceful as ever, the French are turning to science to overcome the truffle trouble. An electronic sniffer is under development, with the help of Manchester University (from observation, I must report that it is some years away from being the match of even the idlest and most olfactorily incompetent pig or dog). At an agricultural college near Cahors, enthusiastic researchers are trying to grow the fungus under greenhouse conditions—dipping the roots of oaks, nut trees and shrubs into a sort of genetic soup—in the hope that, in five or ten years' time, snug under the earth will be a veritable nursery of black diamonds.

There is, of course, something slightly indecent about a food—rather an indigestible one at that—which is so grotesquely expensive. Though little sympathy need be extended to those who are prepared to pay such stupefying prices, one should rather celebrate with the country people in the market who have such little treasure troves on their terrain. And is it all worth it? I would certainly eat truffles again if the opportunity arose. I would not grieve for a second if the opportunity never arose. And never in a million years would I think of buying one.

A SECOND BITE
AT THE CHERRY

GRAHAM LEACH   DENMARK   14 MAY 1993

In May 1993, the Danes went to the polls for the second time to decide whether to accept the Maastricht Treaty on European Union. Eleven months earlier they had narrowly rejected the Treaty, but they won several exemptions as a result of an agreement worked out at the European Community summit in Edinburgh. This, it was felt, would make the accord easier to swallow.

IN THE LATER recounting of the story, I had, of course, flirted with death. Denmark's entire emergency services had swung into action to save my life. It had been a damn close-run thing, worthy of recapture in one of those TV programmes which re-enact heroic, life-or-death moments. In reality the incident had never really approached such dramatic proportions, although it had not been without its moments of genuine distress. Let me explain.

The ferry boat from the port of Aarhus was gently easing out of the harbour, ready for its three-hour passage to Kalundborg. It was a beautifully sunny day, the sea was calm, and we were set fair for a relaxing crossing. A colleague and I found a sea view table in the on-board restaurant, ordered a lager each and made our selection from the enticing *smorgasbord* buffet of herrings, crab, mussels, pickles and so on. No sooner had I started eating than I thought I was choking to death. A lump of food—possibly a piece of corn-on-the-cob—had lodged in my oesophagus, and all attempts to force it up or down only caused more discomfort. My colleague summoned the First Officer. Appeals for a doctor were relayed over loudspeakers: no response. The officer—a hearty maritime figure who looked as though he might have once skippered a Viking longboat—took me to his cabin, bent me over and thumped my back; all to no avail. I couldn't swallow any water because it was diverted straight into my windpipe. The officer radioed to the hospital in Kalundborg. 'Can he still breathe?' they asked. 'If so, he should be OK till you arrive here.' For the next three hours I suffered not a few moments of genuine panic. Several thoughts raced through my mind: memories of lost colleagues over the years who had died nobly in the service of journalism, killed in Middle East wars or conflicts in Africa. How would I be remembered? I could just see it: three lines, tucked away at the foot of the obituaries page in the BBC's in-house magazine, announcing: 'He gave his life while covering the ratification of the Maastricht Treaty.' What a way to go!

We eventually reached Kalundborg, where the local casualty unit clearly had enough spare staff to despatch two of them in a car to meet us on the harbourside. They led us by the quickest route to the hospital. En route, the piece of food suddenly dislodged itself, so there wasn't much for the hospital to do. Nevertheless, after a thorough check-up in the well-equipped, obviously well-funded and not too hard pressed casualty ward, I was relieved to learn that the offending morsel had proceeded into my system via the proper channels and had not found its way into any of the various tubes used for breathing. During my onward journey I pondered how well I had been treated by the various local services involved. I was in no doubt that, had I really been choking to death, a full-scale emergency would have been triggered to get me off the ferry pretty quickly. I could not help but compare my experience with that of a friend in London who nearly died recently during an asthma attack because of the time the ambulance had taken to get to her. In the cold light of day, though, I suppose it is a little unfair to compare the two countries in this way. Denmark has a much smaller population than Britain's; the demand upon the health and social services here is a fraction of that in the UK.

Nevertheless, Denmark does provide an alternative model to the more market-orientated, increasingly privatized public services in Britain. A fellow passenger, on a train journey out of Copenhagen, explained. 'We pay comparatively high taxes, as well as 25 per cent VAT—including on food. Everyone complains about taxes, but we're generally satisfied with what we get in return by way of pensions, health care and so on. No one here wants the American system where you're asked if you can pay before you're given medical treatment.' He admitted, however, that, like health services in many countries, some financial trimming was going to be required. It is unlikely, though, that the Danes will allow their subsidized public services to be curtailed. The train we were travelling on was part of the local system serving the capital city—Denmark's equivalent of Network SouthEast, if you like. The carriage was clean, the stations we passed spotless. 'Do the trains run on time?' I asked. 'Oh yes,' replied my fellow passenger. 'Apart from rare cases when fast trains rip down the overhead cables.' This seemed—to a layman like me—a more understandable excuse for delayed services than 'leaves on the line'.

As our train journey continued, the pleasant suburbs of Copenhagen flashed by. Blocks of flats—owned by local councils—appeared, built to a very high standard, with spacious surrounding gardens: places to live rather than exist in. On the streets, motorists stick religiously to the speed limits; there's a respect for pedestrians and cyclists. Plans for a huge bridge linking Copenhagen with Sweden are being put through the most rigorous environmental appraisal. It struck me that Denmark was a well-ordered society, without being regimented. It is to ensure that it stays that way that the Danes are so dubious about European union and throwing open their borders to what they fear will be an all-round lowering of social standards. Denmark's rejection of the Maastricht Treaty last June raised fundamental questions as to whether it is realistically possible to harmonize a continent with such widely varying levels of prosperity and social costs. If, as the opinion polls predict, the Danes do vote 'yes' next week, it will not be because their concerns on such issues have been answered; rather, that they fear what could be the greater peril: that of being left behind in Europe. They know that the future of the whole European Community now depends on how they vote next Tuesday. It's going to be an exciting day; and I'm relieved that I shall be around to witness it.

THE SPIRIT OF MAY '68

STEPHEN JESSEL   PARIS   15 MAY 1993

A quarter of a century has now passed since of one of the most extraordinary events in Western Europe since the war: the uprisings by students and workers in France in May 1968. For a month the country seemed to be on the edge of revolution. Yet by the summer it was all over. But what legacy, if any, has it left?

IN MARCH 1968, that great newspaper, *Le Monde*, published an article under a title that will be remembered as long as the paper itself: *Quand la France s'ennuie*—when France is bored. The writer lamented the lack of interest of the French people, the triviality of the preoccupations of the young. Within seven weeks, few people were bored any longer. It was a process that, perhaps, began when a cheeky red-headed youth of German Jewish extraction, Danny Cohn Bendit, 'Danny the Red', came to public attention by arguing with a government minister at a university outside Paris. It eventually paralysed France, brought millions out on strike, had the state reeling, and sent President de Gaulle to Germany to consult French generals there. The end came with perhaps a million people on the Champs Elysées, marching to support the General; and an election that gave the right wing a majority similar to that won in the landslide in 1993.

Things happened very quickly. It was the time when, around the world, protests were growing against the American intervention in Vietnam. A relatively minor incident in Paris resulted in a number of students being arrested. Students at the University of Nanterre demonstrated, among them Danny the Red; the authorities closed the university. The focus moved to the Sorbonne, which was occupied. In early May the police moved in; almost 600 arrests were made, and that was the real start of May 1968. I suppose the images that remain in the mind are those of the nightly battles in the Latin Quarter between students and riot police: one side hurling paving stones, the other replying with the liberal use of tear gas and clubs. The whole scene was lit by burning cars, with a soundtrack of exploding gas grenades.

By mid-May, though, the protests had spread, not only to other universities and secondary schools, but to factories and public services. By the second half of the month, economic life had more or less stopped: there was no public transport; petrol stations were closed. By the fourth week of May, Danny Cohn Bendit had been refused entrance to France; the first two deaths had occurred; and the French Communist Party—terrified by a popular movement it could not control—had set about helping to get people back to work. After 25 hours of talks, the government agreed to a series of workers' demands; wages were raised. Parliament was dissolved; although some factories and universities held out, by mid-June it was all over. France hadn't been bored; it had been suffocating. What many people remember from that time is the light-heartedness of so much of it. '*On se parlait*,' Parisians say, in wonderment, of that time: people in this snarling city would engage in passionate discussion with total strangers. Professors and students would debate together. The old barriers and hierarchies were—if not abolished—put into abeyance. With no public transport, the bicycle was rediscovered. It was a time of posters and slogans: 'Under the Cobblestones is the Beach'; 'I'm a Marxist—of the Groucho Tendency'; 'It is Forbidden to Forbid'; 'We Want Everything—At Once'.

1968 was a terrible year: Martin Luther King was killed; so was Bobby Kennedy. In the summer, I watched Chicago's answer to the French riot police in action against young Americans—spiritual cousins of the students of the Latin Quarter. The Prague Spring was turned into winter by the Russians; the massacre of hundreds of students could not, of course, be allowed to interfere with the Olympic Games in Mexico. May 1968, with its serious folly, its hopeless optimism, its high-minded promiscuity, its profound naïvety, was like a small, crazy candle in the night.

Did it leave anything behind, apart from tarmacked roads in the Latin Quarter to replace the cobbles? There are many who think not; that its real effect was to set the cause of the political left back by ten years. Time has shepherded along the leaders of the men and women of '68—the *soixante-huitards* as they are known: Danny the Red is now Danny the Green, an ecologist in city government in Frankfurt; others are civil servants, or directors of art colleges, or architects; or, just occasionally, perennial Trotskyists. Twenty-five years on, the lush economic conditions which made such self-indulgence possible no longer exist; students think about jobs, not reinventing the universe. A right-wing government prepares the way for the election of a right-wing president. Here and there, groups of hippy-like ex-students raise sheep in remote hill villages and remember *soixante-huit*; and the odd pony-tailed teacher asks his pupils to call him *tu*. But it is as if the tide had rolled across a beach, erasing the wonderful castles, the fantastic designs, and leaving it as flat as before.

Yet nothing could ever be the same again, whether it was relations between the teachers and the taught or between men and women. Many would say that the French feminist movement had its roots in the *événements* of May and June; so, perhaps, did the ecology movement. The French state had to realize that there were limits to what it could impose on people. The universities were reformed. Within a year, de Gaulle had gone. There has been decentralization; and the generosity of spirit lives on.

Two years ago, for reasons too complicated to explain, I had to drive the best part of 1,000 miles from the Turkish capital, Ankara, down to the border with Iraq. On the plane I had met two men and a woman in their thirties: a dentist, a physiotherapist and a doctor. They belonged to one of several French voluntary groups whose members give up their time to do medical work in the world's trouble-spots; we drove down together. I met them again, working long hours in a dreadful Kurdish refugee camp. I took them some bottles of wine; I didn't stay to share it, but the toast would have been 'to the spirit of May '68'.

STRATEGY OF TENSION

MATT FREI   FLORENCE   29 MAY 1993

In May 1993 a car bomb exploded in the historic centre of Florence, leaving five dead and 50 injured, and damaging the world-famous Uffizi Gallery. The Uffizi contains works by Italian and Dutch masters, and some 30 pieces suffered. The country was bracing itself for a new wave of terrorism, but no one was sure who was behind the attacks.

THE DIRECTOR OF the Academy of Georgofili held up a singed page from the archives. He was shaking and there were tears in his eyes. The sixteenth-century academy, part of the Uffizi complex of government offices built by the Medici family and later turned into a gallery, is the oldest agricultural institute in Europe. The director showed us around the office of the academy's caretaker. The shelves had collapsed into a heap; a piece of floorboard was embedded in the personal computer; a crunchy layer of broken glass covered everything; the 'phone had been knocked off its hook. Fabrizio Nencioni, the caretaker, his wife and their two daughters used to live on the fifth floor of the adjoining building. Under the glare of emergency lights, their mangled bodies were found in the early hours of Thursday morning on the ground floor. The late-medieval building had collapsed under the blast like a house of cards—and they with it.

Part of the devastation looked like the work of an earthquake. The rest reminded me of Bosnia. Shrapnel had chipped the façades of the honeycombed houses in the narrow Via dei Pulci, the Road of Fleas. Red roof-tiles had been blown off, leaving the bare wooden staves looking like fish bones. Large chunks of masonry littered the street. Amid the whirling dust, sweating firemen in orange rubber suits and white face-masks were picking through the debris. One was engrossed in an old manuscript. A group of six were carrying a lacerated painting to one of the gallery rooms that had been converted into the artistic equivalent of an emergency ward. A group of distraught Dutch tourists were wheeling their suitcases through the rubble: their lodgings had disappeared. The statues of Leonardo da Vinci, Michelangelo and Botticelli looked on morosely.

Three satellite dishes, put up by the Italian network RAI, were towering above the rescue operation. The blast had been turned into a media event as only the Italians know how to stage one. Every few minutes another minister arrived, in a convoy of sirens and flashing blue lights, to pay his respects. The Prime Minister's helicopter landed between the statues of David and Neptune. In the distance, behind a row of metal security gates, tourists looked on in bemusement. On one of the television monitors that had been set up near the site of the blast a game show host introduced his programme with a one-minute silence in respect for the dead; three bunny girls stood with their heads bowed.

Italy's grief is genuine. A car bomb in Rome two weeks ago had prepared people for another explosion, but not here in the heart of Florence. It was a deadly and barbaric attack on the soul of Italy. So far, only one group has claimed responsibility, the so-called Armed Phalange. No one knows much about them, apart from the fact that they always claim to have planted a bomb whenever one goes off. The Italian government has pointed the finger at the Mafia. The organization certainly has a motive: most of its known bosses have recently been arrested by the police, thanks to the state witness protection programme which has encouraged repentant *mafiosi* to betray their godfathers. But the Florence bomb didn't bear all the usual hallmarks of *Cosa Nostra*. The organization tends to eliminate its enemies with deadly accuracy. It doesn't go in for terrorism, unless it has changed its strategy. Furthermore, the police now believe that a woman took part in the Rome bombing, which is unusual for the male-dominated Mafia with its Victorian family values; executions are left to the men. None of this rules out the Mafia, of course, but it makes the government's argument, that the bomb was the work of the men of honour, less convincing.

The Italian public certainly isn't convinced. As the rubble was being cleared away at the Uffizi, a demonstration of 40,000 people filed past in the distance through the Piazza della Signoria. What had started out as a rally to commemorate the dead quickly turned into a demonstration against the state. People shouted '*Stato Assassino!*'—the state is the assassin. It sounds like the surreal twist in a Pirandello play, but it isn't. Since the 1960s, there have been a number of bombs in Italy which have never been fully explained. Take the one in the Piazza Fontana in Milan in 1969: it killed 12 people; the trial took 15 years. First a group of right-wing extremists was accused, found guilty, then acquitted after an appeal. Then left-wing extremists were tried and convicted. None of it sounded convincing. Many Italians suspected the dark hand of the secret service, in what became known as the 'strategy of tension': an attempt to block political change by terrorizing society to such an extent that the people, frightened and cowed, would rather stick with the devil they knew.

Bombs as a distraction from the corruption and ineptitude of government? It sounds far-fetched but, in the realm of Italian politics, many things are plausible. For instance, Sicilian investigators have implicated members of the secret service in the assassination of the anti-Mafia judge, Giovanni Falcone, last year in Palermo. One of the detectives on the scene of the Florence blast told reporters: 'I'm sure we're back in the hands of those people who are never caught: the men in the shadows who have done this before but who've never come out into the light. The bastards!' Those men in the shadows have a motive for derailing Italy's democratic revolution: they are being thrown out of power. For decades, politicians like Messrs Craxi, Andreotti and de Mita—the *troika* of former prime ministers accused of corruption, bribery and collusion with the Mafia—were used to the absolute power bestowed upon them by the rigid structure of Italian politics. Now they are losing it. Few expect them to go without a fight. It is too libellous to suggest, and too difficult to prove, any direct link between these men and the bomb that peppered the Uffizi; but this is what thousands of Italians believe. However, this time the bombs are unlikely to drive them back to the old guard, who have been discredited and declared unfit for power.

THE GALICIAN CONNECTION

PETER GODWIN   SANTIAGO DE COMPOSTELA   29
MAY 1993

The biggest drugs trial in Spain's history opens later this
summer. The case concerns cocaine smuggling along the coast
of the rural and remote region of Galicia, an area now favoured
by Colombian cocaine barons, whose operations threaten to ruin
the local economy.

ON THE NORTH-WEST tip of Spain, the bit just above Portugal, lies
Galicia. It is the westernmost part of continental Europe, extending to
Cape Finisterre—the legendary end of the earth beyond which, mariners
once believed, you simply sailed over the edge into the great abyss.
Because of its rainfall (apparently it is the wettest place in Europe outside
western Ireland) Galicia is well away from mass tourist routes. It is also
refreshingly free of Spanish Costa del clichés: in Galicia you will see no
bullfights or flamenco dancing; you will hear no castanets and drink no
sherry. It is a rural idyll: fewer than three million people with plenty of
room, small, user-friendly cities, granite-walled, medieval fishing towns
nestling around some of the best natural harbours in the world. Indeed, it
is altogether a most improbable candidate for western Europe's principal
entry point for cocaine. But this is what it is.

   The Galicians have always been consummate smugglers. Grain,
alcohol, arms and tobacco have all, in their day, been landed on the
isolated coves and inlets along the Galician coast; now it is cocaine. The
Colombian drug barons had been salivating at the prospect of a European

Community without internal borders; get into one, and you are effectively into them all. In the Galicians they found the perfect *entrée*; and so a lucrative alliance was formed.

Most of the cocaine comes across in ocean-going ships which anchor 50 miles or more offshore. Speed boats or fishing trawlers ferry it to the coast; they have a more than sporting chance of getting through. Consider the arithmetic for a moment: a rugged coastline some 700 miles long; a Galician fishing fleet of about 8,500 vessels, of all shapes and sizes; and, to police all this, just seven customs launches. The odds are pretty good.

The cocaine bonanza is transforming gentle, rural Galicia. Official statistics confirm its place as one of the poorest regions of Spain; yet the salesman for Mercedes-Benz will tell you that more of their cars are sold here than anywhere else in the country. But long-term damage is being done to the local economy. Take the case of Andrés: he is a mussel farmer. He has eight floating platforms anchored out in the bay of Illa de Arousa. Every year, he and his men go on long expeditions along the coast collecting baby mussels. They bring them back and attach them to long ropes, which are suspended from platforms into the sea. In time, Andrés hauls up the ropes and harvests the mature mussels; then the whole laborious process begins again. If you have eaten mussels, the chances are that you have already tasted those from Galicia; half of Europe's production comes from here. But the industry is deep trouble: the local drug barons have moved in, prices have plummeted, and honest operators like Andrés are being forced out. Andrés estimates that a third of the mussel business in Galicia is now controlled by the barons.

It is an everyday story of money laundering. The drug barons, *los gordos*, or 'the fat ones' as they are called here, have been buying up businesses left, right and centre: hotels, restaurants, fishing fleets, vineyards, mussel farms, whatever they can get their hands on. The businesses don't have to make money themselves; that is not the point: they just have to provide convenient fronts through which to launder drug money. So by running at break-even—or even at a loss—these bent businesses are undercutting honest operators, who are then forced into bankruptcy and have little option but to sell up to the drug barons. The economy has become completely distorted as a result.

The Spanish authorities have had a few, rather ineffectual attempts at closing the Galician connection. Their latest, much-vaunted effort is

'Operation Mago': the arrest of 50 of Galicia's alleged drug barons. The key to the operation is Manolo Padín. He looks as though he's been sent by central casting to play the role of drug trafficker turned supergrass—which is in fact what he is. Heavy stubble, open-necked denim shirt, complete with gold chain nestling in exposed chest. His Ray-Bans look so permanent, you begin to suspect they have been surgically grafted on to the bridge of his nose. He was a middling cocaine distributor along the Galician coast when one drop went badly wrong. Abandoned by his bosses to an uncertain fate, Padín began singing like the proverbial canary, as they say. Now he is constantly accompanied by armed bodyguards, as he nervously awaits the trial.

The trial of the 50 alleged barons will be the biggest drugs trial Spain has ever seen. But don't hold your breath: a number of those arrested were previously arrested and charged with tobacco smuggling, in a famous case which began in November 1984. According to the records, that case is still pending, nine years later.

AGOSTINI KILLED
MY BUDGIE

ANDY KERSHAW   KIRKMICHAEL   5 JUNE 1993

On the Isle of Man—the tiny tax-haven in the Irish Sea—the annual TT motorcycle races get under way in June. The event is controversial because it is thought that the course is too dangerous for the modern, powerful machines that take part, and over the years several riders have lost their lives. But for the motorcycle fanatics, it has a special appeal.

THE OLD LADY was taking the sunshine on the doorstep of her whitewashed cottage, just along from the butcher's. 'Good afternoon,' she said. 'Grand day for practice.' Her two-year-old great-grandson jabbed his finger into the hot engine of my motorcycle. 'Bike! Bike!' he shouted. At this hour of the day, Kirkmichael is a sleepy, picture-postcard village (you wouldn't be surprised to meet the cast of *Trumpton* in the post office). But by late afternoon the street outside the cottage that Mrs Keggan has occupied these last 47 years becomes part of the most dramatic motorcycle road-racing circuit in the world: the last truly white-knuckle spectacle in motor sport.

The Isle of Man Tourist Trophy Races have been run on the 37-mile mountain course since 1911. They began here to avoid mainland restrictions on the closing of public roads for motor racing. That first race, on unsurfaced roads, was won at an average speed of 47 mph. A bend on Snaefell Mountain, known to this day as Keppel Gate and now a fast left-hander, is so named because there was a gate there; in the early days of TT racing, the leading rider was obliged to dismount from his spindly machine and open it; and it was the duty of the luckless rider at the back of the field to get off and close the gate behind him.

Top riders in the event of race week, the six-lap Formula One, will be averaging 122 mph, fickle Manx weather permitting; and TT fans are hoping, this year, that they will see the first 125 mph lap of the island. Some corners on the course—there are so many no one can agree on the precise number—are taken at little more than walking pace. So, to be lapping at nearly 125 mph, riders are dashing through other sections—between dry-stone walls, trees, bus-shelters and lamp-posts—at a shattering speed. Coming down Kirkmichael High Street this afternoon, past the butcher's, the parish church, Quayle's the grocers and, of course, Mrs Keggan's front door, the 750cc hi-tech Formula One bikes will be touching 170 mph.

It is the sort of disruption that proud villagers in other parts of the British Isles wouldn't tolerate. But most Manx people are irredeemable race fans. Not only do they recognize their world-famous motorcycle races as part of the island's heritage, they also value the annual boost that 50,000 spectators bring to the otherwise depressed tourist industry. Many of the hotels along Douglas's splendid Edwardian seafront are boarded up; sorry monuments to the cheap package-holiday boom of the late 1960s from which Manx tourism has never recovered. And though the island needs as many visitors as it can attract, the closure of so many hotels creates an accommodation crisis during TT fortnight. I have already re-booked my ferry crossing and cottage in Kirkmichael for next year.

Park View Cottage, the Kershaw billet, is a race fan's dream, particularly for the early morning practice sessions which start at 5 am. I need only push my bed to the bay window, switch on the Manx Radio commentary, and plump up my pillows, to watch the bikes howl through Birkin's Bends—an ultra-quick right-and left-hander at the exit of the village where the faster riders, using every inch of the road, brush their shoulders against the ivy-covered wall at 140 mph. Birkin's commemorates Sir Tim Birkin, a racer who died at this spot in 1927 after colliding with a fish truck. In those days they didn't bother to close the roads to ordinary traffic during practice.

More than 150 riders have lost their lives on the mountain course since 1911: this grim tally has led to the occasional media outcry; a boycott by several top riders in the 1970s; and the loss of Grand Prix

World Championship status 16 years ago. The nine-times winner, Steve Hislop, and the current lap record-holder, Carl Fogarty, are not taking part this year. Neither has anything left to prove on the Isle of Man; Hislop—though careful not to condemn the TT outright—admits, with characteristic humility, that it was getting too fast for his liking. Two years ago, when he was clocked along the bumpy Sulby straight at nearly 200 mph, he described the experience of rushing between the hedgerows as 'aiming at the piece of light between the green bits'. It was difficult at that speed, he said, to see where he was going. Still, he has not ruled out the possibility of returning to the TT in the future.

The TT races are an anachronism. And they are, undeniably, very dangerous. Falling off a bike at Donnington Park, a rider will slide across the grass and land in a sand trap. On the Isle of Man, a competitor making a similar mistake would be lucky not to hit a gable-end or a telephone box. But there is one overpowering argument against banning the TT: people race here because they want to; nobody makes them do it. Alan Batson, a carpet-fitter from Aylesbury and a contender for a rostrum place, embodies the easy-going enthusiasm that sets the TT apart from the corporate self-importance of Grand Prix racing. 'The more you enjoy it,' he says, 'the faster you go.'

The second-largest TT entry in history—530 riders from 18 countries, including five women and a 61-year-old grandfather—are flinging themselves around the island for the same reason that brought a young New Zealander, Michael Willemsen, to race here for the first time this week. He is going well, coping cheerfully with the biggest challenge of the TT: memorizing the wriggling sequence of countless blind bends. 'Michael, why do you do it?' I asked him in the pub after his first practice session. 'It's costing you a fortune, there are no championship points, and tomorrow you might be killed.'

He looked at me, still wide-eyed from his first practice session that afternoon. 'I love it,' he smiled. 'I've always wanted to race here, and now I'm doing it.'

But some TT fatalities have had no say in the matter. As I turned to leave her at her cottage door, Mrs Keggan seized my forearm. The first riders were just leaving Douglas, 14 miles away, and Kirkmichael was waiting, as quiet as the grave. 'Agostini was always my favourite,' she said, referring to the magnificent Italian MV Agusta rider of the 1960s. 'But then he killed my budgie.' For once I was lost for words. 'Y'see, his bike was so loud,' she explained, 'when he came down the street, the budgie had a heart attack and dropped dead. I've got another one now,' she added, and nodded at a nervous-looking bird in the cottage window.

'What chance do you give him?' I asked, trying not to laugh.

'Oh, he'll be all right,' she said. 'The bikes aren't as noisy these days.'

EASTERN EUROPE

A WEEKEND IN THE COUNTRY

KEVIN CONNOLLY   MOSCOW   3 SEPTEMBER 1992

The dacha *is the much-coveted country residence that many Russians either own or wish they owned. But beneath the romanticized images of rural life lies a harsher, colder reality.*

IT CAN BE anything from a palace with a grand piano in the bathroom to a haphazardly built potting shed under the screaming flight-path of an international airport, but the *dacha* occupies a special place in the hearts of all Russians. Most Muscovites, if they don't actually own one, at least know someone who does. The roads out of the city on Friday nights are jammed with weekending families, squabbling in small cars carrying the family kayak on the roof or the neighbour's Great Dane on the front seat.

Even pleasure here can be a miserable experience. Many *dachas* have no water or electricity, and most seem to be in constant need of repair. As a guest, you might spend Saturday pulling tenacious weeds out of the sticky soil of the vegetable patch which will help to feed the family during the coming winter. But that still leaves Sunday for the glazing, bricklaying, sawing, plumbing, digging and concrete mixing which fill the rest of your relaxing break. The dreamers, though, dream of building their own stately *dacha* from scratch, rather than attempting to slow down the decline of whatever they have inherited.

One Russian friend of mine is doing exactly that, having negotiated his way through the obstacle course of regulations and paperwork which leads to the ownership of a suitable patch of land. He is doing the building work himself in his free time, living in a caravan while the weekend dream-home takes shape beside him. Building materials are acquired, like everything else here, through a network of contacts; there are no normal shops, no sub-contractors, no safety rules. The *dacha* is slowly taking shape just north of Moscow, on the St Petersburg road, in one of the wealthiest and most sophisticated parts of Russia. But when the 'great accident'—as he likes to call it—happened, he found himself caught in the frightening chaos which lurks just below the surface of all Russian life.

A tar lorry, which he was guiding in his own car to the building site, suddenly disappeared from the rear-view mirror, to be replaced by a sheet of flame and a column of black smoke. He returned, fearing the worst, and found it: a traffic accident which might almost have been designed to illustrate life in modern Russia. A tractor driver, using the only vehicle available to collect illegally distilled vodka from the nearby house of a friend, had collided with the lorry which, itself, had been quietly 'borrowed' for the weekend from the government department which owns it. My friend, now parked beside the truck, wasted no time in contemplating the powerful symbolic force of the story; collecting that much tar here is like gathering a bucket of fairy tears. So he climbed on to the burning lorry and tried to kick shut a valve through which the boiling tar was escaping.

He can't remember much of what happened next. When he came to, the rest of the cast of the drama had vanished; he was alone, with third-degree burns to one leg and badly damaged trousers.

Somehow he struggled back to his caravan and to the villagers among whom he has lived for years. Their average age is about 80; no one has a 'phone; and no one was able to make the 1½-mile walk to the main road to get help. He lay in the caravan for a week, in pain that can only be guessed at, with the burns untreated and a fever raging. After two or three days (he is not sure), the neighbours finally went into action: one of them brought him a bag of tomatoes. At this point his temperature was around 40°C, and you could have cooked them on his forehead. But it wasn't until the end of the week that someone thought of fashioning him a walking stick so that he could struggle through the woods to the main road.

It is hard to explain their attitude: partly peasant resignation in the face of death, partly Russian poverty of expectations. However low my friend's expectations might have dropped by this point, they were still doomed to disappointment. He must, it is true, have cut a rather unusual figure at the roadside: a week's growth of beard, an obviously home-made crutch, and a sort of makeshift kilt replacing his trousers, which he hadn't been able to pull on over his appalling injuries. But whatever the reason, it was hours before someone stopped and took him to the local hospital, which promptly refused him admission on the grounds that he came from Moscow, and should return there for treatment. A sympathetic doctor (rather a rarity here) overruled that decision and, eventually, he did have a graft operation.

He awoke—in a pool of what he assumed to be his own blood—to be assured that the operation had been a success; although aftercare Russian-style is more traumatic than accidents in most other places.

We were refused permission to see him at first; then we were left hanging about for what seemed like an eternity while someone who had promised to call him didn't; and finally we were kicked out of a cafeteria where we had bumped into him, on the unlikely grounds that an operation was about to take place in the next room. The hospital, with patients in grubby robes drifting around overgrown gardens, a cratered approach road, and cracked windows, looked like a B-movie mental asylum. The friendlier members of staff were like prison guards and the atmosphere crackled with suppressed ill-humour, rather like the house of married friends who were rowing just before you arrived.

In spite of all that, he is making a full recovery. But this is a very Russian tale: we were surprised that, so close to the capital, it was possible to be swallowed up in such frightening chaos; and he was surprised at our surprise. A neat illustration of the truth that, while Russians may be offhand with foreigners almost all the time, you can bet that they are being much nastier to each other.

ROMANIA—AVOIDING THE BALKAN NIGHTMARE

MISHA GLENNY   BUCHAREST   1 OCTOBER 1992

In Romania, legislative and presidential elections were held in the autumn of 1992. President Ion Iliescu was elected for a second term of office, and his National Salvation Front was the largest party in parliament. Whatever else can be said about the complexities of Romanian politics—and they are many—the country had at least managed to avoid the fratricidal nightmares of the former Yugoslavia.

NO OTHER EAST European city projects as much faded glory as Bucharest. Balkan grime has turned the colourful variety of buildings along its once majestic boulevards into a sandy, grey uniformity. The plaster is so cracked that it is sometimes hard to discern whether a building has been scarred by the many angry, desperate bullets fired during the fall of Ceausescu, or by one of southern Romania's periodic earthquakes, or more simply—and more likely—by decades of neglect and disrepair. Whatever the cause, only the slightest hint of Bucharest's fabled renaissance during the 1920s and '30s, as the Paris of the Balkans, remains. But even if Olivia Manning sometimes appeared to exaggerate its majesty in her memorable *Balkan Trilogy*, glorious it once was.

So comprehensive was the spiritual destruction wrought by Nicolae Ceausescu on the Romanian people and the country's minorities, that it will take many decades of searching into the Romanian soul before we can expect these battered peoples to be at peace with themselves. But for the moment, when Romanians are happy, they are ecstatic; when they are sad, they are apocalyptically miserable. It is a sort of collective manic depression.

Both aspects of the national psyche were on full display last Sunday night as the outcome of the Romanian elections became clear. At the headquarters of Romania's opposition movement, the Democratic Convention, two women were in tears and three men were slumped wearily around a large, oval table. At its head, an indefatigable preacher of politics expounded, more in sorrow than in anger, about why the Convention's presidential candidate, Emil Constantinescu, had failed so spectacularly to realize the opposition's euphoric pre-election hopes of removing Ion Iliescu from the Romanian presidency. You could smell and taste the despair around the room as if it were a rich, gooey treacle. 'It's time for me to leave Romania now,' said one young opposition supporter; and he went on to add, 'The most terrible things will begin again here.'

In a quieter room, the mild-mannered, dapper academic, Mr Constantinescu, was putting a brave if deeply unconvincing face on the result. 'We will have to work very hard to prepare for the second round. But we can still win,' he claimed. Very hard indeed! Instead of approaching 50 per cent of the popular vote after the first round, Constantinescu was able to muster only around 30 per cent. To prevent Mr Iliescu scoring the extra $2\frac{1}{2}$ per cent which he requires to reach 50 per cent, and thus to be confirmed as president on 11 October, Constantinescu will need more than hard work—he must hope for divine intervention.

Beaming, bustling and business-like, President Ion Iliescu could barely contain his excitement. 'I knew it,' he boomed confidently. 'This result confirms everything that I was beginning to feel during the last two weeks of the campaign.' It was almost as if, paradoxically, he too had begun to believe the opposition's claims of impending victory. Gathered around Iliescu are his apparatchiks—the rocks upon whom his foundation is built; their rough, fresh features and occasional grammatical errors indicate that most are first-generation intellectuals, who have sprung the confines of their peasant or worker origins. The contrast with the craggy, more sceptical faces of the liberals at the opposition headquarters tells its own story.

How long will it be before Romania's peasants and intellectuals will be able to sit down at the same table without a bitter argument breaking out?

It is very hard to know. Certainly the fear among opposition leaders now is that Iliescu will unleash a wave of retribution against them for daring to challenge him. And who can forget the President's vocal support for the disgraceful, fascistoid mob of miners who terrorized Bucharest's innocent population in June 1990?

The problem for the opposition is that, as this second democratic election indicates, Iliescu does have by far the most substantial political constituency in the country. And although, over the past two years, intimidation and vague threats by Iliescu's establishment have played a role in this delicate democracy, it sometimes seems as though the opposition will be able to win only if the Romanian people is dissolved and a new one elected in its place. But I think the opposition should not be too dispirited. Romanians, often dismissed as gullible, made one thing perfectly clear at the ballot box this time around: the nutty Romanian nationalists, who would drag the country into a reprise of Yugoslavia, were soundly beaten. And for that alone, Romania can be proud of itself.

AN AIRPORT FOR
THE NEW EUROPE

KEVIN CONNOLLY   SUKHUMI   15 OCTOBER 1992

*In the October 1992 elections in the former Soviet Republic
of Georgia, Eduard Shevardnadze was given a convincing
mandate to continue his leadership of the country. The former
Soviet Foreign Minister said the load which he had taken upon
himself was the heaviest ever. Since mid-August, separatists in
the province of Abkhazia had been engaged in conflict with
Georgian forces who were sent in to root out supporters of
Zviad Gamsakhurdia, the ousted president. In the capital,
Sukhumi, there was increasing desperation among those trying
to flee the violence.*

ON THE SHORES of the Black Sea, where the water gleams like polished
iron and the rich land is edged with sand the colour of stripped
pine, Sukhumi airport—bomb-damaged, blacked-out and swamped with
refugees—offers regular flights out of the new Europe. Daylight dwindles
through soft dusk to warm, inky darkness in early autumn, and you hear
the incoming aircraft long before you can see them. Sometimes it is the
dull whine of a Soviet jet which swells briefly into a screaming roar as
the landing-lights pick out the runway and the pilot reverses thrust to
slow the plane to a halt. More often it is the grating, pulsating beat
of helicopter rotors as civilian choppers, adorned with hastily painted
red crosses, hover briefly over their landing points. The new markings
don't stop the loaders packing on bombs in wooden cases and boxes of
grenades, but there is a brutal fairness about the new order in this part of

the world: there is not much chance that they would stop anyone firing on the flights either. They are refuelled wherever they come to rest; the harsh smell of aviation fuel is sour against the faint, sweet scent of the late seaside flowers.

There are no waiting rooms, no departure lounges, no tickets, no timetable. There is no departures board either: the only place to go is out, the only time to go is now. The refugees wait in a miserable crowd, as close as they dare to the point where the taxi-ing plane will stop, then move forward in a ragged wave to surround it. Few of them will ever know more desperate moments. It is impossible to find anyone who is in charge, but heart-breakingly easy to find a drunken soldier or an airline official, at the limit of his patience, who thinks he is. They will promise places on every flight, offering a sudden burst of hope which slowly drains away with the realization that there are five promises, and five passengers, for every seat. The hopeless appeals to reason or charity are still shouted, though. Even people ready to flee their homes, and everything inside them, are desperate to believe that kind of authority, and will keep some sort of reason and order until the last possible moment. Sometimes you will see a child pushed forward, its parents, resigned to their own failure, reasoning that if they must stay behind, at least their son or daughter must have a chance to leave.

For those who do get on the planes there is a moment of silent relief, but often there are also quiet tears. This is the first moment when they are free to dwell on the homes they have abandoned, and the uncertain life to which they are running. Everyone carries a single bag, usually a cheap cardboard suitcase, sometimes just a plastic carrier bag. All carry however much of their lives they were able to cram in at a few hours' notice. The optimists bring food, just enough to keep themselves and their children for a few days; they hope they will soon be back. Others carry rolled-up oil-paintings, treasured ornaments and family Bibles. They, at least, don't believe they will be home any time soon. Many are too old to be thinking of finding new houses to turn into homes, and old enough to realize that, in a Georgia ruined in the economic hurricane that followed the Soviet collapse, new houses will be hard to find anyway. Some of the bags are stuffed with soft toys, but most of the young children are too dazed to reach for the comfort they offer. The first time you see your parents frightened is the first time you realize how frightening a place the world can be.

As long as the planes are on the ground there is a chance that you will lose your seat to someone with better contacts in high places; but the fierce arguments between nervous armed guards and weary flight crews are watched with only a kind of helpless resignation. There is a point at which tiredness can even make it hard to go on being afraid. There are no runway lights to guide the pilot out along the runway that leads into a narrow flight-path between the mountains and the sea. The plane, laden with 100 extra passengers, most of them standing, labours into the air. The backwash from its jets blows leaflets of support, ripped from incoming humanitarian aid packages, into a brief, tattered blizzard.

There were as many soldiers as women and children on the flight we caught; some were frightened by their first, brief experience of war; most were frightened only by what they had heard from their friends. Here and there you would see the empty eyes, the exhausted faces of men who have been in battle and been overwhelmed by it. But more often these were troops, in crisply pressed battledress with polished weapons, leaving a city which their government was pledging to defend. They were not running away, they insisted, but in the confusion of the first days of war there was no one to order them to stay.

They, and the refugees with them, have been badly served by a government which has talked up the level of violence to explain its own failure to put down a small, separatist rising. Abkhazians are a minority even in Abkhazia, but they are starting to get the backing of units of the Russian army left over when the high tide of Soviet power began to recede. Some of the officers are determined to destabilize new countries like Georgia in which, they are angry to find, they have become foreigners. Their men often fight simply for money.

Generating the climate of fear which has created these refugees was easy for the government in Tbilisi, even before the fighting began. This is a land in which rumours appear with the same speed as the automatic weapons and combat fatigues which many politicians now sport at every opportunity. Ending the fighting, calming the atmosphere and persuading these people to return to their homes to rebuild their ruined economy will be much more difficult. For the moment, this is just one more area of obscure hatreds and rivalries, where the settling of ancient scores is more important than the solving of contemporary problems.

THE WORLD'S LEAST FAVOURITE AIRLINE

KEVIN CONNOLLY   MOSCOW   22 OCTOBER 1992

As the Soviet Union has broken up, and its assets have been divided, or squabbled over, by the individual republics, the national airline, Aeroflot, has not been spared this fate. Aeroflot once symbolized the prestige and authority of the former superpower, but even then things were not all they seemed.

IN A COUNTRY where most superlatives were sad—oldest and coldest, lowest and slowest—it was something to be proud of. Aeroflot was just the biggest airline there ever was. It carried more people over longer distances, to more airports, in more aeroplanes than anyone else, spinning the invisible web that held a vast land together. Of course it had more crashes too; but this is not travel as you live it in Western advertizing with its gentle stewardesses, calm, grey-haired pilots and thoughtfully arranged cheese boards. This is travel in a country where you might find an escaped budgerigar flying around in the cabin, a pool table wrapped in brown paper brought on as hand baggage, or even a fellow passenger spending an entire journey perched on your lap because you've both been allocated the same seat. When that happened to me, I remonstrated with a uniformed man strolling unconcernedly past us down the aisle to the toilets at the back. 'Could you tell the pilot?' I asked.

'I am the pilot,' he said.

But foreigners were, in truth, spared most of the worst indignities of the system by a bizarre process of benign apartheid which kept us apart from the travelling Soviet masses. That did not, of course, mean that we enjoyed good service; rather that we got the grim impersonality all to ourselves. Somewhere in almost every airport in the Soviet Union was a room set aside for foreigners to check in; sometimes it was a many-columned room, rich in mosaics recalling the labours of farm worker and factory hand, alongside the efforts of pilot and flight engineer. Mostly, though, it was a shabby, overcrowded office decorated with a dog-eared poster recalling the grand old days before the aeroplanes started to look as though they were being repainted by hand, and the staff had acquired the demeanour of concentration-camp guards asked, at short notice, to work on their day off. Whatever miserable comfort there was, we had. But there is no feeling like the sense of outraged reason which sweeps over you when you are sitting, ravenously hungry, in front of a buffet that is due to open ten minutes after the only flight of the day is due to take off. And there is no uncertainty quite like the nagging sense of doubt which slowly erodes your pleasure in occupying the only decent room in the airport, as time slips away and you wonder, uneasily, if you haven't simply been forgotten. The line, inside all of us, which divides the casual international traveller from the child whose parents haven't turned up to collect it from school, is not as clear as you might think.

But outside our waiting rooms seethed a hell of numbed and sobbing children, blank-faced mothers and gravel-voiced, bawling, airline officials. Almost every airport in the country looked as though it was permanently in the grip of a refugee crisis, with young soldiers slumped in the sleep of exhaustion wherever they could find room to lie, and jostling, shouting crowds gathering around anyone who appeared to know anything about any flight that might be leaving. Even when you finally made it down to the pens from which you were marched out to the planes, you still couldn't afford to relax. Even Aeroflot officials often had only a hazy notion of how well the number of passengers would match up with the number of seats. Frequent fliers mastered a kind of furtive run which allowed you to look as though you were striding unconcernedly towards the aircraft while in fact racing desperately to stay ahead of the pack. On board, the passengers divided naturally into two groups. Not, of course, first class and economy: the Soviet Union was a communist state and reserved such sordid, artificial divisions based on wealth for the airline's international flights, where it thought it might make some money out of them. No, the real division on board was between those passengers who thought they had been allocated a particular seat and those who had been told to sit anywhere they liked. It is by such simple means that real chaos is produced. No flight was complete without at least one operatic argument between a passenger who had thought for months that he was guaranteed, say, seat 7C and someone who had sat down in it, casually having bought his ticket a few minutes before. You were unwise, though, if you were the unlucky one left standing, to press the argument too far; there was always the danger that if you carried on for too long you might find all the other seats full as well. Better to sit down in someone else's seat and thus pass the problem on to him. Even if there was the odd passenger left over at the end of this undignified process, all was not lost. A judicious use of wheedling, threatening, pleading and bribing was often enough to secure you standing room, a seat in the toilet or even—if you were very lucky, very persuasive or very rich—a place in the cockpit behind the flight crew.

But foreigners never quite mastered the lifestyle skills bred in the bone of our Soviet hosts. I once bought a seat in the cramped toilet at the back of a plane, on a six-hour flight to Moscow. I had settled back, as much as one can in an aeroplane toilet, and begun to read when there was a desperate knocking on the door. I opened it, cautiously, to find a formidable-looking woman who had been among the other standing passengers, holding the hand of a small child. 'I'm sorry,' she said, 'he's just desperate to use the toilet.' Courteously, I rose into a kind of polite stoop and inched my way around them in the doorway. The door slammed shut; I didn't see either of them again until the plane touched down in Moscow.

That was a long-haul flight; long enough to ensure that those fortunate passengers with more conventional seating would be offered a meal. No point here, though, to pleasant, idle speculation about what sort of meal you might be going to get which helps to while away the hours on more luxurious airlines. On Aeroflot it was always chicken, with the only possibility of variety being in the various stages of its life-cycle at which it might be served; from eggs, boiled to the consistency of riot bullets, to scrawny, skinny old boilers that might have been killed holding their breath. What never varied was the ill grace, bordering on hostility, with which it was served. This was an airline run for the convenience of the staff, who openly resented anything which interrupted their flight. The only sure way to rouse them was to rise to your feet before the crew had left the plane at the end of the flight. You were supposed to stay seated until the pilot and his team had marched down the aisle with the uniformed swagger of an occupying army. I never looked in the cockpit to see if they left anyone behind minding the shop; but Aeroflot suffered a rash of on-the-ground hijackings at the end of the 1980s, which suggests that perhaps they did not.

And yet, for all its inadequacies, somehow I miss it. Aeroflot has been broken up now, like so much else here, and its fleet has provided the planes for the airlines of the new republics, struggling to life in the ruins of the old Soviet Union. Still its standards live on; I recently caught a plane designed for 165 passengers which was carrying more than 280. I miss Aeroflot most when I'm back in the West, where the experience of flying is marked by what now seems to me a level of concern about safety which is positively disconcerting. Is that seat-back entirely upright? that table folded away securely enough? that hand-baggage fully under the seat in front? It is all designed, of course, to make you feel safe and, to a certain extent, I suppose it does. But I feel safer still knowing that an airline can break the rules, ignore them or not even know of their existence, and still, somehow, survive.

REQUIEM FOR CZECHOSLOVAKIA

MISHA GLENNY   MARTIN   22 OCTOBER 1992

In October 1992, Czechoslovakia celebrated its foundation for the seventy-fourth and last time. Following elections in June, the politicians of the Czechlands and Slovakia decided—for good or ill—to end the federation and to form two independent states in its stead; this, in spite of a majority of the population in both republics being in favour of maintaining a single, unitary state.

UTTERING THE NAME Martin in Prague provokes the same reaction among people in the Czech capital as would a stranger entering a saloon in the American Wild West. There is a dramatic silence, broken, perhaps, only by a coin dropping or an audible gulp from the less courageous present. 'What d'ye want to go to Martin for?' my friends would repeat under a raised eyebrow. Martin is reputed, among Czechs, to be the great fortress of militant Slovak nationalism. It is also here that, despite pressure from Prague, the United States and some West European countries, the local heavy machine engineering complex has been completing an order of tanks bound for Syria. All in all, it would seem that Martin represents the antithesis of all that those who participated in Prague's user-friendly revolution of 1989 had struggled for.

Needless to say, all those who warned me against the demons inhabiting this town in north-western Slovakia had never been there. It is set on a flat plain, surrounded by hills on either side. The day I drove into town there

was no wind, so the motionless wisps of cloud created the illusion of a
Hollywood film backdrop. I felt neither welcome nor happy—sentiments
which were underlined by the initial suspicion with which I was greeted
by managers at the factory. They assumed that I was there to write
another sensational story about the Slovak arms industry. When we began
discussing the topic I was interested in (which was, what effect the
break-up of Czechoslovakia would have on Slovakia and its industry),
they dropped their guard. It was a catastrophe, they said, thought up by
politicians in both the Czech and Slovak republics for their own political
ends. The overall impression they gave was that the end of the federation
would accelerate the collapse of the factory. If this was militant Slovak
nationalism, I was beginning to like it. When discussing the future, the
deputy director hung his head. 'The whole town lives off this factory
and, if it goes, there is nothing left for Martin.'

The gritty realism of the factory stood in stark contrast to the bureaucratic
excitement which has been generated a mile away, atop a hill. Martin
was where Matica Slovenska, the main motor of the Slovak national
awakening, was founded at the end of the last century. What looks like
a small, modern hospital houses dozens of administrators, librarians,
academics and secretaries, whose main function in life is to uncover the
mysterious minutiae of the Slovak soul. These men and women seem to
wear a slight smile stuck like glue to their faces. The drug which induces
this mild euphoria is the prospect of an independent Slovak state, the
goal which they thought would never be realized. Taken for too long,
this toxin not only prevents rational decision-making, it also seems to
dull the faculties assessing the profound problems of those people who
will have to live in an independent Slovak state—ordinary Slovaks.

For the division of Czechoslovakia is a preposterous affair. Although
the Czechs and Slovaks do come from different historical traditions,
they have extracted tremendous gains from one another—economically
and culturally—during their association over 74 years. Unlike the Serbs
and Croats, theirs is not a history stained by blood, but by respect
and mutual assistance. According to all opinion polls, a majority in
both republics does not want the common state to collapse (although
the same surveys say they are resigned to its collapse). Yet it is being
sacrificed to extremes. One is the ruthless obsession with the free-market
economy cradled jealously by Vaclav Klaus, the Czech Prime Minister,
whose steely grimace puts one in mind of Blofeld, James Bond's arch

enemy. The other is the ill-disguised lust for power nurtured by the pudgy features of Slovakia's Prime Minister, Vladimir Meciar.

Already recriminations and bitterness are clouding the relationship between these two peoples whose democratic traditions during the inter-war years were the envy of the neighbouring peoples of Eastern and Central Europe. The break-up of the federation on 31 December represents a sad, dirty little end to a state which has earned better.

The great victims of the collapse will be ordinary Slovaks—hard-working men and women from places like Martin—whose economic future is in serious doubt. Surrounded by relatively powerful states, notably the Czech Republic and Hungary—both increasingly drawn into a German sphere of influence—Slovakia will have enormous difficulties overcoming its various historical complexes. The division of Czechoslovakia represents an unnecessary destabilization of Central Europe; but even sadder than that, nobody, except for a few committed Czechoslovaks—almost all of them over 50—seems to care.

SPITAK—A BITTER PLACE OF REFUGE

KEVIN CONNOLLY   SPITAK   10 DECEMBER 1992

October 1992 was the fourth anniversary of the 1988 Armenian earthquake in which 25,000 people died. The anniversary passed with little public ceremony. For those who survived, there is little prospect of life returning to normal.

IT DOES NOT take long for Maria Gellarian to show you round her home; converted freight trailers are not as big as they look from the outside. There is not much to see, either: just a little bedding and a pile of clothes, and not enough of either to keep her two children warm. If you want to see the photographs of her nephews who died in the earthquake, you have to go back out into the street; there is not enough light inside and, she tells you apologetically, the sour air from the wood-burning stove takes a bit of getting used to. The smudgy black-and-white prints are creased and worn (she takes them out almost every day) and, almost every day, her eyes still fill with tears at the sight. They were seven and nine years old. No one knows how long it took them to die when their apartment building collapsed with them inside it, the day the earthquake tore Spitak apart.

People describe the violence as the earth began to shake and the dull, muffled roar of the falling buildings; but one or two remember more clearly the silence afterwards—it can't have been more than a fraction of a second—before the first screams and cries for help came from the rubble. Maria did not live in Spitak then. She came here later—a refugee from the war in Nagorno-Karabakh for whom this devastated town, where the grief still seems to hang in the cold air, was a place of safety. From the high ground of the graveyard, where most of the earthquake victims are buried, you can see how the tidal wave of destruction swept through Spitak, laying waste to half the town. But your eyes keep wandering back to the polished, black-marble gravestones that bear the faces of the victims.

The winds that whip across Spitak are raw with an edge of dampness from the stinging snow; but on the day of the anniversary there was someone at every grave, pressing his or her face, wet with tears, against the pictures of the children, the brothers and the sisters who were lost. The process of etching the faces of the dead into the headstones somehow ages them; children look like teenagers, 20-year-old women are middle-aged. It is hard work in the deep, soft snow going up the steep hillside to where Maria's nephews are buried, but it is worth the walk. Their faces are bright and cheerful. Their parents felt that was how it should be. They had never seemed solemn in life, so there was no reason why they should seem so in death. They left behind them enough solemn faces. They are exchanging roguish grins, much, you can't help thinking, as they might have been in the seconds before the earthquake first buried them.

You can still see where the building in which they died once stood. One day it may even be rebuilt. The local authorities had tried to persuade people that it would be better to move the town, but without being able to explain why. Families who had lost their homes wanted, at least, to be able to live again where they had always lived. For the moment, anyway, it doesn't matter very much where they want the new buildings to stand. In Spitak nothing is being done. When I arrived, the building sites were so quiet I thought they must be at a standstill, as a mark of respect for the dead. But some have been silent for two years; the cranes that rear above the frames of housing blocks, not even one-quarter finished, are rusting where they stand. When the Soviet Union collapsed, the building gangs from other republics simply went home; they must have left suddenly, with work still in hand, almost as though they were knocking off for lunch. The Armenians cannot finish the work themselves because the entire economy, crippled by blockade, has ground to a halt. There are no building materials, and there wouldn't be enough fuel to transport them here even if there were.

Most days, Spitak gets about two hours of electricity. It has no heating fuel and there is never enough food. For a tiny handful there is black market petrol: half a tankful of a watered-down petrol-and-diesel mixture goes for about two months' ordinary wages; not that that seems a particularly appropriate way to measure cost, in a town where unemployment is said to be over 90 per cent. The people of Spitak know that there is no point in hoping for help from the rest of Armenia: the situation there is hardly any better. The capital, Yerevan, which has a population of more than a million, looks at night like a city blacked out in anticipation of a bombing attack. There is so little traffic that people stand chatting in the middle of main roads, allowing the occasional passing car to swerve around them. This time last year, you were taking your life in your hands using pedestrian crossings, even when the lights were in your favour. Schools are closed for the winter; cavernous hotels, built by the Soviets to entertain the hardy tourists who used to come here, are cold and dark. There is little food in the shops and most people can hardly afford to buy what there is.

Armenia's flair for trading is of no use to it now. Its economy was designed by Soviet officials who thought that their system would last for ever, and who laid this country's lines of supply through Georgia, which is itself now in chaos, and Azerbaijan, with which Armenia is fighting a bitter, undeclared war over Nagorno-Karabakh. Now those lines of supply have been cut, and the Armenian economy is dying. Only a small, corrupt, dollar black market flourishes, and the people who run that—like such people all over the world—help only themselves. My hotel might have run out of food and hot water, but the private shop, now run beside the reception desk, could offer a selection of three different malt whiskies.

Nowhere in the post-Soviet world has the experience of independence been more bitter or more hopeless than here. The Armenian earthquake appeal helped to open up the Soviet Union to the West. Moscow's frank admission that it needed help brought aid workers flooding in. The stickers they left behind, advertizing the organizations for which they worked, are still on mirrors and windows in every bar and restaurant in town. But the bars and restaurants now are deserted—symbols that the latest crisis to grip Armenia is a quiet tragedy which will not dominate headlines in a world preoccupied with the problems of Somalia and Yugoslavia. But if nothing is done—if there is no airlift of food and fuel—some foreign relief agencies are warning that more people may die of cold and hunger this winter than were killed in the earthquake.

For Maria Gellarian, shivering in the temporary shelter she now expects to live in for ever, Armenia is sliding back into the Stone Age and has to turn to the outside world for help. 'I just hope,' she said, 'that something will be done. My family has already lost some of its children. What good is our freedom and our independence if they can't grow up to see it?'

RUSSIA'S LINGUISTIC REVOLUTION

BRIDGET KENDALL   MOSCOW   14 JANUARY 1993

*Since the advent of perestroika, and especially since the
collapse of communism and the first moves towards a market
economy in Russia, more and more English and American
words have found their way into the Russian language.*

WALK DOWN ANY of the main streets in Moscow, and you will soon find
the English signs. Both in Latin script and translated into Cyrillic, they
make clumsy new Russian tongue-twisters, many of them monstrously
ugly. 'Night Shop' becomes '*naeet shop*', even though the Russian
translation is quite unmistakable: '*Nochnoi magazin*' in Russian. A new
firm is a *Korporaishn*, even though for years there has been a perfectly
good word which even declines properly in Russian: *korporatsiya*. But
who wants to use Russian words these days, if the goal is to sound modern
and Western? I had it explained to me once: *magazini* are Russian shops,
smelling of dead chickens, with long, anxious queues and bad-tempered
assistants. Whereas *shopi* are the new kiosks that sell Western imported
goods at outrageous prices and of questionable quality. In *shopi* the young
spivs behind the counter will rob you blind, and the exotic liqueurs in
rainbow colours may give you food poisoning.

Some of the new borrowings are false friends. They sound the same,
but they don't quite mean what they do in English. Take *biznes* for
example. It is a common term in Russian, except that it doesn't mean
'business' in our sense of the word. That would be another word, *delo*.
Biznes means shady dealings in back stairways, involving shoddy products

and quick profits all round. Or there is *miting*, another term that has had a lot of use here in the last few years. But it doesn't refer to a nice, calm, everyday meeting between friends or colleagues over a cup of tea. Quite the opposite: *miting* means a political rally with angry slogans and chants, and hundreds of police armed with guns and walkie-talkies, and the possibility of violence. So if you tell a Russian friend that you are going to a *miting*, their reaction will be: 'Oh, I wouldn't risk that, if I were you!'

Many of these new borrowings from English are recent. When I first arrived in Moscow as a journalist three years ago, I still worked in a *kontora* (an office); I used to drive to the Kremlin to attend sessions of the *Verkhovny Soviet* (or Supreme Soviet, as the parliament was called) which in those days was run by a *Predsedatel*, or chairman—Mikhail Gorbachev at that time. Now everyone uses different words. I work in an *ofis*, the parliament is called the *parlAment*, and it is chaired by a *speeker*.

In fact, it was the politicians themselves who first promoted these borrowings to update Russia's fast-changing political lexicon. I well remember looking up in astonishment, the first time I heard Mr Gorbachev dismiss some suggestion from a parliamentary opponent as a *nonsens*; and in the same speech he came out with another foreign borrowing, *feefty-feefty*, to indicate that something hung in the balance. Not that these imported words did Mr Gorbachev any good. One of the main complaints levelled at him by his critics was that he spent too much time abroad talking to foreigners and didn't give enough thought to his own people. After all, it was with reference to President Gorbachev that Soviet politicians first began to drop into their speeches another English word—*impeechment*. Not surprisingly, his successor, President Yeltsin, has tried not to make the same mistake. Boris Yeltsin wants Russians to speak Russian. He even publicly reprimanded one of his ministers for making a speech at the United Nations in English. And he instructed his cabinet to seek out Russian equivalents for any foreign vocabulary needed to explain economic reforms.

Part of the problem is that some foreign words are, to a Russian ear, derogatory, because the communists used them to denounce the degenerate, bourgeois life of the West. *Fesheneblny* and *komfortabelny* do mean 'fashionable' and 'comfortable', but in a rather disapproving way. The other problem is that it is not always easy to find sensible

Russian equivalents for modern Western economic concepts. How do you explain 'public relations' or 'broker' or 'marketing' in Russian? The result can sound quite ridiculous. In Moscow you quite often hear *broker*, or *brokeri* if there are more than one of them; *pablik relaeeshns*, and *markEting* or, even more incongruously, the adjective, *markEtingovy*. No wonder President Yeltsin wants to avoid them if he can.

Quite recently he called in his privatization minister and asked him to stop using the English term to describe the new vouchers being issued to the population so that they can buy shares in Russian industry. *Va-ucher* was such an ugly foreign word, President Yeltsin argued, which would put people off the government's privatization programme. So instead he ordered all government ministers to use that good old Russian word, *chek*. Russian word? *Chek* doesn't sound very Russian to me. And, of course, no one is using it. Go down to the underpass by any metro station and you will find the touts with their cardboard signs that say, quite plainly, that they will buy up *va-ucheri* for 6,000 roubles a piece.

NOT A STEP BACK— STALINGRAD REMEMBERS

KEVIN CONNOLLY   VOLGOGRAD   4 FEBRUARY 1993

In February 1943, German commanders surrendered to the Red Army in the Russian city of Stalingrad, bringing to an end one of the bloodiest battles of the Second World War; it had lasted for 200 days. At one point, Nazi officers were so confident that they sent a telegram announcing victory to the High Command in Berlin. But, against all the odds, the soldiers and civilians held on, even though between them the two sides suffered nearly two million casualties. In the city—now called Volgograd—younger Russians are wondering whether they were told the truth about the cost of their country's great victory.

IT IS NOT cold—not the way it gets cold elsewhere in Russia—but the grating wind, which sweeps across the high ground on the edge of Volgograd, is sharp enough to make you wonder at the miseries that the millions of soldiers who fought here once endured. It is not a good view, but there is a lot of it. The city clings to the banks of the Volga for miles: a miserable ribbon of shabby apartment blocks and factories the size of small towns. The river, bright and grey as steel, cuts through the rich, flat land which stretches as far as you can see through the mist in every direction. It is hard not to look at it all as the soldiers must have done 50 years ago: nowhere to shelter; nowhere to hide; nowhere to run.

The fighting raged for six months and, at one point, the city seemed to have fallen. The Germans had battled their way, room by room and corridor by corridor, through almost every building on the western side of the river. The Russians, after months of ceaseless bombardment, clung on to a handful of burning warehouses and half-destroyed blocks of flats. One German commander even prepared a telegram announcing that the city had been taken; at about the same time, one of the young officers whom he led was writing to his wife: 'Surely, in all the history of war, there has been nothing as terrible as this.'

His wife never saw the letter. It was found—burned and bloodstained— in his pockets by the Russian reinforcements who killed him, as they arrived to relieve the rag-tag army of exhausted soldiers and starving civilians who had fought, for what must have seemed to them an eternity, in unimaginable misery. They had eaten raw fish from the river, poisoned by thousands of corpses and tons of explosives; what bread they had, crumbled in their hands like damp sand. And yet, on what was left of the buildings in which they had fought, their replacements found that they had written slogans of defiance which are still familiar to many young Russians today. 'There is no land for us beyond the Volga,' read one. 'Not a single backward step,' said another.

The stuff of heroic legend—and yet, with Soviet communism as dead now as the other totalitarian system over which it triumphed so bloodily, the old heroic legends are no longer quite enough. The stirring words, 'Not One Step Back', were not simply a last outpouring of defiance from a brave young soldier facing hopeless odds. They were also the title of War-Directive 227, a chilling document written, it is said, by Stalin himself; it made it a crime punishable by death to retreat, or even to seek cover, in battle. The regulation was savagely enforced. Some 13,500 soldiers were tried for offences under that Article during the battle of Stalingrad. Half were executed, the rest transferred to special battalions which were deliberately exposed to enemy fire to help identify gun-positions, or forced to march over minefields—unarmed and under fire—to clear the way for second-wave troops.

For Russians, this new vision of the battle is a bleak one. Are the men who walked so fearlessly towards enemy guns the less heroic because they knew they faced death at the hands of their own commanders for doing anything else? Was their courage wasted by a High Command desperate to show that the Red Army could meet and overcome the Germans head-on?

It is said that Hitler became obsessed with Stalingrad, determined to prove that his forces would not repeat (what he believed to be) the mistake of relieving the pressure on the beleaguered French garrison of Verdun during the First World War. He could have chosen another route to the rich farmland and oilfields in the south; and the Russian generals could have opted for tactics that might have spared their men some of the bloodiest head-on attacks. But they didn't. At the huge and sobering war memorial on the edge of the town, inside a hall of remembrance, a mosaic containing thousands of names is a reminder of what happened because they didn't. You think, at first, that the casualties are not as many as you would expect, even though they stretch—thousands of them—in columns down the wall, all around the building: that is until you realize that they are the Russian casualties from one day's fighting out of six months.

The veterans are unimpressed by revisionism. 'We fought,' one told me, 'like no one else has ever fought before or since. We always respected the Germans and, after Stalingrad, they respected us, too. Since the end of the old system, they've robbed pensioners and veterans of any chance of a decent future. Now they want to rob us of our past as well.'

LEST WE SHOULD FORGET

JULIAN BORGER   WARSAW   15 APRIL 1993

1993 marked the 50th anniversary of the Warsaw Ghetto Uprising. Although only a few hundred Jews were left alive there, they mounted a spirited resistance to Poland's Nazi occupiers. Their brave fight, in the face of such overwhelming odds, became a rallying point for Jews the world over.

THERE ARE ONLY fragments left of the ten-foot-high wall that used to encircle the Ghetto. The biggest section, about 15 yards long, runs between two new apartment blocks. Its rough, red brickwork looks out of place, wedged between the concrete of the surrounding flats, and most of the local people would like to see the whole unsightly structure torn down. But the old man in flat No. 20 refuses to let it happen. His name is Mieczyslaw Jedruszczak. He is 72 years old and the sort of person that every community needs: the old busybody who will pester the local authorities until they fix the drains or the leaking roof, or go out fearlessly in the middle of the night to scold rowdy teenagers or stumbling drunks.

Mr Jedruszczak is not Jewish and he didn't take part in the Ghetto Uprising, but he will defend the wall to his last breath. He became involved quite coincidentally. When the Ghetto was burning in the spring of 1943, he was fighting in the main Polish resistance movement, the Home Army. He had his own pressing concerns. He survived the underground war against the Nazis, only to be thrown into a Siberian prison camp for three years by the conquering Red Army, which saw the

Polish resistance as a dangerous rival. After he was released, he became
a relentless archivist and historian of the war period. As he traced the
outline of the Ghetto over a map of the capital, he found that the wall
used to run right alongside his flat; in 1978, with a bit of careful scraping
through the layers of paint and plaster, he found the original bricks.

For Mr Jedruszczak, a meticulous historian, it was an unforgettable
moment. These bricks were the same that had held nearly half a
million Jews prisoner from 1940 until 1943. The Nazis penned them
in like animals, and those who survived the epidemics and starvation
were herded on to cattle trucks and taken to be exterminated in the
Treblinka concentration camp. They were all taken except for a few
hundred tough young Jews who decided to make a fight of it. They
ambushed the SS squadrons who moved into the Ghetto to carry out the
final round-up in time for Hitler's 44th birthday on 20 April. They held
out for more than a month—longer than some of the countries overrun by
the German *blitzkrieg*. A handful of insurgents escaped through the city
sewers when the Ghetto was finally razed to the ground. All that remains
of the Uprising are their memories—and Mr Jedruszczak's wall.

When he looks at the bricks now, he says he can hear them cry out
about what they have witnessed. But the town authorities clearly haven't
heard what they have to say. To this day, the wall does not have the
state protection usually accorded to a national monument. The fact that
it is still there—with a brass plaque, a map of the Ghetto and a little
commemorative garden in front of it—is due solely to Mr Jedruszczak.
His neighbours, and even some of his former resistance comrades, call him
a Jew-lover. Hooligans have smashed the glass covering his carefully drawn
map of the Ghetto; but he goes on firing off letters to local councillors in
his attempts to turn his little section of wall into a monument, alongside
the bold socialist-realist statue of the Ghetto fighters that marked the
post-war Polish state's recognition of the Uprising. Mr Jedruszczak has
kept the military bearing he acquired from his days in the underground.
He is firmly unsentimental about what drives him. 'It's a question of fact,'
he told me. 'The wall wasn't five metres this way or five metres the other
way. It was here, and you can't change that. History is precise.'

Perhaps what is harder to explain is the apparent indifference of the
people around him. The Poles lost six million people in the war: half were
Jews, half were Catholics. Not only were they fellow-victims, but Polish
Gentiles were also the principal witnesses of the attempt to eliminate

the Jews as a race. They saw the smoke rise from the crematoria at the concentration camps. The Poles, more than anyone, should have learnt the lesson of where racism can lead when taken to its logical, inhuman conclusion. Yet anti-semitism is still widespread. At a recent demonstration against market reforms outside the government's cabinet office, protesters started yelling, 'Down with the Jews!' and 'Go back to Israel!' It was a surreal scene in view of the fact that there are no Jews in the cabinet. In fact there are fewer than 10,000 in this nation of 38 million.

The idea of Jewishness seems to have taken on a symbolic meaning that allows it to survive even in the absence of Jews. As one journalist told me: 'The Jews are no longer a nation, but a nomination. You nominate as a Jew someone you dislike.' But the story of Jews and Poles has always been studded with bright, shining exceptions, like the Polish Catholic families who defied death penalties during the war by sheltering Jewish refugees. And, of course, there is Mr Jedruszczak.

As he showed me around his beloved wall, workmen were putting down new paving-stones in front of it, in preparation for the ceremonies to mark the 50th anniversary of the Uprising. It is the first time the authorities have shown any interest for years; it put Mr Jedruszczak into a good mood, as he poked the new pavement with his stick and gave unsolicited advice to the workmen. 'Maybe if we had a big commemoration every year,' he said to me, 'we might just get somewhere.'

RUSSIA'S RAILWAY CHILDREN

BRIDGET KENDALL   MOSCOW   24 JUNE 1993

*As Russia's economic problems intensify, a crisis of homeless-
ness is beginning to affect the country. The problem was
common in the years of turmoil that followed the Bolshevik
Revolution of 1917, and again after the Second World War.
In Brezhnev's Soviet Union, police were under orders to
detain and imprison any adults caught sleeping out or in
stations, and to round up homeless children. But now the
old Soviet regime has gone, and the new Russia, with its
uncertain reforms and collapsing economy, is unable to cope
with mounting welfare problems.*

SLUMPED ON A stairway in Kursk station, the thin-faced woman stared
up at the doctor and his foreign visitors, barely mustering the energy
to speak. 'I'm from the North Caucasus,' she said in her sad voice. 'I've
been living here since June last year.' Her filthy legs were covered with
sores. The doctor said that it was the commonest complaint among the
homeless at Moscow's stations—that, and the lice and TB, the result of
bad hygiene and lack of sleep, not enough time spent lying down.

Next to her, waiting to have his leg bandaged, was a man so dirty that
it was hard to tell his age. I asked his name. 'Vyacheslav Yakovlevich,'
he answered, drawing himself up tall. He said that he was a local man
and had spent ten years in prison. When he came out, all his relatives
were dead; the family flat had passed back to the state and he had
nowhere to go.

Suddenly there was a commotion behind me. A woman with a bruised face pushed forward. 'They beat us like dogs,' she sobbed, tugging at my arm. 'They do it every night. I just popped into the pay toilet at Yaroslav station, paid my ten roubles. When I lay down, in they came—the police—and dragged me out by the legs.' Her name was Roza. She too was from Moscow, homeless after a spell in prison. The irony was that her only crime had been to be unemployed, which was against the law under the communist regime of the old Soviet Union. By the time she had emerged from prison, the Soviet Union had vanished and her crime with it. But that didn't help Roza: her Moscow flat had also been confiscated. All she could do was to join the down-and-outs at the stations. 'Tell the police not to beat us,' she pleaded, as she finished her tale.

I hadn't come to Kursk station at 11 o'clock at night only to talk to Roza and her unfortunate friends. I also wanted to meet the 'railway children'—the bands of Oliver Twist kids weaving in and out of the crowds of grown-ups, avoiding the gypsy families encamped in corners, and living their own secret station life. For that I needed a guide, 14-year-old Yasha—though he looked no more than ten. After two years' dossing as a vagrant, he had been picked up by Russian charity workers who persuaded him to swap his hideaway under the station stairs for a bed in a children's sanctuary. He was revisiting his old haunt with us by way of an outing. Yasha was small, wiry, with a big grin and quick eyes. The kindly ladies at the charity home warned us to keep an eye on purses and other valuables; Yasha, it seemed, was an experienced pickpocket. As we wandered past the fruit machines, Yasha explained how he had ended up living rough. He had run away from a mother who used to beat him and a father who was always drunk. There were hundreds and hundreds of kids at the stations, he said. They lived by stealing and selling ice-cream.

At that moment, 16-year-old Andrei strolled up. If Yasha looked like Oliver Twist, then sturdy Andrei was the Artful Dodger—surveying the world with a confident swagger in a jacket just a little too big for him. His pockets sagged from the weight of books—a Russian–English phrasebook on one side and a handy volume of science fiction on the other. Andrei proudly listed the merits of station life. He had negotiated a comfortable corner as a permanent bedroom; his education was in hand, since he was learning English and first aid from the charity doctors; and he had several lucrative jobs. 'Excuse me,' he added politely, 'but I must be off, or I'll be late for work.' Work, it turned out, was running a newspaper stall in the bustling, sordid underground passage near the railway tracks. As weary travellers discovered that their trains were late again, there was Andrei—smiling from ear to ear—waiting to proffer a well-thumbed magazine to while away the time.

Around the next corner, we stumbled on Garik, a small, stern boy of about ten. Garik was sitting on his holdall munching sunflower seeds. He had just smuggled his way up from Armenia, a stowaway on a plane. He was 16, he lied boldly, and was looking for a job. 'It's bad back there in Armenia,' he announced in his high-pitched, childish voice. 'They've cut down the trees and there's nothing to eat.' Garik was streetwise. To impress us, he pulled out a jackknife and two guns, letting his sleeve fall open to reveal several electronic watches wound round his arm like silver bangles.

If the Moscow police catch a boy like Garik, they take him to the police detention centre for homeless children; it is hated by the street gangs. I could see why; I had been there the day before: high concrete walls, topped with barbed wire, surround the bleak buildings; the staff are uniformed policemen and women; children with fleas and lice, and, worse, young girls with venereal disease are instantly put into quarantine. A policewoman in a steel-blue uniform unlocked the door to the girls' section to let us in. She locked the door again. Thin, obedient girls shuffled up in a crocodile and chanted, 'Hello.' Half had been deloused—their heads shaven bare like convicts'.

The chief warder pushed forward one tiny, angelic-looking girl with tufty brown hair and a clean, red dress. Ten-year-old Katya perched on a chair, dangled her feet and confessed her sins. 'I'm here for the fourth time,' she whispered. 'I was living at Kursk and Leningrad stations, but the police picked me up. Me and my friend, we were just having a look around. It's nice at the station,' she added wistfully, staring at the floor. 'We sleep in the trains; the police don't find us there. We buy things to eat and have a good time.'

At that, the warder interrupted: 'Go on, Katya, tell the lady what you're really like. Tell her you smoke and thieve and tell lies.' Yes, she did smoke, she admitted; she had started when she was seven. In a loud, disapproving voice, the warder went on: Katya had run away from her children's home so often that no orphanage would take her any more. Her mother was an alcoholic, a degenerate.

'No she wasn't,' Katya objected.

'And Katya is the worst child in the orphanage,' the warder added. 'There's none worse than this little girl,' a second policewoman joined in. But they admitted that no one knew what to do with her. By law, she could stay locked up for no longer than a month. After that—wherever they sent her—she was sure to steal away to rejoin her station friends.

Back at Kursk station, young Garik from Armenia twisted his knife thoughtfully. 'It's not good here at night,' he volunteered. 'People get beaten up. You wake up in the morning, and you've lost your cap and your knife. They steal everything.'

'Come back with us!' The proposal came from our guide, Yasha. 'Come to the children's charity refuge. It's not the police, and they won't lock you up. You can have supper, sleep and leave tomorrow if you want.'

Garik looked doubtful. Then Andrei, the Artful Dodger, appeared. 'You should go,' he told the younger boy. 'You'll be all right there.' But he shook his head in amusement at our suggestion that he come, too. He had work to do.

At the station entrance, the Artful Dodger shook our hands and proudly waved goodbye—standing in the doorway in his dirty, baggy jacket like the lord of a stately home. In the car, Garik was having second thoughts. 'I'm not coming if I have to give up my weapons,' he warned. His new friend, Yasha, reassured him that he could stay armed, and begged one of his many watches as a gift. Young Garik began to settle down. Sinking back into the seat, still clutching his bag, he started to sing a clear melody in his high voice. 'One, two, three, four . . . ' he sang in English to please us. Then the words changed to Armenian—a slow, mournful lullaby. And we drove through the black Moscow night to the children's charity refuge.

RAPE, PILLAGE AND THE MARKET-PLACE

JULIAN BORGER   WOLIN   8 JULY 1993

In most people's minds, the Vikings are associated with Scandinavia. But experts believe that the ancient citadel of Jomsborg—one of the main centres of Viking culture—was near what is now the Polish town of Wolin. The town, on Poland's Baltic coast, hosted a Viking festival in July 1993, attracting would-be Vikings from all over Europe, including a contingent from Britain. The British hoped that the trip would be something of a spiritual homecoming, but things didn't turn out quite as they expected.

A LARGE, BLACK Mercedes was parked in the middle of Wolin's main square, and four of the town's bright young things were dancing to the pop tunes booming out through the car's open doors. It was enough to put Colin off his beer. 'This is the problem with capitalism,' he said. He fingered the engraved shaft of his Viking sword, as he considered pouncing on the revellers and plunging his weapon into the heart of the car's imported stereo.

Hours earlier, he had wielded the same sword to devastating effect, as he and his friends had staged a mock invasion of the town: jumping out of longboats to lay low a handful of poorly armed defenders, while thousands of local residents looked on in awe. Colin and his friends had gone to great lengths to ensure that every article of clothing, every ornament and weapon was as authentically Viking as possible. They even had an authenticity officer, called Russell, who made sure everything looked historically right. So now, having gone to all that effort, they felt that their hosts had somehow failed to live up to expectations. 'There's nothing Polish about this place,' Colin complained. 'You could go into one of these shops and you could be anywhere. You could be in Milton Keynes.'

The truth was that, as the Viking longboats had appeared out of the morning mist, Poland's enterprise culture had seen them coming. The park was covered in stalls selling everything from kebabs to oversize garden gnomes. A giant banner, advertizing a brand of chewing-gum, hung from the ruins of Wolin's old church. Worst of all, the price of beer seemed to rise exponentially from the moment the invasion force stepped on to Polish soil. Russell, the authenticity officer, was so furious that he stormed into the mayor's office. 'I wouldn't leave until they did something about it,' he said; by the third day of the Viking festival, the price of beer did seem to have stabilized somewhat. When I talked to the mayor later, however, he denied any intervention. 'Of course prices rose,' he said. 'It's the law of the market.'

Lurking beneath these misunderstandings there was a fundamental clash of cultures. A backward-looking, nostalgic Britain collided head-on with a dynamic, modernizing Poland. The British Vikings were hoping to see something of life as it had been behind the Iron Curtain, and to share their legends of a common Viking heritage. Wolin's town fathers, on the other hand, had seen an opportunity to extract maximum revenue for minimum cost. It made for awkward relations between the British contingent and the mayor's office, made worse by the fact that the Britons were not invited to the festival banquet, despite their special links with the town.

What the mayor had failed to appreciate was the perfect historical symmetry of the Jomsvikings' arrival. They took their name from the Viking citadel of Jomsborg, which Nordic sagas place at or near the modern town of Wolin. Almost 1,000 years ago, a war party set sail for London. They had heard that there was trouble brewing in England and, being soldiers of fortune, they were keen to get a piece of the action. First of all, they sold their services to Ethelred the Unready to help him defend London. Then they switched their allegiance to Canute the Great, and were last seen fighting on the losing side against King Harold at Stamford Bridge in 1066. As we all know, Harold, his forces weakened by that battle, went on to lose his next encounter, at Hastings.

Five years ago, Philip Burthem, who arranges fight sequences in films for a living, decided to set up a Jomsviking society, having been impressed by their exploits as told in the sagas. 'They were the most exciting Vikings I'd read about,' he said. 'They were a cosmopolitan, international band of outcasts; they were exiles from courts, they were outlaws and pirates; they were a mercenary, military brotherhood. A thousand years ago, I would have joined the Jomsvikings.' These days they are every bit as multi-cultural. There were Danish and Dutch members, an Italian from Parma, and a Chilean. The last two played the roles of freelance soldiers from Byzantium.

After recapturing their spiritual home, they all swaggered around their tented camp with all the self-assurance of born warriors. In the end, not even cultural misunderstandings with the local councillors could dampen the irrepressible high spirits of the festival. In the evening, the Vikings played tag with the local children and, as night fell, they tried to chat up the kids' elder sisters, relying heavily on sign language.

'They're just a load of plonkers really,' was the immediate reaction of a BBC producer when he heard about the festival. I suppose he had a point. Here were a bunch of young-to-middle-aged men and women who play-acted their way through their weekends and summer holidays and, in some way, did actually believe they were Vikings. 'I try to live my life according to a Viking code of conduct,' Philip told me. His Viking name was Ulf-Eirik. He said that the very act of lunging at one another with cold steel every other week had forged a tight bond among the society's members. 'We've shared blood together,' he said. 'We've sweated together, we've shared personal strife, as friends do.' This is clearly not without its dangers: I met one Jomsviking whose nose had been broken by a metal axe, wielded by a friend who had slipped on damp grass. Another had had a spear rammed home to within a centimetre of his eye. But if they had been less ready to believe in what they were doing, they would probably never have captured Wolin's imagination the way they did. 'This is three great days for people here,' a local man told me. 'Normally we have nothing.'

After two world wars and Stalin's mass deportations, few of the region's original inhabitants still live there; it would, then, be going a bit far to say that the Jomsvikings' symbolic return had reawakened any ethnic link between Wolin and London. But there was one 17-year-old girl there, whose red hair and green eyes set her apart from her friends as a potential Viking descendant. Her name was Dominika Wlodarczyk, and she firmly believed that she was a Viking, ' . . . not in my mind,' she said, 'but in my heart.' There was a young Jomsviking warrior by her side who was keen to take her at her word. As I was leaving, he was trying to convince her to go back to London with him, to live the life of a true Viking—if only at the weekends.

THE BALKANS

AN ARTIST'S IMPRESSION

ALLAN LITTLE   LONDON   22 JULY 1993

*Covering the conflict in the former Yugoslavia has posed
numerous problems for journalists. The physical dangers are
considerable: the BBC's Martin Bell is one of many who have
been injured. There are moral and ethical questions to be
addressed as well. When the official war artist, Peter Howson,
visited Bosnia and subsequently depicted a journalist as a pig,
Allan Little was prompted to reflect upon the lot of those who
report regularly from the region.*

IT IS UNSETTLING to find oneself depicted by the official war artist as
a pig. Some, at first glance, have mistaken it for a teddy bear, big and
round, with floppy ears—a benign if, in the context of central Bosnia,
puzzling figure. But it is not a teddy bear. It has an unmistakable snout.
It is, unmistakably, a pig: a pig on its hind legs, with a long-lensed camera
on a strap round its neck, an expression of malicious intent on its face,
and—just in case you should, even now, miss the point—a badge on its
chest with the word 'Press.'

Rebecca West went to Sarajevo in 1937 and wrote that she had been glad
that the spring had come late because this had enabled her to see snow on
the roof of a mosque, and the incongruity of the image had excited her.
Bosnia is again a place of incongruous images, of mountain-top garrisons
and of unspeakable brutality. Unspeakable, but not unpaintable. Peter
Howson was commissioned, by *The Times* newspaper and the Imperial
War Museum, to spend a couple of weeks in Bosnia as a guest of the

British army, and to produce a 150 canvases for a one-man exhibition. He is no stranger to brutality. He is from Glasgow. Much of his previous work is about the brutalization of working-class life. His figures have big, calloused hands and broad, crude features. But they are romantic figures: shipyard poets, noble proletarians, whose rough-hewn exteriors do not disguise a yearning, righteous spirit.

But there is something pernicious about this: something that lies at the heart of so much of Scotland's contemporary art and literature: the myth of the Big Man, the working-class hero, the overly insistent masculinity, the romanticization of some glorious, radical, visionary past. It is a very Scottish thing—a wilful self-deception that constricts and distorts our sense of ourselves. To the extent that a nation defines itself though its art and literature, this seems to me to be debilitating. We cannot seem to get beyond this Red Clydeside nonsense. I know some of Peter Howson's work, and it appeals to the Scotsman in me—to the wilful self-deceiver—and it is for that reason that I have never really liked it. And now these eyes were coming to Bosnia. I was excited by the incongruity of this.

Peter Howson came to central Bosnia at a time when things were about as tense as I can remember at any time since the war began. He was so disturbed by what he saw that he left after a few days. He had not taken a single sketch. He hadn't needed to. The images were strong and had burned themselves into his artistic mind. He will have no great difficulty recalling them; but he may have some difficulty putting them away. He said, later, that his sleep had been wrecked by those images and that—and this is what seems to me to be worth waiting for—he would never be able to paint in the same style again. I hope that the illusions about the romantic tragedy of suffering, which seem to me to inform all his previous work, will not creep into his paintings of Bosnia.

Those of us who go there with the more mundane task of reporting the war day by day also know what it is to have our sleep punctuated by the grotesque, haunting images of war; to be visited in the reaches of the night by intense, unfocused fear or inconsolable grief; to look, sometimes, into the dark places of the soul, and not to know how to explain, how to tell with force that what you see there deserves to be told. Peter Howson has his remarkable talent. He may be able to put some of it on canvas. We have only our journalism, and we do our best.

I am a little amused to have been depicted as a pig, but also a little sorry. The image of snow on the roof of a mosque led Rebecca West to a whole way of thinking about Bosnia, as a place almost defined by incongruity. The image of the journalist as pig with its snout, presumably, in the trough of human suffering, gorging itself on misery and loss, is a similarly provocative one. I cannot let it bother me. I cannot remember how often I have seen colleagues crying with pity for what they had chanced upon, crying sometimes with the frustration of not finding words sufficient to tell it like it really is. I cannot remember how often I have seen colleagues vomit with disgust and loathing. I cannot remember how often I have whispered a silent little prayer in my head, when a rumour has taken wing that another of us has been killed in some awful, unexpected turn of events. Please, please don't let it be true.

But you harden yourself. You discipline your imagination. You restrict your emotional responsiveness because, if you did not, you would not stay. Peter Howson did not impose any such restrictions on himself. I do not mind that he thinks that my colleagues are like pigs. I am proud of them anyway. But I do not mind *because* I think the war artist—even in a couple of days—may have seen things that I no longer permit myself to see. I cannot wait for his exhibition.

COMPASSION FATIGUE

MALCOLM BRABANT   SARAJEVO   17 OCTOBER 1992

Aid agencies in the former Yugoslavia negotiated a so-called 'tranquillity week' at the beginning of November 1992, during which they hoped that hostilities would be suspended in order to allow relief supplies in. One of the greatest dangers for those caught up in the civil war was creeping complacency in the West.

SHE SQUATTED ON the bed; her black hair was perfectly coiffed; she pouted her lips and smiled. She peeled back her black leggings and said, 'Take an erotic photograph.' But her words were laced with irony: beneath her leggings were white net under-garments rather like the mini string vest that covers the better cuts on a supermarket meat counter. These particular net stockings were hiding what is left of Fika Hadzovic's legs. They were blown away above the knee by a mortar blast. Fika, a vivacious Serb woman of 25, was going to get milk for Bosnian fighters when she was cut down in the prime of life. Doctors at the French hospital attest to her courage and determination to resume as much of a normal life as possible. Not many of Fika's fellow patients in the ward share that fighting spirit. One woman lay on her broken back, looking blankly at the ceiling and moaning in disbelief that her life had been so cruelly shattered. Fika, however, refuses to be consumed with self-pity. She wants to learn to walk again; to get married; to have children.

Fika's name is on a list of 300 war-wounded patients whom Bosnian doctors would like to transfer to foreign, specialist hospitals. Among them are other amputees and paraplegics. There are 70 men with eye injuries whose sight could be saved by treatment abroad. United Nations officials promised the Bosnian government in July that they would come up with a plan to move its war-wounded adults. But, more than three months later, nothing has been done. The scheme has fallen victim to that well-known United Nations disease, 'bureaucracy and buck-passing'. One senior UN official said that they were no nearer sorting out the problem now than they were three months ago. The UN's dithering is forcing doctors in Sarajevo to make some brutal decisions. The hospitals are almost drowning under a never-ending tide of new casualties.

The past week has seemed extraordinarily quiet, but a quiet seven days in Sarajevo have yielded 69 killed and 456 people injured. Most new casualties need beds; doctors are reluctantly telling partially recovered patients that they must leave. They are sending men with one leg missing out on to the most dangerous streets in the world. Some have been hit by snipers as they hobbled across intersections on crutches. Others have died in refugee centres because of a lack of proper aftercare. It will be worse when the snows come in a month or so, when the amputees will make easier, slow-moving targets for the Serb gunmen in the hills.

'Sarajevo is a city of cripples.' These are the words of a doctor who has acquired the equivalent of 20 years' experience of emergency surgery in the past seven months of war. He was slumped in a chair, with a glass of red wine and an American cigarette, at the end of depressing day when he had lost an elderly patient who should have survived. 'Most of the cripples are hidden away in the hospitals,' he said. 'Soon they will all be out in the open, and there will be many tears as we realize just how awful this war has been.' What is so appalling is that there is even worse suffering to come this winter. The medical crisis centre here estimates that 40,000–50,000 of Sarajevo's remaining 400,000 citizens will die from the effects of cold, hunger and disease—that is if they are not killed by the bombs and bullets. To put this figure into perspective you have to realize that the official death-toll in Sarajevo alone, since the war began in April, stands at about 2,500, with another 7,500 missing, presumed dead. Throughout Bosnia, the figure is more like 80,000 dead, including some 60,000 missing persons.

What is also disturbing is that, after seven continuous months of murder, massacre, mutilation, rape, ethnic cleansing, concentration camps and so on, compassion fatigue has well and truly taken root in the West. A friend from a British newspaper called me the other day and said that he had conducted a straw poll at dinner parties in the

Thames Valley; he had come to the firm conclusion that people were bored with Sarajevo. 'The problem with Yugoslavia,' he said, 'is that it's a war being fought by people whose names we can't pronounce; we can't remember who's the good guy and who's the bad guy; and it's a long way from home.' Maybe the so-called average man in the street in Britain, France or America doesn't think that he can change anything; but public opinion can force politicians to act, to cut through the sort of red tape that is preventing the likes of Fika Hadzovic from getting the treatment she deserves.

As I write, I can hear the sound of a sniper taking pot-shots at cars driving at high speed along Sarajevo's main road, just 100 yards from the front line. So far there hasn't been the equally chilling sound of a car horn blaring, which normally indicates that the driver has been hit. Ten days ago, a high-velocity explosive bullet from a sniper's rifle hit our vehicle just inches from my head. There was a deafening bang and a blinding flash; it knocked out my hearing and disorientated me for a few seconds. Maybe that is what the moment of death is like, without the pain. After that incident, and a couple of other close calls, I was feeling decidedly shaky and considered pulling out. But then a mortar fell on a children's playground, killing four of them and wounding nine others. I made up my mind to go to the mortuary—something I had avoided until then. I saw the shattered body of a girl called Sonila. She had died after doctors amputated her right leg; she was seven—the same age as my daughter. Seeing her lying there—wax-like, on a slab, surrounded by scores of other corpses—sickened me, but it gave me the strength to carry on. I intend to return to Sarajevo in December; *inshallah*, conditions will have improved, but I doubt it. They certainly won't if people become bored with Bosnia.

SUBSISTENCE
IN SARAJEVO

BOB SIMPSON   SARAJEVO   2 JANUARY 1993

When the United Nations Secretary-General, Boutros Boutros-Ghali, visited Sarajevo at the end of 1992, people there showed their impatience with international efforts to end the conflict by heckling him. The UN Secretary-General certainly didn't help matters when he said he could think of ten worse places in the world. Meanwhile the continuing siege meant that life—even for those who used to live a comfortable existence—was becoming increasingly desperate.

MUCH OF THE attention focused on the plight of the people of Sarajevo picks out the weak, the obviously vulnerable—the children, the sick and the elderly—but they are not the bulk of the population. That is made up of people who were jogging along quite nicely, thank you, before the barricades went up and the siege developed.

Such a couple are Omar and Ezma Hadziselomovic. They have two daughters, one aged 18 and at university in Massachusetts, and Dina who is eight. Omar is a professor at Sarajevo University. He did his MA in Ohio and came back home to do his PhD. His subject is English and American Literature and Culture, but he now spends only two hours a week in his faculty. Ezma is a graduate too. Her degree is in German and she studied international trade after university. She still manages to work a few hours a week at the Chamber of Commerce but, without 'phones or faxes and with only manual typewriters, there is not much that can be done. Although she is an adviser on trade with Western Europe, she feels that when the war is over (and she is sure it will end) Bosnia-Hercegovina should seek to trade with Turkey.

She expounds her reasons in her living room over coffee and delicious home-made bread, cubed and sprinkled with pepper. It would have been cake and biscuits in better times; there was brandy too. For these Bosnian Muslims are Muslim in name only: they have visited the mosque only out of curiosity and, as for dress, diet and demeanour, they could slip unnoticed into any Christmas drinks party or academic gathering anywhere in Europe or North America. The room where we chat is warm, heated not by the now useless electric storage heater under the window but by a crude but surprisingly efficient stove that Omar bought in a market. It cost about £25, four months of his professorial salary. Every day he spends at least an hour and a half scavenging for fuel, mainly twigs and wood chips. Ezma wraps the chips in the agendas and minutes of long-forgotten Communist Party committee meetings, which she brings home from work. 'Our patent fuel,' she says. Omar must be one of the few professors who can hold forth on the relative qualities of shoes as fuel. All good, he reckons, but go for man-made soles and heels every time; they give much more heat, even if they don't smell as good as spruce twigs. It took two or three parcels of wood chips, along with some of the shelving out of the hall cupboard, to boil the coffee. The water came from a standpipe across the river, no more than a couple of hundred yards from the front line. Others waiting for water told the professor that, on the previous day, a woman had been killed and two people injured by gunfire on the route he had taken. So why go there? 'More interesting,' he said. Even the most gentle of men can become fascinated by war. Another hour and a quarter of Omar's day was consumed by the water expedition; even if the car hadn't been stolen it wouldn't have speeded things up: there is no petrol available except on the black market, and that source has all but dried up.

You *can* get other things, though. You might come across the food that should, by rights, have gone to Omar, Ezma and Dina. It has been stolen somewhere between where the UN handed it over to the government distribution agent and where they should have delivered it to the public. Some UN officials say as much as 70 per cent leaks out of the system. That theft has meant, though, that our family has had only a reasonable supply of bread, flour and rice from the UN. On top of that they have had only 24 American forces MREs (meals ready to eat), two half-pound cans of meat, three cans of mackerel (dreadful, says Ezma), just over a litre of cooking oil, three pounds of cheese and a pound of dried milk for Dina, in the nine months since the siege began. If it wasn't for additional help from the charity CARITAS, they say they don't know how they would survive.

Despite all this, they say that what they miss most is the company of their friends. They have mostly left the city; some have turned up as leaders of the Serb besiegers, others live too far away for socializing. Dina's school is closed, so she doesn't see her friends either.

There was no shortage of company, though, at the old people's home I visited. It used to be a model of its kind, but it has turned out to be in the wrong place: in a front-line suburb of Sarajevo. I had seen the bed-ridden, hunched under blankets in their freezing ward; I had heard how all the water had to come from across a sniper-infested rat-run; how it was impossible to get washed bed-linen dry because of a complete absence of electricity. I was chatting to some of the 100 or so residents in the one warm room where a stove was constantly tended; we spoke about fighting with the partisans, of how they were desperate for cigarettes, or of how futile the fighting was, and about how they all managed to get on together. Both they and the few remaining staff come from all of the groups involved in the war. Then the word went around that Ilija was in trouble; a spritely 79-year-old, he had been chopping wood by the cookhouse door to heat the food the French UN troops had brought. He was turning to reach for his wheelbarrow when a sniper's bullet entered his forehead. He was dying as we put him into the French armoured car to take him to hospital.

He died like that simply because the old people's home was in a Serb-held area surrounded by Muslims. It could easily have been the other way around. He is the 16th resident of the home to die violently and futilely since the fighting started.

IMPOSSIBLE MANDATE— THE UN IN BOSNIA

MARTIN BELL   NEW YORK   6 FEBRUARY 1993

In New York, the talks on a settlement of the conflict in Bosnia-Hercegovina—which had been taking place in Geneva—reconvened at the beginning of February 1993. But some officials said that the proposed agreement stood little chance of success until it received the full backing of President Clinton's new administration in Washington. Already the President had indicated that he had reservations about the Vance–Owen plan and wanted the Russians to be involved more closely. But the problem seemed to be that the United Nations wasn't given enough power to try to control the crisis.

THERE SEEMS AN iron law of Bosnia: the worst that can happen, does happen. This was my sixth time back since last March. Sarajevo was then untouched by the war that has since engulfed it. To be sure, there were forebodings and rumours and refugees pouring in from neighbouring Croatia, but that was seen as something of an example and a warning to be heeded: 'No Vukovars here' was one of the slogans at the city's rolling peace rallies. The reference was to the town in Croatia, levelled by shelling, like a Stalingrad on the Danube. Dr Alija Izetbegovic, then, as now, the President of Bosnia, or parts of it, assured his people that reason would prevail. The danger of war was over.

But it wasn't then, it isn't now, and, ten months on, the city lies in ruins. Its people, some 380,000 of them, scrabble for survival, braving sniper fire to fetch their water and mortar fire to hack their wood from the few remaining trees. Most of the city, most of the time, has no electricity, no water, not much food; aid convoys can be suspended for a week at a time; an egg costs DM5 on the black market, a can of soup, DM20. Everything is running short, including hope, excluding ammunition. This is thanks to the late Marshal Tito's stockpiles: there seems enough ammunition to run the whole of World War III.

You can live through the scale of the tragedy, from month to month, as I have—and on both sides of the line since it began. You can share the experience, but still lack the words to express what it is like to live through a day like the recent one, when Sarajevo was hit by 852 artillery shells. Those were just the ones the UN military observers counted, along with more than 1,000 mortar shells and some tank rounds in the same bombardment. In a cave by the riverbank, once a restaurant and now returned to its original function as a primitive shelter, a woman described what it meant to her. 'During the first three months,' she said, 'whenever an artillery shell was fired, my daughter would ask: "Mummy, is this one going to kill us?" It would have been a hundred times easier to bear,' she added, 'if we were being attacked by a foreign power.' She, a Muslim, said of the Serbs: 'It is very hard to fight against people with whom you sat drinking coffee only yesterday. Almost our own people, our brothers, our neighbours.'

Now the casualties have filled up the city's parks and the graves are overflowing on to the football field. The scale of the dying is one of the few points about which there is no dispute. The Serbs put the total across Bosnia at 139,000, with another 6,000 of their own people missing. The Bosnian government confirms 100,000, but says the true number could be double that, and it is rising every day; the war intensifies and widens, now pitting former allies against one another. Croats are fighting Muslims in central Bosnia, along the borders of the cantons proposed by Mr Vance and Lord Owen under the Geneva peace plan. This, after all, is the Balkans, where the rules of Geneva don't run; the only truth is a lie, and a peace plan provokes more war. Touring the war zones these past three weeks, at a less rushed pace than usual, talking to the military and political leaders, the generals, the ordinary soldiers, I have come away more convinced than ever that this is a disaster with a momentum of its own, unstoppable by the usual peace-making mechanisms. It is certainly no stalemate. The front lines are fluid and changing, even around Sarajevo.

The mainly Muslim government side, after nine months of siege, is drawing strength and heavier weapons from somewhere. Their army commander, Safar Halidovic, tells me that a military victory is absolutely possible. It is also possible, and in time they will do it, to break the siege from the inside. Certainly the Serbs, for the first time, are on the defensive and are losing some ground; they are fighting, as they see it, for their own land, not giving an inch but under the heaviest pressure, and responding to the increasing attacks on their positions, not in kind with infantry which they don't have, but with artillery which they do. As for the threatened intervention, they vow to resist it with all their force—which is considerable. Outside the café of the Chetniks, a log cabin and fire-base on the escarpment south of the city, one of their sector commanders puts it chillingly: 'They,' he said, 'the outside powers, cannot muster enough troops to send here, and I wonder what the Americans will say when they start receiving a convoy of coffins. Let them not come, but play their war games somewhere else—Somalia, Kuwait or Iraq.'

Here in New York at the United Nations, where most of the main players have gathered for what seems the last diplomatic push, it is all a world away. Only the mediators, Mr Vance and Lord Owen, seem moved by the urgency of finding a settlement now. It is as if they have to drag the combatants to the conference table, where they argue endlessly over maps and cantons, and, day by day, the casualties of war accumulate. We are now at a point where the situation on the ground is simply no longer tolerable. Specifically, the UN force, with 7,000 men from 11 nations, has an inadequate mandate and an unworkable force structure. Its men are allowed to save lives by escorting convoys of aid through the war zones; they are not allowed to save lives by standing in the way of ethnic cleansing or stopping the civilians around them being shot. The time has come, in the absence of an unexpected success in the New York talks, for the world community to cut and run, or else to act much more assertively and, admittedly, at great risk. For the Europeans, the dilemma is especially acute. The first war in Europe for nearly half a century, it is as if we had a fire in one of our outbuildings; the choice before us is whether to retreat to an inner room in the hope that it will burn itself out, or to form a fire brigade and fight it. The present force, with its present mandate, does not do that.

CARRYING THE TORCH FOR FREEDOM

ALLAN LITTLE   SARAJEVO   18 FEBRUARY 1993

Despite the fact that most of the semblances of normal life had disappeared from the Bosnian capital, the city's newspaper, Oslobodjenje, *continued to publish. In February 1993 it won the 'What the Papers Say' award for Newspaper of the Year.*

IT IS A short but terrifying journey, and they have to make it every day. You emerge on to the main six-lane highway from behind a little petrol station. The road is deserted. This is the part of Sarajevo known to us all as 'Snipers' Alley'. For three-quarters of a minute you are exposed, in a direct line of sight, to Serb gun positions in the suburb of Nedzarici. You are driving a little red Volkswagen Golf that is pitted with bullet- and shrapnel-holes, and dented from where it has driven off the road. There is plastic sheeting in place of the windscreen, which has long since been blown out. And you hobble across the crater-pitted highway, up over the central reservation, across the tram lines, down from the kerb again, and your back suspension creaks with the strain of it until, at last, you take shelter behind what is left of the newspaper building. But you are carrying a precious cargo that has not once, in ten months, failed to reach its destination. It is a battered, brown envelope that contains tomorrow's news from downtown Sarajevo: reports from the hospital, the military command, the streets, the market, the presidency, the government, the city parliament.

'The brown envelope comes to me first,' says Fetah Ramovic. The fingers of both hands are stained with nicotine and his voice is thick with tobacco and lack of sleep. In better days he was the newspaper's Bonn correspondent, and in appearance he is every inch the stereotyped, boozy, careworn newspaper man. Now he is duty editor—working a seven-day shift around the clock with ten others, mostly subeditors. The brown envelope is emptied of its stories, typed by reporters in the city centre office, and allocated.

We are standing in a nuclear shelter beneath the *Oslobodjenje* twin-tower building; it has been converted into a cramped newspaper office-cum-dormitory. About a dozen narrow beds line the walls. 'We come down here and stay for seven days without leaving the basement,' says Ramovic. 'We have fluorescent light, so we never know whether it is day or night.' There are three teams working in rotation; each works one week in three. None has ever failed to bring out the paper. 'We decided this at the start of the war,' says Emir Habul, who writes a regular column. 'The editor, Kemal Kurspahic, called us all together to decide what we should do. We all wanted to keep publishing. One of our colleagues joined the other side. But the paper has kept its pre-war ethnic mix. Of the seven people in this room now, two are Serbs,' he says.

But the geography of the city could not have been worse for *Oslobodjenje*. From the beginning, it found itself on the front line. Serb forces occupied the suburb of Nedzarici on to which the building backs. Senad Gubelic, a photographer, has a graphic way of demon-strating its vulnerability. We climb to the first floor of the annexe and wind through corridors that are blackened and charred and pock-marked with shrapnel- and bullet-holes. 'I call this the disco corridor,' he says. 'Some nights the whole place is lit up by tracer fire. It looks like a nightclub, and the noise is deafening.' He leads us into a south-facing room and we crouch behind a pallet of unused newsprint. The south wall is completely blown away. We look out across a stretch of wasteland. 'Now you can see the aggressor positions,' he says. 'They are 50, maybe 100 metres away. I can hear them singing their patriotic songs at night. Sometimes they drive a tank into that playground and fire at the building. We're a favourite target. I think they like us a lot.'

And to great effect. The building was destroyed by increments, from the top down; it caught fire six times. The last blaze, at the end of October, finally caused the twin towers to collapse completely, forming two piles of rubble 60 feet high. Only the elevator shaft and stairwell, which ran between the towers, remains, together with a low-rise annexe where the print works are installed. 'It must be my bad luck,' says Ramovic, 'but each time the building caught fire I was on duty. We stayed down here in the basement trying to work. We were determined to get the paper out. Over a thousand shells have hit us since the war began. They're trying to silence us, to kill the truth. That's what gives us strength to carry on. *Oslobodjenje* means freedom, liberation.

'On the night, at the end of October, when the towers collapsed, we didn't get the paper out in the morning. But it was on the streets by one o'clock in the afternoon. One of the Serbs from Nedzarici 'phoned us and asked: "Did you publish today?" We told him we had. "OK," he said, "here comes another RPG," and they started to hit us again.'

The print room is all that survives above ground level. Two weeks ago they installed natural gas heating for the first time, in three stoves made from customized oil drums. The room is hideously exposed. 'Behind this wall there is nothing between us and the Serbs,' says Gubelic. 'We had a tank round in here two months ago,' he adds, indicating the boarded-up cavity it blew in the brickwork. 'Fortunately it didn't explode.'

Fortunately, too, it takes only 15 minutes to print the 3,500 copies that come out daily. But problems of supply have become more pressing as the siege persists. In December and January, the printers ran out of regular newsprint and had to shift production to a smaller, much older print-machine that could accommodate lower-quality paper. 'We started producing multi-coloured newspapers,' says Ramovic, leafing through the bound library copies. 'One day yellow, one day pink, one day blue. Even, occasionally, two colours in one eight-page issue. The French charity, Équilibre, took up *Oslobodjenje*'s cause and delivered a supply of paper—enough to produce the paper for a month. When that runs out it will need a new sponsor.'

The paper's reporters are billeted in a tiny office in the city centre that used to belong to the railway company. 'Before we got this office, the reporters used to work anywhere they could—in the street, even,' says Dzelana Pecanin, an *Oslobodjenje* staffer. When the war began, Dzelana stayed at home; she decided to return to work after her father was killed in the bombing of a water queue in October. 'The dangers are clear to everyone,' she says. 'Two of our reporters have already been killed. Our correspondent in Zvornik was killed right at the start of the war. He was shot in the back in his office. They knew exactly who he was.'

'They know who we all are,' adds Habul. 'They certainly have lists of our names, I'm fully aware of that. But I'm no longer afraid. I'm just trying to be a good, objective journalist.'

Oslobodjenje has a tradition of objectivity to uphold. In this respect it was by reputation the best paper in Yugoslavia before the break-up of the country. It was founded in 1943, at the height of the partisan war against the Germans, Croatian collaborators and Serb Chetnik guerrillas. Its vision of Bosnia owes much to those wartime roots. This is one of the few corners of former Yugoslavia where Tito is still regarded with affection. There are portraits of him hanging everywhere in what is left of the building.

If *Oslobodjenje* stands for anything, it stands for the idea of civil society in Bosnia, and against the ethnocentric nationalism that, in different ways and to radically different effect, is espoused by the Croat and Serb militias which are tearing the republic apart. It seeks to represent the war, not, as it is widely and erroneously seen in the West, as a civil war between three tribes fighting over the same land, but as a war between the idea of tribalism and the idea of civil society. *Oslobodjenje* is Sarajevo's way of keeping that idea alive; its way of proving that ten months of siege—twice as long as Saddam Hussein was allowed to stay in Kuwait—has not reduced the city's sense of itself.

A YEAR IN BOSNIA

ALLAN LITTLE   SARAJEVO   8 APRIL 1993

The World Court in The Hague ruled in April 1993 on a request from the Bosnian government for emergency protection from what it described as Serbian genocide. The Court is the judicial arm of the United Nations, and it was the first time that it had considered a complaint under the 1948 Paris Convention Against Genocide. The ruling in favour of the Bosnians further isolated Serbia. But a year after the capital, Sarajevo, came under siege, there was no end in sight to the conflict.

IN A BATTLE-SCARRED café in central Bosnia, almost within earshot of the artillery that has been pounding Sarajevo for a year, a young German photographer sits, waiting. He has just spent two months in Srebrenica, besieged, under bombardment, and—like the 60,000 Muslims who are trapped there—unable to leave. The waiter brings him his dinner. It is the first good food he has seen in weeks. He stares at it and, inexplicably to those with whom he is sitting, he begins to cry. He is carrying the knowledge that those whom he has just left—the Muslims he has come to know personally and with whom he developed the kind of intense friendships that flourish between good people in bad places—will soon be dead. It is an impossible burden, and it finds expression in tears of despair and rage and a crushing sense of impotence.

It is a year since the war began. From the perspective that an anniversary bestows, the central dynamic of the war stands out in sharp relief. The Serb nationalists, armed and supported by the former Yugoslav People's Army, began their campaign of military conquest a year ago, aiming to build an ethnically homogeneous Serb state on Bosnian territory. They began in north-east Bosnia and eastern Hercegovina. They moved across northern Bosnia, driving hundreds of thousands of non-Serbs from the homes that they and their ancestors had occupied for generations, forcing them into exile and impoverishment. Nothing any Western government or the European Community or the United Nations has said or done has deflected them from their purpose—not even for a day. And now they have almost finished. Eastern Bosnia is the last remaining ethnic grit in their otherwise pure territories. They must flush out the Muslims there. The military imperative is clear and openly stated. The tears of the young German photographer spoke of the terrible inevitability of the fate awaiting eastern Bosnia.

We have been here before. The central Bosnian town of Jajce fell a few weeks after Serb political leaders had promised, in London, to concentrate all their heavy weapons there, and to place them under international supervision. It was presented at the time as an important breakthrough. It was, of course, nothing of the kind: no weapons were concentrated; no UN inspectors were ever deployed; no one, it seemed, ever mentioned it again except the Bosnian government, whom the international mediators had, by now, reduced to the status of a 'warring faction'—morally equivalent to the armed insurrectionists whose explicit aim was the destruction of the state.

Jajce was taken. The men who had signed the paper felled the city. I went to see the resultant exodus. From the last safe Bosnian position, the road to Jajce rises in a gentle curve and disappears behind a little mosque and then up into the wooded mountains beyond. Down this road came the saddest procession I had seen anywhere in former Yugoslavia. They walked—some singly, some in straggling little groups—holding one another up. They were covered in mud. Their feet were sodden. Some looked as though they had died already. Their journey had taken two days.

The first was a man of about 60. He was carrying a little girl in a red anorak on his shoulders. Her chin was resting on his head and her face was without expression. Her eyes, though open, appeared not to be seeing anything. I asked the man some questions:

'How far have you come?'

'From Jajce.'

'How have you got here?'

'I've walked.'

'How far?'

'Seventy kilometres.'

'Who's the little girl?'

'She's my grand-daughter. Her father—my son—was killed on Sunday by a grenade.'

'How old is she?'

'She's two. Today is her birthday. She's two today.'

He clambered aboard a waiting bus and was taken to Travnik, to be registered as a refugee. Then a lone man appeared from behind the mosque. He was carrying what looked like a Gladstone bag. His progress was painfully slow.

'How old are you?'

'I'm 80.'

'How far have you walked?'

'All the way—70 kilometres.'

'How long has it taken?'

'Two days, I think. I fell and hurt my head. I slept in the woods.' Then he began to cry. 'I've left all my instruments behind.'

'What instruments? Medical instruments?'

'No. Musical instruments. I was a music teacher. I had a violin and a grand piano. I wanted to leave them to my grandson. He's a fine pianist.'

For a few moments we stood in silence. We were a small group of four: two journalists, one interpreter and an old man whose instinctive civility, even at the moment of his greatest pain, was clear to us all as he stood patiently answering our questions. But at this moment none of us could speak, and he too clambered aboard the bus and into exile.

This week, a letter arrived in Sarajevo from a man driven from his home a year ago, a former professor of philosophy at the university. He spoke of the refugee condition—not material but spiritual. 'I have learned to live without sense of place, without a home, without friends, without family, without my city, without knowledge, without feeling, without hope. Please, if anyone remembers who I was, whisper to him my name.'

And now it is going to happen all over again in eastern Bosnia, where there are perhaps 200,000 waiting to be cleansed; 60,000 are immediately at risk in Srebrenica. Last week, the Foreign Minister of the Serb forces here addressed his parliamentary colleagues. They had been calling on their leaders to pull out of peace talks and to get on with conquering the lands that the Serbs want. The Foreign Minister thought the first part foolish. 'We must continue to attend peace talks,' he said, 'because our presence diminishes the case of those in the West who want intervention against us. But we must take part in these talks rather as extras take part in a movie.' It is a revealing simile, all the more so for the openness with which it is stated. There is, at least, nothing deceitful about the bad faith with which Serb leaders take part in the earnest efforts of the international mediators. Thus the Serb Deputy Commander, General Milan Gvero, was able to attend peace talks here on Tuesday and promise to uphold the ceasefire; in the east, his men were preparing to pound Srebrenica town centre, their front lines closing, in the words of one senior UN official here, 'slowly but surely on the town itself'.

The UN commander here, General Philippe Morillon, cares passionately about Srebrenica. When he went there three weeks ago, he promised never to abandon it. The people renamed their streets: Marshal Tito Avenue became Philippe Morillon Street. Commentators declared him a latterday de Gaulle. Now he is going back to Srebrenica, hoping to take with him 150 Canadian troops and an international hospital. The humanitarian case is urgent. But he will have to ask the Serbs first, and—if precedent holds—he will have to ask them nicely. They may say no, they may say yes; but the decision will be theirs. The mandate under which General Morillon has to operate permits no other course. If his flamboyant mission today fails, General Morillon may come to resemble, not de Gaulle, but a fictional character, less glamorous but, in the end, more subversive: the character in Czech literature, the Good Soldier Svejk, who so wanted to please his masters that he carried out their instructions to the letter, thus revealing, inadvertently, their absurdity. If General Morillon's mission today fails, it will nevertheless have done a great service in revealing—in the most explicit way to date—the powerlessness of the UN force here to alter the course of the war.

THE THIRTY YEARS WAR REVISITED

MISHA GLENNY · SARAJEVO · 22 MAY 1993

The Bosnian town of Mostar, which until 1993 boasted some of the finest examples of Ottoman architecture in Europe, became the latest victim of the destructive insanity which had consumed a large part of south-eastern Europe. The suffering in the former Yugoslavia appeared to have no end. But there was, perhaps, a glimmer of light at the end of the tunnel.

WITH THE FEATURES and figure of a supermodel, but wearing the uniform of the Croatian Defence Council and with a semi-automatic slung across her shoulder, Maria tells unwanted journalists to turn their cars around and get their 'you-know-whats' out of Herceg-Bosna, as the Croats call their mini-state in Bosnia.

'But we have permission,' came the reply.

'No permission is valid here any more. There is shooting in Mostar and there's going to be more!'

Back in Zagreb, I and my friend Alija Hodzic, a Muslim sociologist, sit in a cheerful café trying to overcome our deep depression by smoking and drinking too much. 'The Croats are now behaving in western Hercegovina just as the Serbs did a year ago in eastern Bosnia,' explains Alija Hodzic, who comes from the once beautiful little town of Stolac, some 20 kilometres south of Mostar. 'They have interpreted the Vance–Owen plan as a right to clear their regions of Muslims.' He goes on to tell me a remarkable tale in order to illustrate how Bosnia has now descended into inexplicable, anarchic chaos. In Gornji Vakuf last month, Muslim and Croat units were engaged in a merciless artillery battle under the watchful eye of a neighbouring Serb unit. When the Muslim guns stopped firing, the Serb commander radioed his Muslim counterpart and asked why.

'We've run out of ammunition,' he said.

'Give me the Croat co-ordinates,' the Serb warrior replied. The Serbs then obliterated the Croat positions in four hours of heavy shelling. As dawn broke the following day, the Muslim commander ran up the Yugoslav flag instead of the Bosnian fleur-de-lys to express his thanks for the Serbian help.

'The situation is rapidly becoming like the Thirty Years War,' says Alija Hodzic, 'where nobody is sure who their enemy is, and where your worst enemy can become your best friend if you happen to run across another enemy unexpectedly.'

Yet for once, however appalling the events in Bosnia may appear, it is beginning to look as though a rather hideous sculpture of peace is to be fashioned out of the molten republic in the Balkans. President Slobodan Milosevic of Serbia and his Croatian counterpart, Franjo Tudjman, are beginning to work overtime in an attempt to stabilize Bosnia. The hot-lines between Zagreb and Belgrade are again buzzing with discreet delegations putting out feelers which would turn Croatia into a federal state. Serbia would recognize Croatia in exchange for the granting of full political autonomy to the Serbs of the Krajina. The Vance–Owen plan would be amended to turn Bosnia into a confederation, allowing closer links between the Serbs and Croats and their respective motherlands. Tragic though it is for the Muslims, the victims of a joint grab for territory both within and without the framework of the Vance–Owen plan, they must now bow to the inevitable and accept the carve-up. If they do not, the Serbs and Croats will quite simply liquidate them.

'It is only the Serbs and the Croats who can stop this war,' the leader of the urban Serbs, Milorad Pupovac, believes. 'And that is why a political agreement between Milosevic and Tudjman is the only way out. It's a terrible thing for the international community to swallow, but it must prepare to accept these two as the peacemakers of the Balkans.'

It is still a long, hard road to peace, and the Croat and Serb leaderships will encounter tough resistance among many of the hardliners whom they have nurtured and encouraged. But the signs that they are determined to do so are growing by the day.

This will not be the end of the Balkan story, however. On the contrary, it is just the beginning. If the international community fails to learn the lessons of the Yugoslav tragedy, it will have new and even more dangerous wars to confront in years to come. If the sticking-plaster of a Serbo-Croat deal, with the grudging backing of the international community, is to work, then the United States, the European Community, Russia and Turkey must be prepared to invest some real money to develop a preventative political mechanism in order to stop the whole region going up in flames.

Preventative measures will come too late to save my dear friend Lenka Raos, who was shot dead last Sunday night in a Belgrade restaurant. Lenka was a Croat who had been living in the Serbian capital for many years. After leaving the news agency, Tanjug, she began working for Reuters Television. Her death was a freak accident, but she was nevertheless a victim of the insane gun culture of the Balkans. All those journalists who have worked over the years in the former Yugoslavia are now mourning her death deeply. Mercifully, her six-year-old daughter, Una, was visiting Lenka's sister in Canada when her mother was killed. I pray that Una will now stay across the Atlantic, where she may at least be permitted to escape, for ever, from these ghastly statelets of death in the Balkans.

GARRISON SOCIETY

ALLAN LITTLE   KNIN   24 JUNE 1993

*The Serb enclave of Krajina is where the fighting that led
to the break-up of the former Yugoslavia began. The territory,
home to some 300,000 Serbs, effectively cuts Croatia in half.
In the capital, Knin, as in the rest of the republic, economic
life has virtually ceased—it has become a garrison society.*

WE CLIMBED THE steep-sided peak above the town to the white stone
walls of the medieval fortress that dominates the valley in which Knin sits.
Zoran wanted to be away from the streets where he could be overheard.
This is the story he told.

'I was nineteen when I killed for the first time. We were taking the
village of Donji Zemunk, near Zadar airport. I came round the corner of
a house. A Croat soldier was standing at the other corner. I went into a
state of shock. I knew I had to kill him. I pulled the trigger and, without
realizing what I was doing, I pumped 30 rounds into him, over and
over. When the magazine of my gun was empty I was still pumping. I
don't know for how long. You know, when you kill for the first time
you are in shock. After that, it's normal. You kill men as though they
are sheep. Now I have images in my head that will not go away. I will
never escape them.'

In Krajina it is not rare to have killed before you are out of your teens:
it has become a rite of passage. One man told me how he had crossed
enemy lines at dawn and found himself observing, from a distance of
100 metres, a group of about seven Croatian soldiers. 'I chose the one I
wanted to kill,' he said. 'He must have been about 25 years old.
I took aim and fired. The rest ran away and, of course, so did I.'

Krajina has been a garrison society before. For centuries it was the land across which the frontier between the Ottoman and the Austro-Hungarian Empires ebbed and flowed. It formed a movable fault-line across the Balkan peninsula, separating Catholic West from Byzantine East. It is a garrison society again. Every able-bodied man between the ages of 18 and 60 is a soldier. There is total mobilization, and everyone expects a summer offensive from the Croats.

Knin is an ugly place, a miserable dust-bowl of a town. Its people, like Serbs everywhere, are hospitable, kind; but when you go among them, you go through the looking glass into a world in which Serbs are only ever the victims of atrocities and conspiracies, never the perpetrators. We visited a man whose name is legend across the territory of the former Yugoslavia: Captain Dragan is a former sergeant in the Australian army, and is regarded in Croatia as a war criminal. He ran his own militia during the war in Croatia. He is, uniquely, an English-speaking Serb warlord. Now he runs a training camp in Krajina which, he says, aims to instil into a civilian army an edge of military professionalism. The war in Croatia, he says, is fought not by professional armies but by civilians carrying guns. Civilians are not motivated by discipline and defined strategic objectives. They are motivated by either fear or hate. When they are afraid, they desert. When they hate, they massacre needlessly. Captain Dragan wants that to change. Striding across the gentle slopes of his hillside training centre, he is in his element. His men salute him as he passes, and it struck me that it was the first time, anywhere in former Yugoslavia, that I had seen soldiers salute an officer. In a garrison society, men like Captain Dragan rise to the top.

Knin has produced a generation of such people; it was the cradle of war. Serb nationalists here erected the first barricades when Croatia declared independence, arguing that, if the Croats had the right to secede from Yugoslavia, then *they* had the right to secede from Croatia. Their leader was Milan Babic, a dentist by profession and—the joke runs—an irredentist by political inclination. He persuaded his people that the choice they faced was stark: they must fight or die—there was no third way. It was the sovereign right of the Serb people to live in a single state. Unity is the Holy Grail of modern Serb politics; it has a powerful resonance. It must, the argument runs, be achieved, even if the price of unity is a perpetual state of insecurity, constantly having to resort to armed readiness and permanent impoverishment. These prices are worth paying because the alternative is less palatable still: the alternative is annihilation. The very name of the place reveals the identity that the Serb leadership has adopted: 'Vojna Krajina' means 'military frontier'; their chosen destiny is to defend the Serb nation. The Krajina Serbs *are* the military frontier, and their mystical nationalism (in which the Serbs speak the most perfect of all human languages, and in which the Serbs are the genetic centrepiece of the human race) is rendered all the more intense by the proximity of the enemy. They are frontiersmen, literally and psychologically.

And the power and status, in the garrison society, of men like Captain Dragan and Milan Babic depend on the perpetuation of the lie that there is no third way; that the choice is to fight or to die. But they are dying anyway. The garrison society cannot survive without a sponsor. Mystically, the people of Krajina are bonded inseparably with their Serb compatriots in the other republics. But economically Krajina needs the Croatian coast. More importantly, Croatia needs Krajina. The main road and rail lines between Croatia's two main cities run right through Knin. Croatia wants it back: without it, the Croats are cut in half—economically unsustainable and perpetually insecure. As long as the Krajina Serbs argue that there is no third way, that the only solution is to draw a thick, fixed border between Serb-occupied lands and the rest of Croatia (across open, flat land that is not divided by any natural frontier), they are leaving Zagreb little choice between capitulation and a war of redemption.

And if, as every Serb believes it will, that Croat war of redemption begins, the garrison society will have to pray that the nine million Serbs elsewhere—whom these 300,000 in Krajina purport to defend—share their mystical faith in the Holy Grail of unity. Zoran, who knows what it is to have killed before you have reached your 20th birthday and who will never escape the pictures in his head, says thousands like him have had enough of Serb unity. Living in a garrison society is too high a price to pay for a young man who does not want to kill again.

THE MIDDLE EAST

MEMORY OF A MASSACRE

TIM LLEWELLYN   LONDON   18 SEPTEMBER 1992

September 1992 marked the tenth anniversary of the massacre in the Palestinian camp area of Beirut called Sabra-Chatila. There were hundreds—perhaps as many as 2000—Palestinians, mostly defenceless, civilian men, women and children. They were put to the blade and the bullet for three days by Christian militiamen, while Israeli forces, occupying the surrounding area, either looked on and did nothing, or actively helped the marauding Christians. One of the first reporters on the scene was the BBC's former Middle East Correspondent, Tim Llewellyn.

FOR THREE DAYS before our ghastly discoveries on that Saturday morning, many of us journalists, aid and medical teams and diplomats in Beirut knew, from our hotels and missions a couple of miles or so away, that something bad was happening in Sabra-Chatila. We received uncheckable, ominous 'phone-calls from Palestinians and Lebanese: there were rumours, and edges of scary intelligence were making themselves known. But those inside the camp, who had the evidence and had survived—Palestinians and foreign doctors and nurses alike—could not, without great difficulty, escape the camp. Those who could escape were afraid to make themselves known to the foreign reporters in Beirut, for fear of arrest (and worse) by the Israelis and their allies in the Lebanese army and Christian militias. Though we tried, on the Thursday and Friday, we could not reach the camp interior.

Quite simply, the Israeli army—which had moved into West Beirut on 15 September, after the long summer onslaught against the PLO and the

Lebanese—was at the gates of the camp, dominating its main exits and entrances from raised positions on the perimeter. One fact that became immediately apparent to all of us who finally trekked into the camp and picked our way through the human detritus in shock, nausea and anger was that the massacre could not have happened without Israeli army knowledge, and most certainly the active collaboration of some of its soldiers. A blemish on Israel's record, the memory of that massacre can never be erased. And, indeed, two of the most senior men in charge of Israel's defence forces on that day are still prominent, even popular, figures in its political life.

To be fair, some rather diluted blame and criticism was meted out by an Israeli judicial commission a few months later; and it was the Christian Lebanese, mostly Maronite militiamen, who carried out the savagery. The organizer of those murders and his supporters are now political operatives and hit men for the Syrians in Lebanon; and the Syrians—to be fair again—have, with their allies, killed and displaced their fair share of Palestinians during the past ten years. History has moved on; more daily horrors, no less bloody and cynical, are served up to us; and I do not intend to describe again here—in what, to me, would be almost pornographic detail—the events and the sights of that day at Sabra-Chatila. Since then, more that is as bad, and maybe worse, has happened in the Middle East.

Now, at a time when the Israelis and the Palestinians, and other Arabs still at odds with Israel, are beginning to gnaw tentatively at the edges of peace deals, it's worth trying to assess what Sabra-Chatila, and the whole Israeli intervention of that year of '82, might have done to and for the Palestinian movement.

The Israeli invasion that year was successful, in the end, in emasculating the organized, armed body of the PLO in Lebanon; the Syrians helped by finishing off the job for them in 1983. Now only a rump of Palestinian guerrillas remains in the country—most of them under strict control, and very limited in their operational ability. The PLO's armed presence in Lebanon, however, had never really been much more than an irritant to the Israelis. It was much more of a problem for the Lebanese Christians, Shi'ites and Syrians, at different points; and in any case, in the year preceding the invasion of '82, the PLO had carried out no attacks of any consequence over the border. This was all part of an understanding, brokered by the United States and Saudi Arabia, between Israel and the

PLO. What the departure of the PLO's central core and armed units from Lebanon *did* help to achieve (a process already under way but now accelerated) was the realization among Palestinians that diplomacy and pressure—the attempt to work with the international community, the superpowers and the Arab states—should replace motley, armed groups of limited effectiveness as a bastion of the struggle for Palestinian rights.

But there was another bastion: the Occupied Territories, which were also directly connected to Israel's invasion in '82. Ariel Sharon, then Israel's Minister of Defence, reckoned that a crushing defeat of the PLO in Lebanon would crack the morale of a new generation of Palestinians, on the West Bank and in Gaza, who were showing themselves to be less docile than the generations that had been displaced and crushed by the Six Day War, 15 years before. He was wrong.

In 1987 began the *intifada*, the uprising which brought the Palestinians back to being the prime focus of international concern and cast the Israelis, again, in an aggressive and law-breaking mould. The experiences of the United Nations peace forces in South Lebanon, Sabra-Chatila and the battering of Lebanon in 1982 had done much to change Israel's reputation. It changed from that of beleaguered little democracy to regional bullyboy in the eyes of many important former supporters—especially in Western Europe and the United States. Conversely, youngish PLO men I had known on the barricades in Beirut, in the 1970s and early '80s, wearing olive drab and carrying guns, were now in pin-striped suits on the steps of the chancelleries of Europe, and even the United States Embassy in Tunis. Only Arafat kept up his Guevara-esque garb and elaborate chequered bandanna; but even in that rig he was being publicly heard to acknowledge the state of Israel and the two-state solution, and to disavow the use of terrorism.

All this was vital. But perhaps most important of all—from those very Occupied Territories which were to have been subdued beyond recall by Ariel Sharon's Lebanon *putsch* of '82—was emerging a new, reasoning, civilian, academic, legalistic, internationally respected and respectable team of negotiators. They carried the PLO's imprimatur without any of its doubtful legacies. They are now in the front line. The United States is the dominant agent in the peace process, working with the Palestinians—as with everyone else—and no longer simply emblemized by them as a one-sided supporter of Israel.

No solutions are imminent: it could all go badly wrong: a new American

administration next year might drop the ball. But it looks a lot more
evenly balanced than it did when I tramped—ten years ago—through the
bodies, the blood, the rubble and the tormented widows and children of
Sabra-Chatila; and I wonder how many Israelis regret the consequences
of that mad summer of '82.

GALVANIZING GAZA

ALEX BRODIE   GAZA   15 JANUARY 1993

When Israel deported more than 400 Palestinians into South Lebanon, it intended the gesture to be a powerful blow to the fundamentalist group, Hamas, in the Occupied Territories and, especially, the Gaza Strip, where most of the deportees come from. As things turned out, the deportees served as a rallying point for opposition and international condemnation and had a far greater effect than if they had stayed at home agitating.

THE WALLS OF the Gaza Strip are the notice-boards of the *intifada*. Five years of instructions and exhortations from the leaders of the uprising against Israeli occupation have left hardly a gap that is not covered in red, green and black writing. The stars of the show now are the Islamic group, Hamas, to which most of the deportees are said to belong. Its claims of responsibility for attacks on Israeli troops are daubed everywhere, as is the slogan: 'We Are All Hamas Now'. The new graffiti are about solidarity with the exiles and unity among the Palestinian groups. Activists of the secular PLO parading through the streets for the first time include their rivals of the Islamic Hamas in chants of unity. In the past they have fought and killed each other; that is unthinkable now.

Far from driving a further wedge between them, the Israelis have thrown them together; the banishment to no-man's-land of Hamas activists has converted their peripheral demand to abandon the peace talks into mainstream Palestinian policy—temporarily at least. The Palestinian negotiators have in the past been vilified and even threatened by Hamas. There is no criticism of them now, because they say they will not go to any more talks until the deportees are returned. It is the only line they can take, such is the feeling on the street.

Dr Haider Abdul Shafi, the head of the negotiating team, is depressed at the lack of progress in over a year of talks with the Israelis, and he is close to giving up. On his desk at the Red Cross clinic in Gaza, which he has run for the past two decades, is a book, *The Birth of Israel*. He fears that the collapse of talks will take the Palestinian cause out of the hands of moderates like himself, who believe in a Palestinian state alongside Israel, and put it in the hands of those like Hamas who are pledged to destroy Israel. He says that so many young men are joining Hamas, not out of belief in radical Islam, but out of support for armed struggle, born of frustration with the peace process. Similarly, the fact that all women in the Gaza Strip now wear the headscarf is a sign of the advance of Islam, but it is also partly a political statement: the veil as a symbol, as another barrier that the Israelis cannot penetrate. Israeli attacks on the Islamicists seem to strengthen, not weaken, their popular appeal. They are deeply involved in the community—for instance, in medical clinics—so their expulsions are seen as an attack on social welfare, as well as on religion.

At the Islamic University, to the background sound of mid-day prayers being conducted in the corridor, one of the administrators explained how virtually all the teaching staff of the department of medicine had been deported; in the separate women's section of the university, the wife of one protested his innocence of any political involvement. In fact Hamas activists themselves do not necessarily know who else is a member, since the movement is made up of clandestine cells.

The Gaza Strip has got to be one of the most desolate and hopeless places on earth. On a stormy winter's day, rain poured down from dense, black clouds, a rough sea pounded the shore, meeting and carrying away the torrent of grey water which poured on to the beach from the open drains of Gaza City. Unpaved roads, rutted like ploughed fields, were reduced to mud across which slewed the ubiquitous, ancient Peugeots—the car of Gaza. Several main roads were closed completely by huge, standing lakes of water. There is no local council, no services, one of the highest birth-rates on earth; three-quarters of a million recalcitrant Palestinians kept under by Israeli soldiers who, doubtless, ask the same question as the bemused outside observer: what on earth are they doing here?

It is getting worse; Gaza is seething. At checkpoints where troops used to be merely alert, now as you drive up and stop you will have at least one rifle pointed directly at you from very close range, and the soldier's finger is on the trigger. This certainly intimidates me; it does not seem to intimidate my Palestinian companions, who claim it as a victory. They say that when an Israeli soldier points his gun at them it makes them proud, as it shows that the soldier is afraid of them. Across a main road in Gaza City, the Israelis have built an enclosed bridge to allow them to go from their base to a prison without venturing into the street. The Gazans call it 'fear bridge'.

To most Israelis Gaza is a closed book: the only ones who see it, do so through their helmet visors, through the stone-proof grilles on the windows of their jeeps, or down the sights of their guns. Between the Israeli Jew and the Gazan Arab—the occupier and the occupied—there is virtually no understanding or human contact, only confrontation; and that is not sporadic, it is continuous.

In the fading winter light of mid-afternoon, ten little girls, seven or eight years old, with satchels on their backs, dancing from one to another and chattering away, dawdled home from school. Where the mud path narrowed to squeeze between the corner of a house and a piece of railway track—stuck into the ground to hold up the fence of the army camp—the girls had to go through in single file; but they were soon in gossiping clusters again, apparently oblivious to the commonplace ritual being performed around them and over their heads. To one side boys, the youngest about ten, were trying to hurl stones over the high fence at two soldiers inside the wire. The soldiers, visors over their faces, rifles at their shoulders, postured; tensing, aiming, first in one direction then another. As the guns swung, the boys skipped behind a wall. This is routine at the perimeter fence of the main Israeli army base, slap in the middle of Jabaliya refugee camp. The soldiers do not cool things by removing themselves from view, just as the boys do not bow before their guns; the Israelis feel it necessary to display their power and command, the Palestinians their bravado and defiance.

Today the stones missed; the soldiers didn't shoot. But often they do: stone-throwers are routinely wounded, sometimes killed. One teenager proudly displayed his scars where he had been shot four times and, no, he did not think it was advisable to stop. What if he should be killed? Well—that would be God's will.

THE SPECTRE OF WAR

CAROLE WALKER   KUWAIT CITY   21 JANUARY 1993

Tension was high in Kuwait in January 1993 following Iraqi incursions across the border and the subsequent punitive strikes against the Iraqis, launched by Allied forces. American troops from the 1st Cavalry Division moved up near the border to take part in unscheduled joint exercises with forces from the emirate. For its part, Iraq made a unilateral ceasefire offer which was met with guarded optimism by the Allies. Among ordinary Kuwaitis, there was a mood of collective panic.

AS I RACED across the car-park at Kuwaiti television, with minutes to go before the satellite booking to get my story on the *Six O'Clock News*, two portly Kuwaiti gentlemen began running after me as fast as their traditional Arab robes would allow. 'Madam, Madam, is it Scuds? Is it bombs?' They were convinced that I was making for the air-raid shelter, fleeing from an Iraqi attack. Over the past week Kuwaiti fears of renewed aggression by Saddam Hussein have intensified to the point of hysteria. At the height of the Allied strikes we were inundated with 'phone calls from people asking the BBC if it was true that a Scud missile had hit the airport, or that Iraqi troops were once more invading from the north. I did my best to reassure my companions.

Given the almost obsessive fear and hatred of Saddam Hussein here, two years after the liberation, it is perhaps surprising that they have done so little to secure their northern border with Iraq. When we drove there, seeking evidence of the six Iraqi police posts on Kuwaiti soil, which were finally removed this week, we almost drove straight into southern Iraq by mistake. After the Gulf War the United Nations decided to guarantee the inviolability of the new border, which runs about half a mile north of the 1963 line. It was marked out last November and declared effective from 15 January. But it is quite hard to find; you have to look for what appear to be upturned oil-drums, painted blue with 'UN' in white letters. There is one of them every two kilometres along the border in an area of flat, almost featureless desert. The demilitarized zone is a corridor running its entire length; ten kilometres wide on the Iraqi side and five kilometres wide on that of the Kuwaitis. The few hundred unarmed UN monitors are very thinly spread indeed; very little aggression was required on the part of the teams of Iraqis who breezed on to what is now Kuwaiti soil to collect their missiles and dismantle their warehouses. These were the border raids condemned for their provocative flouting of UN resolutions. There are just two tarmacked roads in this area, and a network of unmarked dirt tracks. Given that patrolling Kuwaiti and Iraqi border guards are in danger of running into one another, skirmishes are hardly surprising. Now some Kuwaitis talk of building a sort of Berlin Wall to keep the Iraqis out. The UN is considering the deployment of some 3500 peace-keeping troops. One wonders whether a simple fence might be worth contemplating before such a costly measure is approved.

The border zone, littered with debris from the war, is the one area that appears to have been overlooked in the programme to restore Kuwait to its former, rather brash, oil-rich glory. Returning after almost two years, it is quite a shock to drive past endless limousines, along well-lit streets; to find that the blackened shell which was the International Hotel, now has not only power and running water but also a gleaming marble lobby, three restaurants and two swimming pools; to find the beaches empty of mines and tank traps, and the skies clear of the heavy, black clouds from the burning oilfields. Much of this was achieved, of course, with the help of coalition countries. Kuwait has emerged relatively unscathed while still commanding sympathy for its suffering during the Iraqi occupation. International condemnation for its ill-treatment and expulsion of thousands of Palestinians was short-lived.

Once again the government can rely on the Allies to defend the sovereignty of the country. The 1st Cavalry Division is rumbling through the desert; Patriot missiles have been deployed in case of a Scud attack. One of the few Palestinians still here joked, rather scathingly, that Kuwaitis could not really be expected to go out and defend their own country as there was no air-conditioning in their tanks. But for all the talk of border incursions and UN violations, this latest Gulf crisis does appear to have been driven by the animosity between Saddam Hussein and George Bush. Kuwait has wholeheartedly endorsed the American-led strikes against Iraq, while rather nervously taking a back seat.

TAKING UP THE VEIL
STEPHEN SACKUR   CAIRO   6 FEBRUARY 1993

1993 saw a number of attacks by Islamic fundamentalists on tourists. The attacks served further to undermine the government's claim that it had crushed the militant threat. Indeed, the activities of Muslim gunmen are but one element in the broader Islamic trend sweeping across Egypt. In other, less newsworthy but significant ways, Egyptian society was changing—and not in a way that pleased the government.

THE WOMAN AT the lectern was a picture of Islamic piety: her body was swathed in a long robe, her hair hidden by a headscarf of the purest white. She spoke before an audience of 60 women in one of Cairo's well-to-do suburbs. 'In my former life,' she told them, 'everyone constantly stared at me. I could feel the contempt in their eyes.' The woman broke down, racked by convulsive sobs. In front of her, half of the audience was also crying, deeply affected by the fall and subsequent rise of one of Egypt's most successful and best-loved belly dancers. The speaker was Hala Safi, known to millions of Egyptians for her sensual gyrations on stage and screen. But for Miss Safi the days of diamanté bras and ruby-red lipstick have gone for ever. Now her only public performances are devoted to the propagation of Islam. Her message is infused with all the emotion and zeal of the born-again believer. 'The Prophet came to me in a dream,' she told her audience of middle-class Muslim women, after the first rush of tears had subsided. 'The Prophet covered me, and from that moment I knew I would never feel naked again.'

    In Egypt they call it 'taking the veil': dozens of well-known belly dancers and actresses now make a very public display of their Islamic modesty, much to the annoyance of the Cairo government, which is more determined than ever to resist the Islamic trend sweeping the country. The semi-official Egyptian press never misses an opportunity to undermine Safi and her Islamic sisters. There are allegations of underhand financial deals, and Saudi princes are said to have offered certain actresses hundreds of thousands of dollars to give up their careers and adopt Islamic dress. Popular culture is fast becoming a battlefield. State television has attempted to defy the Islamic tide by refusing to employ female presenters or newsreaders who insist on keeping their hair covered. As a result, Egypt's television viewers are confronted by women sporting gravity-defying bouffant hair-dos and day-glo make-up, in a perverse imitation of Western fashion.

Not only on television does Egypt seem to be a society ill at ease with itself. For months the government of President Hosni Mubarak has been conducting heavy-handed security operations against a disparate band of Muslim militants. Isolated acts of religious violence are nothing new in Egypt, but in recent months the gunmen have begun to pose a more serious threat to the status quo by targeting foreign tourists. The recent bomb attack on a South Korean tourist bus was typical: a mix of desperation and incompetence which did little damage but which will doubtless frighten off thousands more potential visitors, thereby robbing the Mubarak government of yet more sorely needed foreign currency. Officials in Cairo would like to believe that the upsurge in violence has been prompted by foreign meddling. The Interior Ministry claims that there are as many as 20 terrorist training camps in northern Sudan, financed by the Iranian government. As yet, however, no evidence has been produced to substantiate the Iranian link.

Instead, a more potent foreign influence seems to come from New York City, from the seedy Brooklyn apartment presently occupied by Sheikh Omar Abdel Rahman, a blind theologian said to be the spiritual guide of the Egyptian militants. Samizdat cassette recordings of his venomous sermons have been found in safe houses used by the Egyptian gunmen. The Sheikh refuses to acknowledge any direct involvement in the military campaign, but in a recent interview he told me: 'President Mubarak is a corrupt oppressor. In fact, he's worse than Ceausescu in Romania; and we all know what happened to Ceausescu.' Mass arrests, brutal interrogation techniques and blanket policing of militant strongholds have, for the moment, contained the militant threat; but neither the

Egyptian government nor its overseas backers should assume that the broader fundamentalist challenge has been overcome.

The real strength of the Egyptian Islamicists lies in their peaceful, community-based activities. As with Hezbollah in Lebanon and Hamas in the Israeli-occupied territories, the Egyptian fundamentalists—this time in the form of the Muslim Brotherhood—offer an impressive range of welfare, health-care and educational services to thousands of people neglected by the secular state. Um Ahmed, an exhausted-looking mother of two children in the Talbia neighbourhood, west of central Cairo, is a fine example. She has no deeply held political or religious beliefs, but for a woman living in poverty the Muslim Brotherhood represents her only source of support. Abandoned by her husband and without independent means, she relies on an Islamic clinic for medical care. The doctors know her and charge only a nominal fee for treatment. A nearby butcher with Brotherhood connections gives her cheap meat and sometimes, when she is really desperate, the Brothers send her small amounts of cash. 'The Muslim Brothers have helped me; they have always stood by me,' Um Ahmed said, sitting in her tiny, bare-brick tenement flat. 'They showed me a compassion that I never even found in my own family.'

Um Ahmed and thousands like her represent the challenge facing the Egyptian government. The Islamic trend is exploiting the cracks in a society close to collapse. The time for cosmetic repairs has long since passed. Without massive structural reform, Egypt's secular edifice could come tumbling down—sending shock-waves to the furthest corners of the Middle East.

FREEWHEELING THROUGH LEBANON

PENNY YOUNG   BEIRUT   4 MARCH 1993

After many years of civil strife and foreign invasions, peace has now been restored in Lebanon. But as Penny Young found when she cycled from the Syrian capital to the Lebanese coast, it is something of an uneasy calm.

I CYCLED OUT of Damascus before the sun was up. It is 25 miles to the border with Lebanon; I was a little apprehensive. I knew that the Lebanese embassy in Ankara had made a mistake with my visa. According to the entry in my passport, I should have entered Lebanon during the preceding month. I was sure that I could argue the toss, but I kept thinking of all those people who had been detained at sensitive borders because their papers weren't in order. Fortunately, the big chief at the Syrian border was charming and spoke excellent English. He let me out of the country. I cycled through the gate into no-man's-land; the Lebanese border post is some way beyond. The hills were suddenly green and beautiful; in the far distance the mountains of Lebanon reared up. Shocking, by contrast, were the crashed cars every few yards among the trees and rocks—a legacy of 15 years of civil war.

I was marched off to see the head man at the customs post. He questioned me at great length, but finally I got a permit to stay for a month. I battled past the sweating queues waiting to enter the country: taxis, Syrian businessmen and Western diplomats popping over the border to do some shopping. Gangs of money-changers clutching enormous bundles of notes waylaid us. I was to find the dollar is used for everything, from buying cheese to paying hotel bills; better not to change at all.

Off I went down the pot-holed road, past ancient posters of cowboys advertising American cigarettes, through fields strewn with plastic, past black grape vineyards, more crashed cars and into the Bekaa Valley. It isn't a valley at all, more a huge, fertile plain stretching between the mountains separating Syria and Lebanon on one side and the mountains of Lebanon falling to the Mediterranean coast on the other. I turned off the Beirut road up the valley towards Zahle. The people of Zahle spent part of the early '80s in their cellars as the Syrians and Phalangists battled it out. The old Catholic town is still beautiful with its French-style châteaux built on either side of a ravine. Tucked at the top, under the hills, is an area of restaurants, bars, casinos and funfairs. Families were strolling, eating, chatting: a relaxed, sunny day. From the hills above Zahle the views are vast over the Bekaa Valley. I was adopted by a little girl and her young uncle. They drove me into the hills to a ruined Crusader castle. A Bedouin family was camped in the middle, their goats leaping up and over the walls. In the distance I spotted a stone hut which had obviously once been used for target practice.

The Christians of Zahle shook their heads when I talked about cycling 25 miles north to Baalbek—Hezbollah country. It was obvious that I was leaving the Christian sector. There were wall-paintings of bloody swords, rearing horses silhouetted against the sunset, blood dripping from a Star of David. I passed through a gateway draped in flags; a full-length picture of Ayatollah Khomeini stared solemnly at me. I lost count of the Syrian checkpoints. And, suddenly, there was the Roman temple—one of the finest in the world. From the shadow of its columns I could see the empty camp of the Hezbollah on the hilltop dominating Baalbek. Opposite the temple is the Palmyra Hotel, where anybody who *was* anybody used to stay: General Allenby, the Empress of Abyssinia, Charles de Gaulle. The manager told me that I was the first English guest for 18 years to stay there.

The constant sound of gunfire was a little unnerving, but I was told that it was only people hunting birds . . . and it was. As I cycled off next morning through a thick mist, scores of young men dressed as cowboys were, indeed, banging away; their spent cartridges littered the road. Meanwhile tanks loomed out of the mist and I passed what seemed like half the Syrian army out on a morning run.

Up and up I went, though Maronite villages dripping with crucifixes and shrines, to the foot of the real mountains. I took one look at the ascent and hitched a lift on a passing lorry. A perpendicular corkscrew up above the clouds, over the bare peak, and a vertical corkscrew down—the surviving cluster of cedars of Lebanon visible down below. You can forget where you are in Lebanon: from fundamentalist Islam and its veiled women, to the Christian areas with miniskirts; French spoken everywhere; cafés and pâtisseries; and then only shell-pocked roads and buildings marked with bullet-holes.

I took the sea road to Beirut and bumped in via Martyrs' Square. It is now a heap of rubble and weeds; even trees are taking over. The boulevards look like a two-dimensional film set. People live in squalor, without electricity or water—their washing hanging up in charred shells of rooms. Soldiers are billeted in ruined apartments; you can see their sleeping bags on their bunks through the holes in the walls. Beirut rumbles and rocks to the sound of private generators. Rubbish is heaped in the gutters and on the pavements. By night, people stumble along, using torches to avoid the pot-holes. I passed a shop filled with coffins, the shopkeeper sitting alone in the gloom. And yet they are trying to re-create a normal life. The coastline may be destroyed, but people sit on the beach, ignoring the heaps of rubble and rubbish. There are restaurants and casinos; some hotels have re-opened; and in the Chouf mountains you can eat lunch overlooking countryside reminiscent of southern Italy.

As dusk fell, I caught the ferry to Cyprus from Junieh, just north of Beirut. A Palestinian who had been staying in Baalbek told me the tales of cellars and attics still stuffed with guns and rocket-launchers. Lebanon—the land of war and contradictions; the chance for peace balances on a knife-edge.

TIGHTENING
THE NOOSE

STEPHEN SACKUR   BAGHDAD   11 MARCH 1993

In March 1993 the International Committee of the Red Cross launched an appeal on behalf of a quarter of a million Iraqis, said to be suffering as a result of the sanctions imposed upon the country by the United Nations. Medicines and foodstuffs were running short and, in some parts of the country, sewerage and sanitation—damaged during the Allied bombing of Iraq—had yet to be restored.

ON MY SECOND night in Baghdad I decided to go to the theatre. I asked a couple of local acquaintances for their advice and was told that there was something on at the Al Khaime playhouse that I simply had to see. It was called *How to Become a Millionaire*. I bought two tickets, one for me and one for my government minder—a big, humourless man who bore a striking resemblance to Boris Yeltsin. When we got to the theatre it was immediately apparent that something was wrong: dozens of cars were already leaving the car-park. A group of people were standing aimlessly in front of the main entrance. This, I discovered, was the cast.

'There has been a terrible accident,' one of them told me. 'One of our colleagues has just been killed in a car crash.' I heard a couple of stifled sobs. Feeling awkward, I said how sorry I was and turned to leave.

'Come back tomorrow night,' somebody said. 'We're sure to have found a replacement by then.'

Iraqis have turned resilience into an art form, and here was proof. On the following night *How to Become a Millionaire* went ahead in front of a large and highly appreciative audience. Even Boris Yeltsin, who hadn't produced a single smile in the previous 48 hours, emitted the odd chuckle; during one scene of high farce, his broad shoulders appeared to be heaving with mirth. The story was a moral fable about life under sanctions. A millionaire merchant with contacts in the ministries makes vast profits by siphoning off government rations. He is protected by a coterie of corrupt officials, until a lowly employee in the Ministry of Agriculture exposes his crimes. As this was Iraq, it came as no surprise to see the profiteering merchant killed in the final scene.

Iraq has indeed become a sanctions-obsessed society: the siege mentality, established during the daily bombardment of the country two years ago, is now fostered by the material hardships of life under an economic embargo. President Saddam Hussein, having effectively pauperized one of the region's wealthiest countries by engaging in disastrous wars—first with Iran and then with the Gulf War Allies—now uses the sanctions issue as a shield to deflect popular criticism away from his government—and it works. It is impossible to visit the Qaddisiyeh hospital in the sprawling, overpopulated Baghdad suburb of Saddam City without feeling the depth of Iraqi anger at the outside world. In the dimly lit paediatric ward, doctors are engaged in a daily struggle to revive babies rendered grey and lifeless by months of malnutrition. One mother, shrouded in black robes, attempted to bottle-feed her six-month-old boy. The baby stared, eyes wide, refusing to swallow. A steady stream of milk ran down his cheek. 'The mother has no milk,' a doctor told me. 'She, too, is malnourished. At home she can't afford the milk formula, so the baby doesn't grow, and then he picks up infection.'

It is a familiar story throughout Iraq. Infant mortality has increased tenfold as a result of malnutrition and diarrhoea. In the southern city of Basra, the post-war misery into which Iraqis have been plunged is all-pervasive. A foetid smell hangs over almost all parts of the city as a result of a comprehensive breakdown in the city's sewerage and sanitation system. Lakes of raw effluent disfigure many neighbourhoods. Infants can be seen paddling in the shallows. More than half of the city's residents have no piped water. All drinking water has to be taken from tanker trucks which lumber around Basra's streets early in the evening. According to the city's director of water supply, the problems could be put right within weeks, if hi-tech pumping and water-treatment equipment could be bought from overseas. But it can't; so municipal workers continue their efforts to lash together a home-made system while typhoid and cholera begin their inexorable march across the city.

It is perhaps worth remembering that just two years ago Basra was in the hands of Shi'ite rebels, determined to overthrow the Ba'athi regime. Basra is not, and never has been, a city instinctively loyal to Saddam Hussein. But in 1991 the rebels received not a single scrap of support from the Gulf War Allies: indeed, their uprising was greeted with ill-disguised horror in Washington and Saudi Arabia. Hardly surprising, then, that Basrans are now utterly bewildered by a Western policy which still characterizes the Iraqi President as a menace but which does nothing to remove him, save for the imposition of a sanctions regime that brings discomfort and disease to the very people who tried to rebel.

UN sanctions are, in a technical sense, tied to the ceasefire resolutions imposed on Iraq at the end of the Gulf War. When the Iraqi government has destroyed all its weapons of mass-destruction, when it has agreed to a long-term monitoring programme and when it has stopped oppressing civilians in the north and south of the country, then sanctions will be lifted. In the meantime, however, Western diplomats tacitly express hopes that the economic pain inflicted on the country will sow seeds of dissension in the armed forces. A clean, clinical coup is just what the doctors in Washington would like to order.

But President Saddam Hussein, for the moment at least, still appears to be one step ahead of his opponents. Not only does he divert popular anger towards the Western powers, but he has also created a convenient class of bogeymen at home. In this regard, the plot of *How to Become a Millionaire* is instructive. The villain of the piece, the corrupt, profiteering merchant, is a character constantly referred to in official propaganda. The fact that rampant inflation has been caused by the collapsing value of the Iraqi dinar is glossed over; instead, the ever-rising price of basic foodstuffs and clothing is blamed on treacherous speculators and merchants. Last year more than 40 traders were executed after being accused of manipulating prices and exploiting the poor.

Soon the United Nations Security Council will once again review the sanctions imposed on Iraq. They will not be lifted; but perhaps the members of the council should consider the realities of life in Iraq. Saddam Hussein has rebuilt his ministries and security installations; he has, for the moment, maintained the loyalty of his army. And perhaps most important of all, he has manipulated sanctions to ensure that those who are hurt most, matter least: the poor, the weak and the vulnerable. And even in their misery, these victims are no longer sure who their real enemy is.

FIN DE RÉGIME?

STEPHEN SACKUR   DAMASCUS   15 APRIL 1993

In the spring of 1993 it looked as though President Hafez al-Assad of Syria, for so long a bitter enemy of the Jewish state, was about to make a momentous peace with Israel. At the same time, this strongman of the Arab world was, according to some reports, not in the best of health.

A BRONZE BUST of President Hafez al-Assad stands next to the headquarters of the Ba'ath Party Workers' Union in central Damascus. Syria's leader is depicted as a bare-chested man of toil: his torso is a study in virile masculinity, his lower half is clad in a traditional pair of baggy pantaloons known as *sherwarl*. With a shovel in his hand and the spring sun on his back, this bronze President cuts an impressive figure: a man seemingly rooted in and devoted to the Syrian soil.

One can only imagine how galling it must be for the real-life Hafez al-Assad—62 years old, diabetic and extremely frail—to see this absurd representation of his own body on his rare forays into the heart of Damascus. The Syrian President is old beyond his years. A decade ago he had a heart attack which almost killed him; late last year there was another heart scare, which laid him low for several weeks. At least that is the story being peddled by 'reliable sources' in the Syrian capital—sources which, needless to say, must remain anonymous in this most secretive of all Levantine cities. Government officials have done their best to scotch the persistent rumours about Mr Assad's health. One senior apparatchik looked me squarely in the eyes and said, 'I know from personal experience that our President can work for ten hours without a break. He works harder than any other leader in the world.'

Perhaps such slavish loyalty keeps sagging spirits up. It does not, however, stop Syrians and foreign diplomats from speculating about the power struggle that is sure to follow the demise of the dictator. Assad's likeness—with the unmistakable high forehead and the sharp, foxy eyes—still dominates public buildings, shops and restaurants. Now, though, the official propaganda often refers to him in the traditional Arab way as 'Abu Basel'—'Father of Basel'. It's a deliberate attempt to link Assad's 30-year-old son with the continuation of the regime. Basel is, in fact, a relatively junior army officer; but in recent months he has been given a significantly higher political profile, reportedly enjoying his father's confidence in matters of intelligence and national security. But experienced diplomats in the Syrian capital do not expect Abu Basel's dreams of dynastic rule to be fulfilled. The President's authority is intensely personal, based on the loyalty of the armed forces, the intelligence agencies and the all-pervasive *mukhabarat* or secret police. In a country where there is no political process, only the most senior generals can hope to make a bid for ultimate power when the time comes.

Almost all the President's closest, uniformed advisers are—like their leader—Alawites: born into a sect which is an offshoot of Shia Islam and which claims the loyalty of just 10 per cent of the Syrian population. For 23 years the Alawite community has imposed itself upon the Sunni majority. Nothing would do more to upset this fragile status quo than a damaging power struggle between rival Alawite pretenders to the presidential office. 'When Assad goes,' one ambassador told me, 'nobody knows what will happen. We could get more of the same, or we could get a bloody mess, involving all sorts of religious and tribal vendettas. The one thing we know we won't get is any move towards pluralism or democracy. The best we can hope for is stability.' It is ironic, to say the least, that a man directly responsible for thousands of deaths in his own country, a man heavily implicated in attacks on Western targets in Lebanon and deemed responsible for a plan to blow up an airliner flying from Heathrow Airport, is now viewed with a respect bordering on admiration by some Western diplomats. But 'stability' has become Assad's great strength in a region assailed by Islamic militancy and ethnic tensions.

In springtime Syria can present an extremely pleasant face to the outside world. Around the capital city, acres of sprawling orchards are in bloom; in the foothills of the Lebanon Mountains the winter rains have produced a riot of wild flowers. Compared with Iraq to the east or, indeed, Lebanon to the west, the military presence is relatively discreet. But any temptation to hail a kinder, gentler Syria in the twilight years of Hafez al-Assad should be resisted. Everything is still viewed through the prism of dictatorship. When interest-groups—be they religious, economic or ideological—are perceived to be dangerous, they are crushed.

The President has built himself a new palace on one of the imposing hills that overlook Damascus. It is a vast, angular, concrete creation which hangs over the city like a giant spaceship. Mrs Assad is said to hate it so much that she refuses to sleep in it. Whatever its merits as a secure presidential bunker, it is most certainly not the home of a man who feels confident of his people's affections.

Before leaving Damascus, I allowed myself time to wander around the Hamidiya souk in the heart of the old city (one of the few places in the capital from which the grey menace of the presidential palace cannot be seen). In these narrow streets, choked with spices, gold and fine cotton, it was possible to believe in a Syria free of spies, prisons and crude ideology. Here was a city of grand tradition—a sensuous haven for all the Arabs. Full of such romantic nonsense, I joined a queue of Syrians waiting patiently to buy tickets to enter the Azem Palace, a fine old relic of Ottoman rule. A moment later, two men barged their way to the front of the line. Both wore sunglasses and self-consciously casual clothes. The old man in the ticket-booth started to shout, then suddenly stopped. In Syria men from the *mukhabarat* do not need tickets: as long as Assad is alive, the country is theirs.

THE BATTLE FOR HEARTS AND MINDS— NINTENDO TAKES ON THE MULLAHS

STEPHEN SACKUR   TEHERAN   17 JUNE 1993

As was widely expected, President Rafsanjani of Iran won a second four-year term of office in elections in June 1993. He did not, however, receive the overwhelming popular mandate he had hoped for. Among young people, above all, there was a distinct lack of interest in Iran's revolutionary slogans.

WHEN IRAN'S SUPREME leader, Ayatollah Ali Khamenei, cast the first vote in Iran's presidential election, earlier this month, 17-year-old Sohrab was fast asleep in his parents' comfortable, middle-class apartment. By the time voters had formed an orderly queue outside one of Teheran's central polling stations, Sohrab was sprawled across a couch next to the television, playing with his Nintendo computer game. For six months Sohrab has been pitting his wits against inter-galactic enemies from the edge of the cosmos. According to his father, his obsession threatens to destroy all hope of a place at university. 'You're crazy, it's just a harmless game,' says Sohrab, without diverting his attention from the all-out war taking place on the television screen.

Sohrab is a child of Iran's Islamic Revolution; he was just three years old when the Shah was forced to flee his kingdom, in the face of a religious uprising such as the world had never seen before. This middle-class boy of secular parents was schooled in the Islamic Republic and taught to revere the Great Imam, Ruhollah Khomeini—the inspiration and guide of the revolution. Now he is old enough to vote in Iran's presidential election, to play a part in the shaping of his country's future. But Sohrab isn't interested: politics bores him. Yes, he knows it is election day, but, no, he won't be voting. 'What's the point when we all know who's going to win?' he asks, zapping another video alien.

In Iran, demography and politics have conspired to give adolescence a special significance. The country's high birth-rate and improved infant health care have disrupted the traditional population balance: half the population is now under the age of 16. And, thanks to the desire of Iran's leaders to garner ever greater numbers of votes from the electorate, the voting age has been successively lowered. It now stands at just 15. But the guardians of the Islamic Revolution, including the re-elected President, Hashemi Rafsanjani, have a problem. After 14 years of economic hardship, warfare and international isolation, their theocratic republic holds little appeal for Iran's first post-revolutionary generation. Like Sohrab, many teenagers have no interest in the political intrigues of the mullahs. They want excitement, fresh ideas, foreign influences; in short, they want to rebel. Ali is a 15-year-old high-school student in north Teheran, a young peacock strutting in the early-summer sun, his hair carefully coiffed, his Levi jeans and high-top trainers making their own declaration of style. 'We all come here after school,' he told me as we chatted outside a Teheran shopping centre. 'Our school—the boys' school—is just up the road, and the girls' school is around the corner. So we come here to hang out, to chat to the girls and stuff.'

For Ali and his friends, the Islamic Revolution represents, not a set of values, simply an inconvenience. Western cultural imports are forbidden, so teenage culture has gone underground. Music cassettes and CDs can be bought easily, but not openly. According to Ali, Iranian teenagers can be divided into two camps: rap-lovers and heavy metal freaks. 'Actually,' he confided to me with unmistakable pride, 'I'm into thrash metal myself.' I nodded knowingly, and kept my mouth shut. Soon the conversation turned to clothes. I asked a pretty 16-year-old girl if she resented the compulsory *hejab*, or Islamic dress, imposed on Iranian women. She smiled and said: 'What do you think?' The answer was indeed obvious: in Iranian terms, her *hejab* was very bad; her headscarf was pulled back off her head, revealing a quiff of dark hair; she had applied mascara and lipstick with vigour; and her body was swathed, not in the shapeless black gown favoured by the mullahs, but in an olive-green mackintosh with formidable shoulder pads. 'We all follow fashion,' she told me. 'Right now, all the girls are into dressing as boys, so underneath our *hejab* we're wearing Levis and men's shirts and trainers or boots.'

Some of the fear seems to have gone out of these youngsters' lives. In the 1980s the mullahs imposed their Islamic orthodoxy with fanatical zeal. The revolutionary Komitehs and the so-called Baseej militia were active moral policemen. Now public confrontations are less common. Occasionally boys with long hair are given on-the-spot haircuts; sometimes women exhibiting bad *hejab* are rounded up. But the revolution has lost its fire. New business opportunities have opened up. Almost every Teheran neighbourhood now has a door-to-door video salesman who visits his regular clients with a suitcase full of pirate copies of Western movies. For the wealthy, satellite dishes have suddenly become available and affordable. From a vantage point above Teheran rooftops, it is easy to spot the half-hidden dishes that are beaming foreign news, sport and entertainment into an increasing number of middle-class homes. Corruption has eased the constraints of the revolution. A 21-year-old newly married woman told me about her wedding party. About 100 guests were invited to her parents' home and were treated to a live band and an 'alcohol room'. There was no fear of a raid from the police because the chief of the local Baseej unit had been paid protection money. His men were outside, guarding the ungodly activities inside.

President Rafsanjani probably doesn't worry about the backsliding activities of Teheran's middle-class minority. Perhaps he sees in the inconsistencies a useful safety valve, allowing a potentially powerful economic and political group to reconcile itself to the revolution. If so, he is playing a dangerous political and cultural game—courting resentment from a population who can see hypocrisy and corruption at work. Moreover, in a country where state television is almost universally reviled as unwatchable and where very cheap second-hand video-players are widely available, the obsession with foreign movies and Western culture has spread far beyond the smart confines of north Teheran.

In the '80s, Iranian youngsters lived with the grim reality of war with Iraq. Hundreds of thousands were conscripted to the front; many never came back. Now there is no such terrifying, unifying threat to quell the voices of youthful rebellion. Iran's newly re-elected President has placed economic reform firmly at the top of his agenda for the next four years. Success is vital if he is to win the sympathy of the Islamic Republic's newest voters. In itself, however, material progress won't be enough. The revolution has to capture the imagination of youngsters for whom the slogans of Islamic struggle look increasingly empty. Failure will rob the revolution of the new blood desperately needed to keep it alive.

AFRICA

CHILDREN OF WAR

FERGAL KEANE   JOHANNESBURG   8 AUGUST 1992

*The shooting of a 13-year-old girl in Alexandra township, near
Johannesburg, South Africa, prompted Fergal Keane to reflect
upon how many children become the hapless victims of adult
disputes.*

THE CHILD'S NAME was Lucky. She was 13 years old, and she sang in
the Emanuel Choir. Those who knew her say that she was not a political
child, that she was interested in music and clothes. But this week an
adult, a grown-up, pointed an AK47 rifle at this child and killed her. The
newspapers said that she was 'dead on arrival in hospital'—a sterile phrase
that hides the reality of wailing sirens, voices crying, of blood and dying.
Yes, it has been a bad week for children: first the snipers of Sarajevo
taking their war to a busload of orphans; and then, ten minutes away
from my front door, the gunmen of Alexandra spraying Lucky and her
friends with high-velocity rifles.

When I arrived at the pathetic collection of tin shacks where the
shooting took place, I saw a man approaching his car with a bucket of
warm water and a cloth. I asked him if he had seen what had happened,
and he beckoned me over to the car. 'That is the blood,' he said. 'I am
going to clean it.' The man seemed distracted, and I left him alone.

At that point, a nine-year-old girl approached to tell me that she had seen
everything. 'The people were falling; they were all crying,' she said. The
child was agitated, hopping from one foot to the other and rushing to get
her story out. This was one nine-year-old who had seen too much.

Later on, once the immediate news had been sent to London, I found
myself unavoidably thinking of the other children of war I had known.

Lucky was only the latest in a long line of the butchered and the betrayed. The first I really remember was a young boy named Ande Mikhayle. When I came across him, he was lying in a field hospital, high in the lunar mountains of Eritrea in the Horn of Africa. The journey there had been perilous, weaving down mountain tracks in the night to escape the attentions of Ethiopian MiG fighters, our guerrilla escorts fidgeting nervously with automatic rifles. But the fear and exhaustion were all forgotten when I stepped inside that tent. On a stretcher lay a boy of about ten. He was covered in tin foil and lay face down. As I entered the tent, a soft wind blew in from the valley and the boy began to moan.

It was explained that Ande and his sister had been walking home from a village market when the jets released their cargo of napalm. Ande's sister was burned to death; he survived, but with terrible burns. 'And you see,' said the doctor, 'when the breeze blows through the tent, it torments his skin.' The doctor doubted whether Ande would survive. From time to time Ande tried to answer the doctor's questions about where he came from and how many others were in his family. But his lungs had also been ruined, and the voice was no longer a voice but a strange, wheezing sound from the depths of misery. Unable, any longer, to stand and look, I found my way outside and sat on a rock; but the sound followed me, and for a while I imagined that it was filling every corner of the darkening valley. I am not ashamed to say that I sat and wept for Ande Mikhayle, until the doctor came to tell me that it was time to be on the move while we still had the cover of darkness.

There have been other children of war since then: many in my own country, Ireland. Some who were killed or wounded; still others, like Robert, whose minds were scarred. Robert (I hesitate to use his second name lest he should read this) was the son of a post office worker under whose car the IRA had placed a bomb. The man was the victim of an IRA mistake. He died, yards from his own home, when the explosives ripped through the car: a sudden, deadly thunder, heard by his wife and children. At the funeral, I stood with a television crew near the corner of the street as the procession came into view. Walking directly behind his father's coffin on his own, slightly ahead of the main procession, was Robert. As he passed our vantage point, Robert looked at us. It is a gaze that I will always remember because it looked through and beyond us, to what I surmised was some place of unimaginable emptiness and coldness. Perhaps I was wrong, but it was a gaze that I thought was full of hatred.

We know that what happens in our childhood shapes our destiny; and we are told that all children have the right to happiness, to a loving environment. But let me ask aloud if any right has ever been more shamelessly trampled upon and abused. From Sarajevo to Belfast to Alexandra, the adults are busy making legitimate targets out of children: children like Ande Mikhayle, like Robert and Lucky and all the other lost and broken children of war whose hands reach out to us through the bars of history.

NO HOLIDAY FOR APARTHEID

FERGAL KEANE   JOHANNESBURG   3 OCTOBER 1992

Despite the talk of a 'new South Africa', and the government and the ANC stressing the need to bury the past, life for ordinary South Africans goes on much as before.

NATHANIEL SOKHO AND his wife Winnie live in a two-roomed house in the township of Atteridgville outside Pretoria. The township resembles a hundred others the length and breadth of South Africa: a blur of box-shaped houses and dust. One Sunday morning about a fortnight ago, Nathaniel and Winnie set out for Pretoria, a journey along the freeway with its concrete flyovers and streams of traffic pulsing towards the city. It was early morning, and the sun was starting to creep up behind the hills that seem to act as an outer ring of defence around the Afrikaner capital. As they travelled down the freeway, Nathaniel and Winnie were in good spirits; they were due to meet their friends and join a bus tour to the Cape, specifically to Namaqualand: a wilderness area of improbable beauty where the spring flowers throw a carpet of colours—red, purple, yellow and more—as far as the horizon. It is a wonder of which South Africans justly boast and which Nathaniel had been waiting and saving for years to see. He and his wife are pensioners who worked in the public service all their lives: he a schools administrator, she a nurse. The six other pensioners they were meeting were also former nurses.

At the prearranged meeting place, the Pretoria Holiday Inn, there was much laughter and shaking of hands as the friends talked excitedly of the journey ahead. At this point, it is worth remembering that such holidays are not the stuff of everyday life for black people: they are rare, very rare; for many, a once-in-a-lifetime experience. With their bags on board, Nathaniel, Winnie and friends took seats on the coach and waited for the journey to begin. They waited and waited. The next they knew, the white tour guide was reading out a list of names—the names of all black passengers on the coach—and asking them to get off. Their luggage was immediately offloaded. Standing with their bags on the pavement, they watched the tour buses drive off, bound for Namaqualand, a coach full of white people bound for the multi-coloured beauty of the Cape. After some time (around two hours according to Nathaniel), the manager of the tour firm arrived and arranged for a minibus to take the black group! By this stage, humiliated and angry, Nathaniel and Winnie and a friend decided that they would withdraw completely from the tour. When I spoke to him this week, Mr Sokho told me that he believed an English-speaking couple on the bus had refused to share the same transport as blacks. What galled him was the assumption that, if there was such a dispute, it should be solved by the removal of all the black passengers and not the withdrawal of those objecting to their presence. 'There is still apartheid in this country—it will only die when the old people die,' Nathaniel Sokho said.

At a time when so much is being said about the need to bury the past in South Africa, it strikes the observer that it is the attitudes of the present which are most badly in need of attention. Perhaps it is because I have returned from a long holiday abroad, but in recent weeks I have felt a rising sense of despair, prompted by the lack of humility—the arrogance which characterizes so much of white interaction with black. Like many of my colleagues, I find myself caught between the objective recognition that white and black alike are prisoners of history and deserve all the support the world can give and, on the other hand, a sense sometimes of disbelief at white attitudes. After all the evil of apartheid—the scientific savagery of the Immorality Act, of the Mixed Marriages Act, the Race Classification Act—the majority of those I encounter are reluctant, to say the least, when it comes to expressing any remorse. In fact, you are more likely to be treated to a defensive rant about how standards have slipped, how the ANC is controlled by a bunch of communists, how blacks are not fit to govern, and so on, and so on. Perhaps it is a defensiveness born of guilt, or a justifiable fear of what a black future may bring. Who knows?

The most that many in the National Party can rise to is an admission that, yes, people were hurt and apartheid was wrong; but the official party line remains that it was a policy born of idealism. President de Klerk, who was as much a part of the apartheid past as any other government minister, is one of the chief proponents of this line. Yes, it is true that some of his spokesmen have said 'sorry' publicly, but the President and, it has to be said, the majority of his followers are still a long way from that act of repentance. The overwhelming vote for change in the white referendum was, it is true, a leap forward—a practical step towards building a more just society. President de Klerk himself has shown immense political courage in taking what must be a great leap into the unknown. But one comes back to the words of Nathaniel Sokho: 'Apartheid is alive.' The sorry fact is that, whatever reforms have taken place, the attitudes which forced Nathaniel and his friends off the bus are still alive—draining away the goodwill and fellowship that this wounded country so desperately needs.

EMMA'S STORY

COLIN BLANE   WAAT   15 OCTOBER 1992

In southern Sudan the civil war has claimed the lives of an estimated half-million people over the past nine years. The world had already been shocked to learn the extent of the crisis in Somalia, and relief workers believed that a similar crisis was developing in Sudan.

IT WAS THE sound of singing that caught the attention first, as it wafted across the fields from a low, thatched building. Even on a weekday afternoon, the church choir in the town of Waat was practising, as thousands of other congregations do across southern Sudan. Inside the dark, cool building, light filtered through from one end to where a small boy with a drum beat out the rhythm for the worshippers to follow. Christianity is relatively new in the long history of southern Sudan, but its roots are deep and strong. Religion has become one of the most visible differences in the older animosity between Arab north and dark-skinned, African south. The war has other causes—including the untapped oil wealth of the region—but religion has provided the most potent symbols for both government and rebels to rally round.

Given the size of Sudan—it is the largest country in Africa—few foreigners, and even fewer Europeans, live there these days. One who does is Emma McCune, a former aid worker from Yorkshire who recently married a rebel commander, Riak Mashar. I met them under a fig tree in the vast swampland known as the Sud, which drains into the Nile. They had been walking for two days—often up to their knees in water—on their way to attend a leopard ceremony, an important tribal festival. For Emma, the march was a reminder of the gap between soft, Western ways and the tough, uncompromising life of Africa. As she sat in the shade, in her blue sun-hat and long skirt, she described how cars and planes have robbed most Westerners of the natural strength of their legs.

The man she has married is a Nuan chieftain who set out on a dangerous course when, a year ago, he defected with his troops from the founder of the rebel movement, Colonel John Garang. Riak Mashar travels with a bodyguard of 50 armed men and a solar panel to charge his computer and radio transmitter. His aim is to lead a stronger rebel army against the government; but if he fails to win round most of his former allies, then even the vastness of the Sud may not be big enough to hide him. Not that Commander Riak seemed troubled by such weighty military matters. His discussions with tribal leaders were punctuated by laughter, and the recent defection of another rebel commander may prove to be to his advantage. Like his English wife, Riak has crossed a cultural divide. This large, smiling figure, in soldier's beret and fatigues, went to university in Glasgow.

Emma McCune's adopted country has been devastated by the civil war; many of her friends have been killed. She told me that she had seen more death in three years in Sudan than she had known in a lifetime in England. Much of what is happening in southern Sudan is hidden from the outside world, partly because the region is so huge, and partly because the Islamic fundamentalist government is selective about the places aid workers and journalists may visit. One town that United Nations planes have been permitted to fly to is Waat. It has become a magnet for the hungry from places as far as 150 miles away; local people say the displaced are dying, as they walk for days in the hope of UN food and fresh water. There is no end in sight to Sudan's years of suffering, despite efforts by Nigeria to organize constructive negotiations. The government in the capital, Khartoum, has just announced a new offensive, in the language of a holy war, to bring the south to Islam. There are reports of purges in the southern capital, Juba, and in the Nuba mountains.

The rebels, too, have attracted international condemnation, for an incident last month in which four foreigners were killed in territory controlled by the original wing of the Sudan People's Liberation Army. Two of the four (an aid worker and a journalist) were shot in the back; the other two (both aid workers) were despatched by gunshots to the head, fired at close range. Despite this outrage, aid workers are still keen to help in southern Sudan, and some are pressing for a United Nations debate on the crisis. One man, Dieter Hanurch of the UN World Food Programme, has warned that the signals from southern Sudan are similar to those which led to the appalling famine in Somalia: too many guns and too many young men who don't know any other law.

In the wetlands of the south, I left Emma, the commander's wife, puffing an illicit cigarette as the clouds rolled across the endless green marshes. She might have been hundreds of miles from the nearest tarred road, but she knows—like everyone else—that there are only hard times ahead for southern Sudan.

NATAL—LAND OF HOPE AND GLORY?

FERGAL KEANE   DURBAN   5 NOVEMBER 1992

The South African province of Natal—a stronghold of Chief Buthelezi's Inkatha Freedom Party—has suffered appalling violence. Since the mid-1980s thousands have died in factional fighting. In November 1992, the leaders of Inkatha and the ANC were trying to foster good relations in an effort to put a stop to the bloodshed.

ON THE PROMENADE, where the moist breeze coasts in from the Indian Ocean and the lights of the Ferris wheels flicker green, blue and orange in the water, a saxophonist was playing *Land of Hope and Glory*. He was 15 floors below me, but the notes rose easily, even above the shrieking of the whirling children on the fairground machines. *Land of Hope and Glory*, on the seafront in Durban—a city in the midst of summer revels, on the day that 22 people were being lowered into a mass grave only 20 minutes away, in the village of Mpushini.

Like drifting from day into night, you can leave the glamorous acres of Durban's beach front and be in the murderous hill-country of Natal in minutes. The war is waiting out there in the hills, lying in forests, and in ditches: the war of ambush, massacre and assassination. In fact, drive in any direction from Durban, and you will find communities of frightened, angry people: north to Aesop, where Reggie Hadebe of the ANC was gunned down; east to Mooi River, where the rival gunmen struggle to beat each other in merciless killing; and south to Mpushini, where I found myself last weekend, witnessing a mass burial.

The road to the village swings in from the coast, over the sugar fields and along the edge of steep, terraced valleys, where houses and banana plantations stand staggered above one another. There are the usual cattle and goats rambling across the road, and gangs of children playing football on the few uncultivated patches of ground. But the rustic idyll ends when you begin to pay closer attention to the houses that flash by the car window: there are too many with broken windows, shattered roofs, walls pockmarked by rifle fire. And soon after you enter the area, you will almost certainly encounter military patrols: the mud-brown hulking shapes of armoured vehicles, where young, white soldiers sit—alternately bored and nervous—watching and waiting.

The road to the village is little more than a dirt track, veering round the edges of tiny thatched huts, an old school. I came to the village as the funeral service was getting under way. I passed lines of men carrying spears and clubs; a few had pistols stuck inside their belts. They viewed me with a wary eye: in this part of the world, strangers tend to mean trouble. In the centre of a small field, the coffins of the dead were lined up in front of the bereaved families. They sat on the ground, singing softly to themselves while a young priest moved through the group offering condolences. Then, from behind, came a loud, piercing cry. I turned and saw an old woman being helped along towards the coffins. She seemed to sway from side to side, crying all the time; then others in the group began to call out to the dead, until the entire field was rent by the sound of their sorrow. As the coffins were being lowered into a long, dusty trench, people stepped forward, placing final gifts of clothes next to their loved ones; one woman placed a letter in the grave.

It seemed to me that these people, and the young men who fired wildly into the air, were like people frozen into a nightmare, their world collapsing in the dust of a mass grave, and all thoughts now on the basic question of vengeance. The talk of the young men, and of quite a few older people too, was of reprisal. The ANC was blamed for this attack; the victims were all living in an Inkatha area. It is virtually certain that some other group of ordinary, landless, poverty-stricken people will suffer the same fate as the villagers of Mpushini, because they live in territory controlled by the ANC. For that is largely the way in the war of Natal: most of the dead are South Africa's have-nots, people who can only dream of the golden beaches of Durban. They are frightened people in ragged clothes who move across the landscape in the darkness, dragging their few belongings and their children to some new place of refuge, while Nelson Mandela and Chief Buthelezi argue over the terms for a possible meeting; and President de Klerk emphasizes, again and again, the black-on-black nature of the violence.

Back in Durban, of the blue seas, golden sands and beach-front musicians, I listened back to the tapes of voices crying in the valley of Mpushini. There, in my hotel room, watching the lights flickering on tankers in the bay, listening to the laments on my tape recorder, I felt an intense weariness: with the politics of massacre and reprisal; the endless exchange of recriminations. You will, I trust, understand why the intrusion of the solitary notes of *Land of Hope and Glory*, rising from the street below, brought a wistful smile to my lips.

ANARCHY RULES

TOM CARVER   MOGADISHU   7 JANUARY 1993

The situation in Somalia at the end of 1992, following the ousting of President Siad Barre, had deteriorated to such an extent that 20,000 US-led troops were sent in to the country. But some observers believed the only way to restore order was to disarm the militias.

'TWO WEEKS IN Mogadishu is the equivalent to a year anywhere else,' the American TV producer said on the first day I arrived. And so it soon seemed. Mogadishu is unlike anywhere else I have ever been to. Anarchy is a term used far too easily by journalists, but it is the right word in Somalia's case. When thinking of Mogadishu in terms of a capital city, suspend all judgement. Even in the chaos of Kinshasa or Beirut there are still hotels that work, street lights that flicker on and off, signs pointing in vaguely the right direction. In Mogadishu there is nothing: not one traffic light, street light or billboard. The only water for our first five days dripped reluctantly out of the tap for 20 minutes every afternoon, before drying up with a gurgle that sounded, to my fevered imagination, like a laugh from the underworld. A lot of time was spent cutting the tops off plastic bottles and filling them up: so much for flushing the toilet, so much for shaving, and so on. The building where we stayed would have been called a hotel, had it been anything more than half-built. Instead, bare wires poked menacingly out of the wall; even the flea-ridden mattresses were imported.

In an anarchy, the marketplace goes berserk. For the privilege of this poverty, we had to pay $85 a day each; the same as a hotel room in central London. Two years of internecine warfare have reduced Somali society to its lowest common denominator. Stripped of all altruism, and of any sort of civic responsibility, the only guiding principle in Mogadishu is the dollar. 'They are not all bandits and gunmen,' the head of an aid agency said to me once—but it sounded as though he was trying to convince himself. We soon learned not to let anyone touch our bags; a man had only to lower one case from the back of a truck and he would be jabbing you in the chest, yelling, 'Ten dollars, ten dollars!' One day a young boy came to our room and offered to do the laundry; we agreed a price and he went away with the clothes. The next day he brought them back in a bucket of dirty water which he dumped in the middle of the room. 'Drying and ironing is extra,' he announced. We refused to succumb to such blackmail and hung them up ourselves. But all this was only a foretaste of what was to come.

Our worst experience occurred on Christmas Day. We had travelled down to Badera to cover the arrival there of the Marines. Having been told that transport was in short supply in the town, Andrew Roy, our TV producer, agreed to drive a car from Mogadishu while we flew in ahead of the troops. After some difficulty, he had found a battered Land Cruiser which he had to pay $500 a day to hire, complete with drivers and guards. On Christmas morning, we pulled up outside the UN offices in this vehicle in the centre of Badera when—without warning—we were surrounded by a group of about 40 men, screaming at us. One of them leant inside across the driver and tried to pull out the ignition key. I tried to stop him, and eventually extracted the key from his hand. But then the knives came out, long and double-bladed. They began jabbing at the doors and windows. We got the message; we jumped out and ran. Our drivers were already halfway up the street ahead of us. We were lucky to escape with our lives and equipment. I threw away the key in disgust, but they managed to start the vehicle anyway and careered off, men hanging on to each corner.

It was the last we ever saw of our car. We went to the District Commissioner and told him. But he said that the vehicle had been stolen from Badera in the first place. We said that the owner in Mogadishu had papers proving that he owned it. The District Commissioner said that the owner in Badera had papers, too. When we got back to Mogadishu, things went from bad to worse. As soon as the owner heard what had happened, he did not leave us alone. Every morning he would be in the yard of the hotel, yelling and threatening us whenever we went out. We sat down to talk to him, and pointed out that we had at least saved the life of his son, who was one of the drivers. 'Which do you care about more, your son's life or your car?' we asked him.

'My car,' came the chilling reply, 'I have 20 other sons.'

It was clear that we were going to have to compensate him; but how much? His son had said that the car was worth $30,000. We laughed. Then the owner demanded $200,000 and we stopped laughing. In the end, after bringing in a clan elder to act as a negotiator, we agreed on compensation smaller than either of these figures; but it was still a lot of money.

What made the situation even more bizarre was that all this was going on under the noses of 30,000 American and international troops. The impact of the forces on life in Somalia has been surprisingly muted. For the first few weeks, the military interpreted their role, of providing security for the food convoys, very literally. They were not here to restore law and order, we were told. So all day the Marines would sit atop their war machines, while below them in the streets things went on much as before. Television crews being held up at gunpoint became commonplace: one American network lost five cameras within a week; another had a camera stolen, then bought it back from the thieves, only to be hijacked again within 24 hours. There was a feeling of immense helplessness that can only come from being in a country without any sort of civil authority.

There was no point in going down to the police station: it had long since been emptied and ransacked. There were a few elderly men dressed in uniform trying to direct traffic, but they were utterly ignored by the cars, which drove in any direction they wished. To some people, who feel hemmed in by authority in the West, the idea of anarchy may seem an attractive one. But in real life what anarchy means is the law of the jungle. In Somalia, a few teenagers with the guns prosper, while the vast majority live like animals, cowering under pieces of plastic, scrabbling in the dirt for food, dying of typhoid and dysentery. Worst of all, since anarchy means the absence of any legal code, no one is held accountable for his actions. A man can die for a curse in Somalia and no one would notice.

Twenty-one centuries after the Greeks gave us the concept of civic rule, it sometimes feels as though we haven't progressed very far.

FAREWELL TO EAST AFRICA

COLIN BLANE   NAIROBI   4 FEBRUARY 1993

The Somali famine, the Kenyan elections, reconstruction in Ethiopia—these are some of the stories which have been making the news in East Africa. In the course of the last four years there, our correspondent, Colin Blane, has covered events in 20 countries, including coups, civil wars and a string of political upheavals.

IT HAS BEEN a period of rapid change; a time of vivid images and big political convulsions. The end of the Cold War, the beginning of the multi-party era and the revival of tribalism: these are some of the themes which have transformed the way Africans view their continent.

When I arrived in the Red Sea port of Massawa nearly three years ago, a mound of grain was still smoking and smouldering on the quayside. The town, in rebel hands, had been bombed by warplanes of the Ethiopian dictator, President Mengistu; humanitarian aid, like much else, had been set on fire. Churches and mosques had their roofs blown in, houses were destroyed, the population hid in culverts under the road. But the bombing of Massawa didn't only terrify civilians, it also lit a fuse under President Mengistu himself.

Fifteen months later, Africa's largest army had been defeated and rebel tanks were thundering through the streets of the Ethiopian capital, Addis Ababa. It was Mengistu's ruthlessness and cruelty which galvanized them: those rag-tag troops from the mountains, the sons and daughters of peasant farmers. Away from the gaze of the rest of the world, they fought armoured battles and trench warfare with a ferocity never seen before in Africa. Later, when the guns fell silent, I visited a graveyard for tanks; the future of one of the world's poorest countries mortgaged for a futile war. There were hundreds of American and Soviet machines, barrels pointing at the sky, grass growing over them and a solitary horse grazing among them. Ethiopia's weapons of war claimed victims even after the soldiers had fled. When an ammunition dump blew up in Addis Ababa, four journalists—myself among them—were caught up in the blast. When the dust had settled, our cameraman, Mohammed Amin, was badly injured, and the sound recordist, John Maathai, was dead.

Somalia's civil war erupted six months later; another dictator, Mohammed Siad Barre, was forced to flee. His capital, Mogadishu, had been a place of whitewashed villas and almost Mediterranean charm. A few weeks before the city imploded, I remember speaking to a priest in the cool of the Anglican cathedral, eating lobster in a restaurant by the beach, and playing golf in the grounds of the US embassy. In the frenzy that followed, all that—and a lot more besides—was utterly destroyed. Somalia did have a local administration, and it could have again if the clan elders could shake themselves free of the gangsters' grip. The militias blame each other for the catastrophe in their country, and all trust between them has gone. During one ceasefire ceremony, a shell landed in the compound where the agreement was being signed. Everybody accepts that it was the war which caused the famine; and it was the gunmen who have made it so difficult for outsiders to help.

It has been a similar story in southern Sudan, where ten years of fighting have ravaged towns and villages across the region. One afternoon, in the lengthening shadows, I watched thousands of Sudanese boys trekking across the border out of their homeland into Kenya. It was, for most of them, the third country they had walked to in a year; 1,000 miles of wandering, pushed backwards and forwards by the war. Some had been hit by bullets; a few had been taken by crocodiles in the swamps; the tail-ender, a cripple, limped through the dust with a black umbrella as a crutch. More then 10,000 stray children fled to Kenya from the fighting, many still carrying the school books that they hoped would give them an education. They are part of a generation lost to the civil war, a war which the Islamic government in the north is gradually winning, as Christian pastors in their dark wattle churches fear the worst.

Further to the south, in Kenya, there have been powerful political forces at work as well. When a renegade churchman preached an anti-government sermon on New Year's Day in 1990, few could have imagined that the country's one-party system was in any serious danger. But government critics grew bolder; after that, the abiding opposition image was of the populist, Martin Shikuku, riding on the roof of a pick-up, trying to address a banned rally. Pressure from inside and outside the country took Kenya all the way to multi-party elections. The process may have been manipulated by government, but Kenyan voters still turned out in their millions and rejected some of the country's most unpopular politicians.

In Kenya, as in other places in the region, the most pressing issues remain unresolved. Recession and the burden of debt threaten an already faltering economy. Political rivalry has brought back to life the tribalism whose existence African diplomats used to deny. And a lack of resources is undermining the provision of education and health, to whose development all efforts were previously supposed to be directed.

What happens now in eastern Africa will depend, to some extent, on how the crisis in the southern part of the continent unfolds. I was in the Zambian capital, Lusaka, when Nelson Mandela went to meet his ANC colleagues, days after his release. It is no exaggeration to say that Africa rejoiced. Gradually, trade with South Africa is reviving. Accents from the Transvaal and Durban can be heard across the counter in Nairobi. The success of reform in South Africa is becoming more and more important for the economic survival of the rest of the continent as well.

PLUS ÇA CHANGE

FERGAL KEANE   JOHANNESBURG   4 MARCH 1993

This despatch, recalling the violent death of a black security guard in South Africa, made Fergal Keane the overall winner in the Amnesty International Press Awards, 1993.

THE MINE DUMPS of Benoni loom out of the landscape like mountains on some stark, lifeless planet. They are the residue of deep burrowing in the earth, the hungering after gold which gives towns like Benoni, and others along the Reef, a reason for existing. This is scrubland on which the mine dumps and the acres of suburban bungalows were imposed, as the Witwatersrand was opened up by the settlers in the closing stages of the last century. The gold hunger brought with it the need for a large pool of native labour. They are the people who gaze out at us, like dejected shadows, from contemporary photographs of those years; and today Benoni is circled by the townships which house thousands of black South Africans. You may or may not notice the townships if you travel as a tourist from Johannesburg to the Kruger National Park, but you will certainly see the mine dumps, for they dominate the horizon.

What I am fairly sure of is that Samuel Khanagha saw them one clear, autumn morning, less than a year ago. He was sitting in a car, speeding towards one of the dumps; and one has every reason to believe that he was afraid—very afraid. Samuel was sitting between two white men; another drove the car. Two black guards followed. Samuel knew the white men, Johan Van Eyk, François Oosthuizen and Hendrik Gerber. They were colleagues at the Johannesburg security company where Samuel was a guard. They were taking him to a disused dump, out of the public eye—a place where a man's screams would be lost in the emptiness of the veld. The court records do not tell us what was said in the car, so we can only imagine the scene: a black man and three white men; he accused of stealing £15,000, they determined to make him admit to it. All three white men were former members of the security forces: two had served in a counter-insurgency unit in Namibia; one was the son of the recently retired Deputy Commissioner of Police.

The car pulled up on waste ground and Samuel was hustled out and tied up. Somebody went back to the car and produced an electric shock machine and a plastic bag. Lying on the ground, Samuel would have seen this happening: the muscular white men chattering to one another in Afrikaans, setting up the machine and wires with which they planned to extract the truth from him. Somebody tied a rope round Samuel's feet and put the plastic bag over his head; he felt himself being dragged along, and then hoisted on to the branch of a tree.

Within a few minutes, we are told, the interrogation began. One of the white men pulls Samuel's trousers down and places electrodes on his genitals. The electric shocks start—waves of pain that convulse the body. Soon Samuel is begging for mercy, but he still refuses to admit to the crime. He did not do it, he tells his tormentors again and again. But the white men are thirsty, so they pause; one of the black guards is sent off for drinks. Among the white men there is laughter and bantering. This is hard work, and the day is warm. Eventually the drinks arrive and Samuel Khanagha begs for something to cool his thirst; he begs for mercy, but his interrogators laugh. The worst has yet to come. Of the three, only Oosthuizen is feeling any pang of conscience; he offers Khanagha something to drink. We are not told from the records of the court what the reaction of the two black guards was. The white men appear by now to have run out of patience. They begin to place wood and sticks under Samuel's body. Somebody adds a match, and soon a fire is blazing under the black man's head. Van Eyk, Oosthuizen and Gerber stand back and watch their victim twist in agony as the fire gathers force. They can hear his screams but no one else can. One of the whites pumps several bullets into the dying black man; another cuts off his right hand. This bizarre mutilation is never explained in the subsequent trial. By nightfall, Samuel Khanagha is dead, his body abandoned in the bush, his right hand found on a suburban street in Benoni.

When the case came to an end in court last week, the men were sentenced to periods of 10, 15 and 20 years for Samuel Khanagha's murder. With good behaviour, they could all be free having served less than half their sentences. Had three black men been accused of murdering a white in so horrific a manner, they would doubtless have been sentenced to death. People die in brutal attacks every day in South Africa: nobody—no racial or political group—has a monopoly on the exercise of murder; whites kill blacks; blacks kill other blacks and whites. Yet there is something about the murder of Samuel Khanagha which stands apart: he died at the hands of men who can have regarded him as little better than an animal; men who took their time with the killing; who carried it out in front of black witnesses; and who never even bothered to cover their tracks. All three men were products of a security system that revelled in the casual exercise of brutality over a black underclass.

The system is being dismantled, but the attitudes remain entrenched: what happened to Samuel Khanagha was not an isolated incident; nor was the leniency of the sentencing untypical. Yet the image of this figure—hanging upside down over a burning fire while others laughed at his pleas for mercy—is a challenge to all of us—correspondents, observers and analysts—who speak glibly about a 'new South Africa'.

THE MIRAGE OF PEACE

TOM CARVER   LUANDA   18 MARCH 1993

In Angola, hopes for a negotiated end to the renewed civil war were dashed by the government's rejection of the United Nations' appeals for peace talks with the Unita rebel movement, which had refused to accept electoral defeat in September 1992. Five months on, it was estimated that 15,000–20,000 people had died since fighting broke out in October, and three million—almost a third of the population—faced disease and hunger.

THE THEME OF those selling on the streets this morning appears to be beach-wear. Yesterday it was clocks; the day before, cooking pots. It all depends on which shipping container in the port the kids have broken into overnight. Today's sight is strikingly surreal even for this crazed country. Through the petrol fumes pouring out of a thousand broken exhausts in the Rua de Missao outside my hotel, I watch the kids walking between the vehicles, waving their products: inflatable rubber rings of bright yellow and pink; lilos blown up in the shape of green tortoises with huge smiles on their faces; masks, flippers, beach-towels. Sometimes the smoke and traffic become so intense that the children disappear from view and all I can see is a dozen cheerful tortoises floating through the streets. There are not many takers for the goods; these days, Angolans have more sombre things on their minds than what to take to the beach. Nevertheless the kids have effectively become the capital's shopkeepers. Every morning, Theresa, our indefatigable translator, will ask the children how much a packet of cigarettes costs. As they eagerly thrust their rival brands through the car window, she says that she doesn't smoke; she just wants to know what the level of inflation is today.

This was my first trip back to Angola since the elections last September. The first thing that struck me was how much more relaxed the atmosphere was in Luanda. During the elections, when Unita was in town, life was not easy. Luanda is very much the territory of the ruling MPLA; for the Unita leader, Jonas Savimbi, living in the capital was like inhabiting the lion's den. Ironically, now that Unita have gone back to the bush to resume the war where they left off, Luanda is more peaceful than it has been for a long time.

The tranquillity, however, disguises the fact that Angola is facing its worst crisis since independence. In the six months since the elections, Unita has succeeded in capturing more of the country than it did in 16 years of civil war. Margaret Anstee, the UN's special envoy to Angola, told the UN Security Council last week that the rebels were now in charge of 104 of the country's 120 municipalities. Not only does it control Huambo, the country's second-largest city, much of the diamond-producing areas of the north-east and large tracts of the countryside, but there is now talk of a rebel advance towards the capital itself.

Many Angolans blame all this on what they regard as the ham-fisted intervention of the international community, which insisted on elections and then failed to ensure that the results were observed. The MPLA government is seething with righteous indignation: having won the elections fairly and squarely, it is now in danger of losing everything on the battlefield to Unita, which flatly refused to accept the outcome. And the UN—as in so many other parts of the world—seems powerless or reluctant to do anything about it.

For those who suffered during the long years of war before the elections, the present situation is almost more than they can bear. It is estimated that there are 60,000 *mutilados* in Angola—men who have lost at least one limb fighting in the army against Unita. We found one colony of them in an old hotel on the outskirts of the capital, living with their families in conditions of total poverty. As we approached the former hotel, we could see them milling around in front. Some lay on the ground, fast asleep. Others leant on their crutches, arguing ferociously with one another. A few sat on the wall, cursing the traffic that passed by. It was clear that they were all blind drunk. In the middle, some of the wives stirred a huge tub of frothing liquid. One of the women explained that they made the brew from sorghum and battery-acid. As they doled it out into tins mugs held by shaky, frail hands, I wondered whether they knew that they were killing their own husbands with the lethal mixture; yet this was their only release from their misery and pain.

'We drink to lose our memories,' said Elias Job in Portuguese—one of the few *mutilados* coherent enough to speak. He was 27 and had been in a wheelchair for four years, having lost both his legs to an exploding mine. He had a gentle, open face, but his eyes were bloodshot with alcohol and unhappiness. When I mentioned the election, he shook his head. He knew all about it. He had nothing to say. For a few brief months, these men—the neglected victims of a war in which they didn't choose to fight—had dared to hope that they might not finish their days dying under their old army blankets, forgotten and unthanked. The election represented a gleaming hope: they dreamed of being able to rejoin society, of being reunited with their families. But the cruel collapse of hope and the resumption of war have, instead, added to their demented suffering. 'My family are all in Huambo. I have no idea what has happened to them,' Elias said. 'I want to go back to Huambo, but I can't because of Unita. I hate this place.'

I thought of the contrast with Remembrance Day in Britain, and how our war-wounded are revered and honoured. These men deserve better; their country has voted for peace and received more war in return. I thought of the promises that the West makes to Africa—and of how few of them are ever fulfilled.

THE ALMOST APOCALYPSE

FERGAL KEANE   JOHANNESBURG   15 APRIL 1993

The tortuous negotiation process in South Africa was thrown off-course by the assassination of one of the African National Congress's most senior figures, Chris Hani, in April 1993. The anger among blacks boiled over into violence, and concerns were expressed that law and order in South Africa could be on the verge of collapse. The ANC seemed to have lost control over its young, radical members, who were no longer responding to their leaders' appeals for calm.

THIS IS A strange and frightened hour in South Africa. The voices of reason are being drowned, swept away in a wave of anger and bitterness. For the first time in my experience, naked hatred of whites is in the eyes and speech of those I meet on township streets. I experienced it myself on the streets of Soweto yesterday. An angry crowd surged around my car and chanted the slogan of the radical left, 'One settler, one bullet'. It was no use explaining that, as a foreign correspondent, I was anything but a colonial settler. This was a crowd seething with hatred, and only my black colleague's calming voice soothed the mob. A few minutes later we were swept along to the fence of Protea police station, the township's biggest security base. Then the chaos erupted. I was standing by a wall when a volley of gunfire cut a swath through the crowd. The crowd pushed me back over the wall, probably saving me from serious injury in their attempts to flee the shooting. Tear-gas enveloped the area, and I ran with the surging thousands to the safety of a nearby community hall. Behind me, my BBC colleagues, Glen Middleton and Lee Edwards—cameraman and sound man, respectively—were lying, wounded, on the ground. They were among the 250 people hit by gunfire. They are, thankfully, safe, having had several shotgun pellets removed from their bodies. But others were not so lucky: at least three were killed, and many other people sustained critical injuries. This was a police response which far exceeded the degree of provocation offered. At Soweto's giant Baragwanath Hospital I watched the injured being carried in by the dozen; inside the emergency ward, doctors and nurses struggled to cope with the numbers. The cries and groans of the injured could be heard above the din of ambulances sweeping into the courtyard. Most poignant of all was the face of a woman who watched her husband slip into death and then cried, 'What for, what for?'

But if the police acted with callous stupidity in Soweto, one also has to concede that the ANC was patently unable to control its supporters in many areas. The visions of looting and wanton destruction on the streets of Cape Town and Port Elizabeth will linger long in the mind. So, too, the vision of Nelson Mandela struggling to be heard above the angry shouts of the crowds in Soweto's Jabulani stadium. One could only feel sorry for this gentle and dignified man, as he was shouted down by a generation which wants revolution, not the subtle compromise which Mandela and other ANC leaders advocate. The situation is complicated by the actions of South Africa's huge criminal community—ever eager to ply their trade under the guise of political protest.

As I write, President de Klerk is announcing the deployment of thousands more troops and police, and warning of sweeping security measures to contain the unrest. It is a predictable measure, but it will do nothing to defuse the anger on the streets. For, in essence, what we are witnessing is the rebellion of a lost generation which feels it has waited too long for the freedom and democracy that Nelson Mandela promised when he walked free from the gates of Victor Verster prison three years ago.

In the chaos of these past few days one almost forgets the chilling facts of Chris Hani's murder and the terrible loss he represents, not just to the ANC, but to the cause of sanity and reason. It took only seconds for his killer to strike: one moment Chris Hani was stepping out of his car, the next he was dead. In such a manner was the destiny of a great political figure decided, and the future of South Africa placed in question. I have witnessed a previous emergency—that of 1986—when South Africa again seemed to hover over the abyss. Because the situation was brought under control then, I am reluctant to predict a complete collapse of law and order. It has always appeared to me that South Africa is the land of the almost apocalypse: too often in the past journalists have predicted the imminent demise of the government, or a racial bloodbath. For that reason, you will forgive me if I refuse to make any predictions, beyond the sad certainty that the sound of gunfire and weeping will fill the air for some time to come.

BANDA ON THE RUN

ANDY KERSHAW   LILONGWE   1 MAY 1993

Demands for an end to the years of dictatorship by Malawi's
'Life President', Dr Hastings Banda—both from opposition
movements and from countries supplying aid—was about to
spell an end to years of one-party rule.

THE DOCTOR WAS spluttering with rage. 'Twenty-eight years of independence and we still have to put up with this!' he yelled and swept
an arm at our marooned vehicles. I was driving south down the western
shore of Lake Malawi, hoping to complete a lap of the country, and I
had met the doctor and his four passengers coming the other way. Now
both our cars were stuck in a valley of thick mud. We swapped details
of the grim conditions of the road we had covered. The doctor had a
four-wheel drive. I had been supplied with a small saloon. It was when
the axles of the four-wheel drive began to slip from our view, deeper into
the cake mixture, that I had to face up to the unthinkable: I was beaten;
and I had come so far.

In fact I had come all of eight kilometres. But the rain the night
before had been a downpour of Old Testament ferocity, and those
eight kilometres had taken me five hours to drive. Where the rain
had sliced deep gullies across the track, I had to build my own road
to get through. From the undergrowth I gathered rocks and branches
and, to the amusement of knots of villagers, toiled under a fierce sun
to repair the craters and bridge the ruts. Inching the car forward over
each obstacle, I fancied myself as John Mills in *Ice Cold in Alex*.
The road was marked on my government map as a main highway
and named, playfully, the M5. Everyone I had consulted, in the last

town before the tarmac ran out, assured me that the road was first-class. Reasons of national prestige had lured me into this morass, and the doctor, slithering in the mud in an expensive suit, couldn't defend the charade any longer. There, in a bog, in a jungle, in the middle of nowhere and to a European stranger he had met just a few seconds before, he cursed the *Ngwazi* (The Hero), His Excellency, Life President Dr Hastings Kamuzu Banda, and denounced Banda's self-trumpeted, post-independence achievements as phoney.

Until recently, the doctor would have bitten his lip, fearful of informers from the Malawi Congress Party Young Pioneers—Dr Banda's very own Tonton Macoutes. Like Papa Doc Duvalier, the Haitian daddy of designer-dictators and another self-appointed Life President, Dr Banda came to power as the promising black nationalist hero of his people. But since independence from Britain in 1964, Banda has ruled Malawi with a rod of iron in one hand and his famous fly-whisk in the other. He is the world's oldest head of state, aged somewhere between 92 and 97, and one of its most paranoid. The Father of the Nation is a puritanical, Victorian parent—severe with any insolent advocates of a multi-party system. And he has also got a thing about trousers.

You get your first hint of this at the check-in at Heathrow. The woman on the desk was obliged to read me what the Americans call a 'travel advisory': 'Male passengers, both visitors and residents, are reminded that they are not permitted in Malawi to wear bell-bottom trousers.' Restrictions on women are even more puritanical: trousers on women are banned; skirts must cover the knee. The Inspector-General of Police had a bit of a rant about this recently in a government newspaper. He noted that there was a tendency among women and girls, especially in the cities, 'to wear long trousers indoors or during parties. These lawbreakers,' he said, 'who change the law from their bedrooms will be arrested once found.'

The river of sludge that is the M5 is Dr Banda's real road to democracy. Portuguese and British companies have begun building bridges and a proper highway down the lake shore. But foreign aid to Malawi for projects like this has been linked recently to a move to a multi-party system. The combination of donor countries' insistence on political reform and the sensational outburst last year by Malawi's bishops against Banda's revolting human rights record has pushed the Life President into a referendum, on 14 June, on the future of one-party rule. Ordinary Malawians are going daft with excitement. In the deepest parts of the forest, villagers waved the two-finger symbol of the multi-party movement at my car and yelled, 'Aford!' (the Alliance for Democracy) as I rumbled by. Aford and the UDF, the United Democratic Front, are campaigning together up to the referendum. Their platform is a simple one, but novel for Malawi: civil and human rights, and not being the Malawi Congress Party.

After the referendum, Aford and the UDF may go their separate ways; and herein lies the danger for the Malawian pro-democracy groups. Banda, in the event of a general election, will be pinning his slim hopes of victory on a split in the opposition vote—it did, after all, work for Daniel Arap Moi in Kenya. But it might never get to that: Dr Banda has surpassed himself in his attempts to discredit, divide and destroy the opposition. Orton Chirwa, a former Minister of Justice, was brave enough to speak out against the corruption of one-party rule; he was abducted in Zambia by Malawi security agents in 1981. For more than a decade he was left to rot, chained and naked, in a stinking prison. Last October, aged 73, he died in jail—of strangulation. Banda, in a speech shortly afterwards, expressed his sorrow at Chirwa's death. The trade union activist and Aford leader, Chakufwa Chihana, is serving nine months for sedition. He had the audacity to re-enter the country after Banda, in a speech in February 1992, had categorized opponents returning from abroad as 'meat for crocodiles'.

With Chihana banged up for the referendum, the opposition has a new charismatic leader in a young Presbyterian priest, the Reverend Aaron Longwe. A year ago, Longwe had no intention of becoming a liberation theologian messiah. Then, from his pulpit, he echoed the bishops' unease about human rights. The congregation was ecstatic. Longwe is now a hot contender for president.

This week the government began to gag a flourishing opposition press. Copies of *New Express* and *UDF News* were cutting it too close to the bone, and selling out as fast as they could be printed. A cartoon in one of them caught the referendum euphoria splendidly: a man is returning home from work with a huge bunch of papers under his arm. 'Where are your wages? Where is the food?' his wife is shouting. 'I've got neither,' says the man. 'I spent all my money on newspapers.' Government newspapers and the Malawi Broadcasting

Corporation are cringing servants of the Life President. Lead stories in the *Daily Times* and the *Malawi News* (motto: Freedom Of Expression Our Birthright) seldom varied in my two-week visit: there was the success of the *Ngwazi*'s provincial crop inspections, where every day the old brute was photographed fingering the stems of maize plants in the gardens of what the *Daily Times* referred to as 'ordinary people'. And with the imagination that once characterized the Albanian dailies or the *Pyongyang Times*, there were sad articles detailing the *Ngwazi*'s achievements since independence: unity, peace, stability and prosperity. Of course no one points out that the price of Malawi's stability is terror. Nobody questions why a manifestly fertile country with enormous tobacco, tea and coffee exports is one of the poorest on earth. Not a column inch is devoted to the programmes of the opposition, except to attack the uppity multi-party advocates for having the disrespect to question the *Ngwazi*.

And no one, except perhaps Banda himself, believes this guff any more. Fear was lifting like a fog. Malawians found the confidence to speak out and, apart from government and party functionaries, I didn't meet one person who was supporting the Life President on 14 June. Even the army and, to a lesser extent, the police are quietly pro-democracy.

It should be a landslide. But now the *Ngwazi* is beginning to panic: this week he introduced new laws that give Malawi Congress Party members immunity from prosecution for acts of violence and intimidation during the referendum campaign. Nothing less than the violence of a dictatorship in its death-throes could stop the pro-democracy tide. The turn-out at the Banda rally I attended suggested that his defeat in a free and fair referendum would be humiliating.

The *Malawi News* called it a 'mammoth crowd' in his home town of Kasungu. But if you discount the Mbumba—his troupe of women dancers-cum-bodyguards—party officials and Young Pioneers, the only civilians present in significant numbers were hundreds of children, brought in specially to make up the numbers on the promise of a bus-ride and a day off school. Frightened and bullied by the red-shirted Pioneers, they clapped lamely when told to do so. The Father of the Nation, a control freak, kept the children waiting three hours in the broiling heat beyond his scheduled arrival time. When finally he drove up, standing on an open-top Land-Rover draped in white silk, I got the briefest glimpse of the fly-whisk, the black homburg, the sun-glasses and the dark suit. Then he vanished into a swarm of scowling Young Pioneers brandishing placards: 'Foreign Press, Tell The Truth About Malawi!' and 'Amnesty International Leave The Ngwazi Alone'. (The human rights organization has been refused permission to enter the country).

Dr Banda, showing a flair for supreme self-delusion to the end, prefers not to look beyond the slogans of his party thugs. But the game is up and he knows it. After all, only a deeply insecure president would worry about the political implications of a lame Paul McCartney song: *Band on the Run* is outlawed in Malawi.

SOUL FORCE

TOM CARVER   BHAMBAYI   27 MAY 1993

April 1993 was the 100th anniversary of Mahatma Gandhi's arrival in South Africa, where he founded a community based on his philosophy of non-violence—or 'soul force' as he preferred to call it. Since than, Phoenix Settlement has been turned into South Africa's largest squatter camp, now called Bhambayi.

IT WAS A glorious evening such as you get only in Africa: still and cloudless and full of unbelievable, rich, soaking light which blessed everything it touched and turned even the most grotesque squalor into something of dignity. As I tried to manoeuvre my clean, white, hire car along the rain-eaten gullies of the squatter camp, I felt very conspicuous. The people stopped what they were doing to stare as we passed. In the rear-view mirror, I could see their gaze following each turn and bounce of the little car into the distance. It was an ominous sign; we had entered territory that few outsiders ever ventured into if they cared to stay alive.

This was Bhambayi squatter camp, some say the biggest squatter community in the whole of South Africa. As far as the eye can see, a canopy of tin, ragged plastic and refuse ranged over the hills just north of Durban, a maze of deprivation where only feral dogs and warlords walked with any impunity. Once, however, it looked very different and was known by a different name: Phoenix Settlement. A hundred years ago, Mahatma Gandhi chose this spot, then empty and green, to set up the first community based on the philosophies which were to make him justly famous.

Gandhi was only 23 when he arrived in South Africa from India as an unknown lawyer. He intended to spend only a few months here, but he quickly found himself caught up in the Indian community's struggle against the racist laws. As he became increasingly involved, he developed his philosophy of passive resistance, though that was a term he never liked. He preferred to call it 'soul force': the negation of any form of physical force or violence. 'If a man gives you a drink of water and you give him a drink in return,' Gandhi once wrote, 'that is nothing. Real beauty consists in doing good against evil.'

We arrived at the top of a small clearing, squeezed on all sides by shacks. 'This is the place where Gandhi built his home,' Mawa Rangobin said to me. Mawa had been born in Phoenix Settlement and was once married to Gandhi's grand-daughter. When I told him that I wanted to take him back there to see what remained of the place, he had looked at me nervously. 'Do you know just how dangerous it is?' he said. Now that we were here, he kept close to his car. On the downside of the mound was a small concrete platform. 'That is all that remains,' Mawa said, pointing at it, 'of Gandhi's home. In 1985 the government drove thousands of these squatters on to this land as part of their forced removals programme. It took them just three days to raze the place to the ground.'

I felt an immense sorrow. Here, all around us, were the type of people to whom Gandhi had dedicated his life: the downtrodden, the hungry, the oppressed. Yet they had destroyed his very home with the sort of unconscious brutality that he had worked so hard to prevent. The only building belonging to Gandhi that still stands is the place where he once produced a newspaper, *Indian Opinion*, to disseminate his ideas. Today it is no more than a concrete shell. Above the entrance is written 'Printing Press—Founded by Mahatma Gandhi, 1903'; on the walls below are scrawled more modern messages: 'Viva APLA', 'Viva AK47', 'Kill the police'. There could hardly be a more poignant symbol of the fate that has befallen Gandhi's ideas in South Africa. After 21 years of struggling to create a culture of non-violence here, he decided to return to India. In one of the last editions of *Indian Opinion* he wrote a farewell message to his followers:

'I shall soon be far from Phoenix, and I would leave behind my innermost thoughts. Passive resistance is the noblest and the best education. It will not be denied that a child, before it begins to write its alphabet and to gain worldly knowledge, should know what the soul is; what truth is; what love is; what powers are latent in the soul. A child should learn that in the struggle of life, it can easily conquer hate by love;

untruth by truth; violence by self-suffering. It was because I felt the force of this truth that I endeavoured to train the children at Phoenix along these lines.'

I decided to venture further into the squatter camp to see if any vestiges of Gandhi's spirit remained in Phoenix. I stopped the car and was immediately surrounded by a number of men, heavily armed with sharpened assegais and knives. They looked at me with cold, passionless eyes—eyes exhausted by pain. They told me that they were fighting a war against a group of rivals, and they asked me to come down to the front line. I hesitated but thought it unwise to refuse. As we walked, I began to hear chanting. We rounded a corner and there, in the dying sunlight, were perhaps 120 men standing on a small rise. A ragged cloth of red fluttered on a pole. As they sang, they clashed their spears and knives together. It was one of the most eerie sounds I have ever heard. My companions pointed over the roofs of tin huts to another mound about 200 metres away. There was the rival army, about the same in number, doing the same thing—only it was a green flag which flew above them. The scene seemed so medieval: the soft but sinister sound of metal against metal; the two armies facing each other across a swamp of refuse, armed only with their spears.

Some 200 people have died so far this year in fighting between the 'reds' and 'greens' in Bhambayi. People say that it began over rival witch-doctors; but who cares what the cause was? Alone and unknown in the world, these men stood facing death in a remote squatter camp on the southern tip of Africa. Who cares about these men, singing to keep themselves warm, frightened to face the night alone? Who would raise his voice in protest if there was one fewer of them in the morning? Gandhi would.

ASIA AND THE PACIFIC

THE LAST OUTPOST

SIMON LONG   QUEMOY   5 SEPTEMBER 1992

While the Cold War has been largely consigned to history in Europe, in parts of Asia its legacy continues to be felt. The government of Taiwan still describes its territory as 'The Republic of China', and this includes not only Taiwan itself but also some 80 or so islets in the straits between Taiwan proper and the Chinese mainland. Two of these islands, Quemoy and Matsu, are within sight of the mainland and twice came under heavy attack from the Chinese army in the 1950s—conflicts that threatened to escalate into superpower confrontations.

A MONUMENT HAS been built on the tip of Quemoy closest to the mainland of China: one of those rather grim, grey-stoned Chinese affairs, with an ornate roof of green tiles. From a platform you can peer through the haze towards the thriving mainland port of Xiamen. It is just over a mile away, but to make the journey legally could take you days. Taiwan's government still bans direct contact with the mainland, so you would have to board the plane for Taipei from the military airstrip, which is so narrow our Boeing 727's wings seemed to rustle the leaves of the adjacent trees. Then, after the 80-mile flight to Taipei, you would have to go several hundred miles south to Hong Kong, then take an overnight boat trip, or short flight, back across to where you started from.

Taiwan lifted martial law in 1987, but not in Quemoy or Matsu. Of the 80,000 people on Quemoy, half are soldiers. On quiet, rustic roads, what look like overgrown traffic islands are camouflaged with jungle green and painted palm trees; on top perch soldiers manning double-barrelled machine-guns.

I stood on the monument with an American, Professor Richard Walker, who as Dixie Walker, the former diplomat, is a popular figure in Taiwan; the monument stems from the bygone era when Taiwan and the offshore islands stood at the forefront of a global struggle against communism, and the United States stood four-square behind them. Walker was there in 1958 after China launched its most serious attack on the island, when shells fell day and night around what is now the monument. He was there in 1961 when, following Mao Tse-tung's disastrous Great Leap Forward, famine gripped the mainland again, and the done thing for the visitor to Quemoy was to release propaganda balloons that dropped leaflets on the mainland, urging rebellion against the communist bandits. After the failure of the 1958 bombardment, China kept up occasional, almost ritual shelling of Quemoy until 1979; then it gained American diplomatic recognition, and stopped altogether.

But China never again made a real effort to capture the island. Probably Peking rather likes the idea that Taiwan controls it. Symbolically it fosters the notion that China is still a victim of the Cold War—arbitrarily divided by a line on a map, a bit like Korea. And for some in Taiwan, who fled the mainland when the communists won the civil war in 1949 (or their parents did), the parallel rings true. For most, however, the differences are far greater. In Korea millions of people have close family the other side of the border. Most people in Taiwan are descendants of farmers who left the mainland generations ago. But the government clings to the principle of one China, and Quemoy is its shrine. A tour there is to see testimony to the heroic sacrifices made in the name of freedom. A vast 1,000-foot auditorium is housed underground at the centre of the mountain, hollowed out by dynamite, chisels, pickaxes and bare hands, for shelter in 1958. Miles of tunnels are said to hold two years' food supply and four-fifths of the heavy weaponry on the island. A museum is stacked with whizzing, banging, flashing, mechanical reconstructions of the 40-day war, 34 years ago. Briefings from the military drip with an almost forgotten rhetoric. 'Red China' or the 'Chicoms' is not what most countries now call the People's Republic of China. The first words of an introductory video are: 'Quemoy is a dagger pointed at the heart of communism.' The history you learn on the island is partial, a David and Goliath story. There is no mention of the American naval support that kept supply-lines open during the shelling; nor of the key role of Nikita Khrushchev in restraining Mao Tse-tung from provoking a superpower conflagration over a tiny fishing island.

Like Cuba and Berlin, Quemoy was one of those places where the Cold War got very hot. In November they are opening Quemoy for tourists, but if you fancy visiting the first (and maybe last) Cold War theme park, I don't think you need to rush. The ice is melting; but it's a slow process.

HONOURABLE
WITHDRAWAL

HUMPHREY HAWKSLEY   MACAO   10 SEPTEMBER 1992

Negotiations between Britain and China, over the return of Hong Kong to Chinese sovereignty, have been acrimonious at times. Forty miles along the coast, the handing back of another territory to China—the Portuguese enclave of Macao—has been proceeding much more smoothly.

EVERY 15 MINUTES, bright red-and-white jet-foils back out of their terminal into Hong Kong harbour, rise up on their hulls as they gather power, and head off westwards to the Portuguese enclave of Macao. It takes an hour to get to this backwater of faded yellow and pink colonial buildings, of seedy hotels, nightclub dancing and casinos. China is very close: the land border is just on the edges of the city centre. You can see the mainland from various places, across narrow stretches of murky water, with their Chinese coastal barges and police patrols to catch illegal immigrants trying to swim across to seek their fortune.

Macao is out of step with its neighbours along this swath of the Far East, which holds itself up as the economic engine of the twenty-first century. Its economy is haphazard, fuelled by tens of thousands of illegal immigrants who supply cheap labour, and one of the only steady expansions is in gambling. Macao is a sort of Monte Carlo of the Orient with a raw edge. Eighty-three per cent of the visitors to Macao head straight for the casinos, which at weekends have gamblers three or four deep to a table, in smoky basements open around the clock. This is the character of one of the strangest remnants of European colonialism.

Macao is administered by Portugal, but the real control is in the hands of China.

The Bank of China has already put up the highest building along the skyline, as if to underline its position in Macao's affairs. Just in front of that building is the statue of a former Governor of Macao, JoMo Maria Ferreira de Amaral, warlike and gripping the reins of a rearing horse. He was killed by the Chinese in 1849 when he tried to extend Macao's borders. China has said the statue must go because it symbolizes colonialism, and the Macao government is now expected to take it down within the next few weeks. That, in short, is the style in which Macao is handling China. It has neither the muscle of Taiwan nor the wealth of Hong Kong to put up much of a fight. There is no democracy movement of mass appeal, no candle-lit vigils for dissidents or cries for political reform. The democracy leader (although he hesitates to be called that) is Alexandre Ho, a softly spoken man who trains people to work in the flourishing tourist trade. He simply says he doesn't want to go to the extreme of full frontal confrontation with Peking.

Macao was one of the first European colonies in Asia. Portugal created it in 1557—nearly 300 years before Britain took Hong Kong—and has ruled it with a benevolent but lacklustre hand ever since. Lisbon became so uninterested that it even offered twice to give Macao back. During massive protests at the height of China's Cultural Revolution, the Governor wanted to pull out within a month. Peking refused. Then, in 1974, Portugal's new left-wing government again told China that it wanted to leave, but was unsuccessful. Only in 1987, after Britain had thrashed out its agreement with China over Hong Kong, did Peking and Lisbon agree that Portugal would go in 1999.

Lisbon will leave behind a ramshackle, somewhat corrupt place; but there is a twist to its departure which has not been lost on the Chinese of Hong Kong, 60,000 of whom are leaving every year to qualify for a second passport, as a safeguard against the repressive nature of Chinese rule. Everyone born in Macao before 1974 is a Portuguese citizen. Figures published last week revealed that 101,000 people, 90 per cent of whom are ethnic Chinese, already have passports. That accounts for a third of the population. Many more would probably qualify. Not only could they go to live in Portugal any time they chose to, but under European Community rules they could set up house in Britain. One Maccanese woman—a product of cosmopolitan colonialism with mixes of Malay, Chinese and Portuguese in her blood—had both a Portuguese passport and what is called a Hong Kong British passport. I asked her which she used when she flew into London. Without hesitating she said she used the Portuguese passport. Then she is simply waved through. The Hong Kong passport involved long questioning, humiliation and the possibility that she could be turned back.

The Chinese in Macao talk about their colonial power with far greater affection than those of Hong Kong. There is a feeling that, by giving citizenship, at the end of the day Portugal has done the right thing. And there is a sense, too, that while Hong Kong with its ostentation, glitter and flaunting of wealth is a symbol of Western power and its capitalist system, Macao, with its crumbling churches, cheap wine and strip shows, is more neutral; certainly not a threat. In all probability, after 1999 the jet-foils will still be packed with gamblers. Dancers, fleeing recession in Europe, will be able to titillate at the Crazy Paris Show and, knowing that they have a safety net, the thousands of Portuguese passport-holders will stay; unless, of course, the hand of Chinese communism takes a turn for the worse.

CHINA'S GREAT TRAIN ROBBERS

JAMES MILES   PEKING   1 OCTOBER 1992

China's overstretched rail network—with one train in three still pulled by a steam locomotive—often suffers appalling congestion and delays. But these are by no means the only problems: passengers often risk robbery and assault as well.

FOR THE PRIVILEGED few, travelling on Chinese trains can be a pleasant experience. Take, for example, train No 37, which took me on a recent trip from Peking to the city of Wahine in central China. With my so-called soft-sleeper ticket I was escorted by a white-uniformed attendant to an air-conditioned compartment with cushioned berths for four people. On the green-carpeted floor was a large thermos flask of hot water, and the attendant provided cups and tealeaves free on request. Next door to my compartment was the dining car, where at supper time one could choose from a menu of half a dozen or so quite tasty dishes. As the train made its leisurely way towards Wahine, a journey of about 700 miles, the only complaint I might have raised would have been about the train's broadcasting system. Efforts to relax and enjoy the scenery of paddy fields and picturesque villages were frustrated by the constant blaring of music, news and commentary from a loudspeaker in the compartment. The volume control for our loudspeaker was stuck on maximum.

Tickets for this class of travel, however, are generally sold only to foreigners and officials. Most Chinese rail passengers travel in what are called hard-sleeper or hard-seat compartments, dirty, crowded and distinctly uncomfortable. Sometimes passengers are forced to sit in the lavatories or to stretch out on the floors because of the lack of space. Such people are easy targets for what the Chinese media call 'train bandits' and 'railway tyrants', in other words robbers, acting singly or in gangs, who prey on passengers or plunder freight.

Last month, a senior Chinese official described the law-and-order situation on Chinese railways as extremely serious. Reports of such crimes appear almost daily in the official Chinese press. One story told of how, in one village in southern Guizhou Province, every family was found to be involved in robbing freight trains. The only exception, the report said, was one elderly widow who was too old to loot. In another province, it said, train robbers had developed their own code of ethics, which required them to set aside 30 per cent of their loot in order to support gang members who had been fined or arrested. The gangs also provide pensions for the families of those killed while robbing trains, to help raise their children and farm their land.

There are certainly plenty of convicted train robbers for such gangs to support. According to official figures, nearly 70,000 people have been sentenced in China in the last ten years for crimes committed on trains and at railway stations. In the southern province of Guangdong alone, police say that they have arrested about 1000 railway criminals and uncovered more than 80 gangs since April this year. Last year, the authorities said they had discovered a gang, consisting of more than 90 people, who carried out more than 100 robberies on a single railway line in central China. During one crackdown on railway banditry two years ago, the police seized more than 100 guns, 10,000 rounds of ammunition and 900 electric batons and tear-gas launchers, as well as unspecified quantities of heroin, opium and explosives. Death is certainly a hazard for those who are caught. In July, an official newspaper said that 50 train bandits and railway tyrants had been sentenced at a mass rally in central China. Seven of them were taken directly to the execution ground, where they were shot by a police firing-squad.

The government says that railway crimes are becoming more frequent, partly because Chinese passengers are carrying ever larger sums of money with them. In China, credit cards and cheque books are virtually unheard of among ordinary citizens, and there is a traditional reluctance to keep money in banks. Businessmen and officials sometimes take large amounts of cash to use as bribes or for entertaining.

Train tickets themselves can also be expensive. Although rail travel is theoretically quite cheap by Western standards, tickets are often difficult to buy except at inflated prices from scalpers. Railway stations in China are often scenes of chaos, with hundreds of people queueing and shoving to buy tickets. Many of them wait for hours, only to be disappointed. A Chinese friend recently travelled by train to a scenic tourist resort in the countryside. In China, you have to buy a new ticket every time you break your journey, but when my friend arrived at her destination she found that all tickets had been bought up by employees of local hotels. These people then waited for passengers at the station, and agreed to re-sell the tickets only to travellers who promised to stay at their hotels.

From time to time the Chinese authorities attempt to crack down on this kind of crime. Scalpers are rounded up by the police, who shave the heads of offenders and parade them in the forecourts of railway stations, pressing their heads down in front of the crowds of passengers. Some are then fined, others sent off to labour camps. Often, it is railway employees who are involved in ticket scalping and other railway crimes. In a much-publicized case earlier this year, railway police and attendants refused to help when a group of college students fought to stop a five-member gang from robbing a moving train. Every year, dozens of people are killed or injured by robbers on Chinese railways, and officials say that the number of criminal incidents on trains is increasing by 50 per cent per year. As one official account put it, 'Railway bandits are like wild grass which grows again after being burned or stamped on.'

BRUNEI'S NAUGHTY TEAPOTS

KIERAN COOKE   BANDAR SERI BEGAWAN
15 OCTOBER 1992

In October 1992 the Sultan of Brunei celebrated 25 years as the absolute monarch of his small country, on the western coast of Borneo. The Sultan is believed to be one of the richest people in the world, with a fortune somewhere in the region of $37 billion. Mingling with royalty, though, could be far less glamorous than people are often led to suppose.

TWO MEALS WERE the highlights of Brunei. One was a modest affair in a Chinese restaurant. The food was ordered; then it was a question of drinks. Since last year no alcohol has been allowed, in what is becoming an increasingly Islamic state. The attractive waitress had a teapot in each hand. 'Would you like tea?' she said, pointing to one teapot. 'Or,' she said, with just a very quick wink, 'tea from here, the other teapot?' She then poured beer out of the spout. It was rather expensive, but all the more satisfying for being just a little bit naughty.

There was no hint of naughtiness at the other meal. A few members of the international media had been invited for dinner at the Sultan's palace. It was just us, the Sultan and a contingent of Malay princes and princesses—and 5,750 others—all sitting down to dinner in the one room. Not so much a room, more an aircraft hangar, a cross between the Palace of Versailles and a holiday camp. Sultan Bolkiah Hassanal, still only in his mid-forties, has two wives and ten children, and a great deal else besides. His palace in Brunei is said to be the biggest such building in the world:

it has nearly 2,000 rooms; more than 12 acres of wall are covered with the finest Italian marble; there is enough gold to stage a sunset. The palace has 278 lavatories. There are chandeliers that weight a ton apiece. We sat and waited.

The Sultan is not known for his punctuality. A few lesser potentates arrived; dignitaries glowed up in the tropical heat. A cheery Australian waiter came up; he was one of more than 700 staff flown in from as far away as Sydney and Tokyo; the meat had been flown in from the Sultan's Australian ranch—twice the size of Brunei itself. We had arrived at six o'clock; it was now nine. The food was before us, but no one could eat. No one is allowed to lift a fork until the Sultan gives the signal. There were ugly mutterings from some quarters. The Sultan has his own palace guard, made up of retired Gurkhas; any mutinous behaviour and the kukri knives might be out.

At 9.45 the Sultan and his family finally arrived. Government in Brunei is very much a family affair: the Sultan himself doubles up as Prime Minister and Minister of Defence; one brother is Foreign Minister, another is Minister of Finance. There have been no elections in the country—which has a population of a little over a quarter of a million—for more than 30 years. Brunei became fully independent from Britain only in 1984. A state of emergency has been in force ever since an uprising was put down by British troops in 1962.

We—all 6,000 of us—fell on the food. Inside a sort of glass bubble, the royals tucked in as well, though with considerably more decorum. Brunei has jungle; it has a few roads; most importantly, it has oil and gas. The story goes that, earlier this century, a couple of British geologists were cycling along a path near the coast. They stopped to rest, then one uttered the magic words. 'I smell oil,' he said. Brunei has never looked back. The country now has one of the highest *per capita* incomes in the world—and the richest family. The Sultan—29th in succession in what is said to be one of the world's oldest monarchies—seems a modest, even shy, man, but he is certainly not averse to spending a few dollars: at the latest count, he had 153 Rolls-Royces, plus a whole starting grid of other cars. Then there is the property: hotels in Singapore, London and Beverly Hills; homes in Malaysia, England, the States and who knows where else; air-conditioned stables for his polo ponies. Recently acquired is a jumbo jet, to add to his other aircraft. And plenty of other knick-knacks to play with.

We had been nearly six hours at the palace. By the time the meal was finished, it was nearly eleven o'clock, and not a naughty teapot in sight. Sometimes it is best to be modest. Eat at the back-street restaurant, not the palace; it can be a lot more fun.

OBSTACLES TO PEACE

PHILIP SHORT   PHNOM PENH   12 NOVEMBER 1992

By November 1992 there were signs that the UN was becoming increasingly irritated with the peace process in Cambodia. Officials said that the UN's biggest and most expensive operation was being held up by the intransigence of the Khmer Rouge.

CAMBODIAN MOTORISTS—and there are many more of them these days, clogging the streets of Phnom Penh—don't so much go anywhere as mill around aimlessly. Cambodian politics are a bit like that, too. More progress has been made than anyone thought possible a year ago: but, amidst all the bustle, no one can say which way the traffic is going, which way Cambodia is heading. On the plus side, the repatriation of 300,000 refugees from camps along the Thai border is going like clockwork; registration for next year's elections is under way; de-mining has begun. Banditry is not the problem it might have been: the most menacing sight that I have seen here was on an unspeakably awful road near Sisophon in the north-west. A boy of about five, brown, muddy and completely naked—as is the way with small Cambodian children—was walking down the village street, carrying an AK47 assault rifle that was considerably bigger than he was. In the countryside there are more water-buffalo, wallowing in the mud beside pink-and-white lotus ponds; more cattle out in the fields. And in Phnom Penh and other cities, Thai and Singaporean businessmen are building hotels, opening restaurants and nightclubs and, inevitably, massage parlours; they are refurbishing colonial villas to rent out at $5,000 a month.

And yet—the detail may be clear, but the overall prospect for Cambodia's future is as uncertain now as it was when the UN operation began. For today—just as they were 20 years ago—the Khmer Rouge are the key. Either they have the strength to undercut the Paris accords, remaining part of the peace process but refusing to disarm, thus making a mockery of the 'neutral security environment' in which the elections are to take place; or they are what one official here calls 'an empty shell'—surviving on the aura of fear that they once engendered, but without the means or the support to stop the rest of the country making peace without them. There is evidence to support both views: when the Security Council announced last month that new steps would be taken to force Khmer Rouge compliance, the response was instantaneous: two bridges on Route Six, linking Phnom Penh with the north of the country, were blown up by a Khmer rouge commando, killing six people and wounding 20 others. The UN called it the most serious ceasefire violation since the peace accords were signed. That implies not only intransigence but, much more importantly, a well-organized capacity to strike back. French officers who meet local Khmer Rouge leaders in the mountains behind Kampot, along the southern coast, say that they detect no softening of Khmer Rouge morale: their weapons are in good order, and there are few defectors. On the other hand, the Cold War is over and the socialist camp is in ruins. It is a very different climate from 1975, when the Domino Theory was in vogue, and the Khmer Rouge marched into Phnom Penh two weeks before the fall of Saigon.

Then there is the argument that the Khmer Rouge themselves, and their potential supporters, will be seduced by the good life that a market economy and enlightened democratic principles—nurtured by the UN—will eventually bring. But you only have to travel through the idyllic but god-forsaken villages of the Cambodian countryside to see that, even now—although life is better than it was—Cambodia is still desperately poor, and most peasants have little to lose. After all, it was the townspeople whom the Khmer Rouge slaughtered; the peasants didn't have such a bad time—at least not all of them.

Once again, the towns are corrupt—the more so because of the flood of UN money coming in. And the peace process, on which the UN has staked so much, is walking on water: the foundations on which it was supposed to rest are simply not there. Seventy per cent of the four factions' troops were supposed to have been disarmed and placed in cantonments: that has been blocked since the summer; and the UN can't even gain access to the main Khmer Rouge areas.

Moreover, even the positive side of what has happened in Cambodia over the past year has its limits: de-mining has begun, but only 200 of the 900 Cambodians who have been trained are actually able to work, because most Western governments—including Britain—are afraid that their troops may be injured if they act as supervisors. The French, who are supervising mine clearance, say that the Cambodians work well: but will they continue when the UN leaves? 'Sincerely,' one French officer told me, 'they won't; they have to have someone behind them.' And even in Phnom Penh the recovery is fragile, and there are constant power cuts. The open-fronted, Indian-style shops sell Christian Dior make-up, Dunhill cigarettes at 40 pence a packet and sequined dresses for the higher-class prostitutes to wear. In the hotel book stores, *Vogue* magazine shares shelf-space with books on the Killing Fields. And it won't be until after the elections, and after the UN have gone—probably in three or four years' time—that we will know for certain whose strategy will have been proved right and whose will have been proved wrong.

AND THE MOSQUE CAME TUMBLING DOWN

MARK TULLY   DELHI   10 DECEMBER 1992

In India, in December 1992, nearly 800 people died in four days of religious violence after hordes of Hindu militants tore down the disputed mosque at Ayodhya on Sunday. The repercussions for India's secular state have been enormous. It all began when the right-wing Hindu party, Bharatiya Janata, brought together a quarter of a million supporters for what they said was to be a purely ceremonial demonstration of solidarity; but then things got out of hand.

ON THE MORNING of the Sunday before Christmas, I went to Mother Theresa's prayer meeting at the memorial to Mahatma Gandhi in Delhi. I wasn't the only one to have tears in my eyes, as the small woman, whom so many Indians of all religions regard as a saint, said those beautiful words of Saint Francis of Assisi: 'It's in forgiving that we are forgiven.'

On Sunday afternoon, my eyes again filled with tears. This time I was crying because of the tear-gas that the police were firing to disperse thousands of supporters of the right-wing Hindu Bharatiya Janata Party, or BJP. This is the party which has put the demand to build a temple on the site of the Ayodhya mosque at the top of its political agenda. The BJP supporters were demonstrating against a ban on the rally that they had planned to hold that day. The slogans they shouted showed that forgiveness was the last thing they had in mind. They were rejoicing at the revenge they had taken on the Muslims at Ayodhya. The BJP leaders denied that revenge was their motive. They say that, at

Ayodhya, the pent-up anger of Hindus—frustrated at not being allowed to build a temple on the site which, they believe, is the birthplace of their God, Ram—erupted and could not be controlled. But just before the destruction of the mosque, I heard the BJP President, Dr Murli Manohar Joshi, tell a rally that what he called the 'structure' at Ayodhya was a symbol of Hindu slavery, and that the Muslim emperor, Babar—after whom it's named—was a looter. Hindus, he said, must wash out that stigma. That surely was a call to take revenge.

But the BJP leaders are not alone in trying to disguise the reality of Ayodhya. Secular Indians are attempting to distance themselves from the whole event by making out that the vast majority of Hindus are deeply shocked. But then the leaders of Indian secularism are not in the best position to assess the mood of the nation. As one Marxist member of parliament said, 'While communism is being spread throughout the countryside, secularism is being debated in seminars.' Indian secularists don't need to go far beyond the air-conditioned conference halls in which they hold their seminars to see that the rejoicing over the destruction of the mosque is not confined to the hard-core members of the BJP. When that party's supporters were confronting the police in the centre of Delhi, government servants stood on the lawns of their blocks of flats, egging them on. One broadcaster, dictating his copy to a secretary in the government-controlled *All India Radio*, was warned not to be so hard on the BJP. A guest at a Delhi dinner party attempted to touch the feet of one of the BJP leaders, present when the mosque was destroyed.

Those who are prepared to see reality believe that Ayodhya has dramatically improved the BJP's electoral prospects. The *Times of India*, the breakfast reading of the country's secular élite, at least admitted in an editorial that the central government, parliament, the courts and all those who shape opinion had underestimated the extent to which those who wanted a Hindu India had spread their influence in the body politic. But the *Times of India* made no effort to understand why so many Indians had become what it considered to be 'prejudiced bigots'.

What of the Muslims? One of the two committees set up to protect the Ayodhya mosque has reacted predictably by demanding, if not revenge, not far short of it by saying that the mosque must be rebuilt on the exact spot where it stood. The imam of Delhi's largest mosque, while counselling his followers to be restrained, spoke of the anger burning in his heart. Predictably, the Prime Minister of Pakistan is using Ayodhya to damn India internationally, although he knows that, in doing so, he is increasing the threat to his fellow Muslims across the border. The Prime Minister has strengthened the case of those Hindus who say that Muslims can never be loyal Indians because, in their heart of hearts, they are all Pakistanis. But Abid Hussain, a distinguished Muslim economist who was, until recently, India's ambassador in Washington, does believe that his community should also indulge in some introspection. He is suggesting to Muslim students that they ask themselves why there are Hindus who welcome the destruction of the Ayodhya mosque.

Mahatma Gandhi, while addressing a prayer meeting after a mosque had been desecrated in revenge for an attack on a temple, said: 'I'm grieved when I hear that Muslims have desecrated a temple; but should I retaliate by damaging a mosque? How can such damage save the temple or benefit the Hindu religion?' On another occasion Mahatma said: 'The sword is yet too much in evidence among the Muslims; it must be sheathed if Islam is to be what it means—peace.' The Mahatma would clearly have sided with Mother Theresa, who called for forgiveness. I doubt if he would have had any time for the BJP, the secularists or the orthodox Muslim leadership.

AFGHANISTAN—AN UNLIKELY PLACE OF REFUGE

DANIEL LAK   MAZAR-E-SHARIF   16 JANUARY 1993

The long civil war in Afghanistan caused a massive problem of refugees, five million of them fleeing to neighbouring states, making it one of the biggest movements of refugees of modern times. By 1993, the refugees were returning, and work began on rebuilding the country. Then Afghanistan itself became a place of refuge for more than 100,000 people fleeing the fighting in the former Soviet Republic of Tadjikistan.

THE ROAD RUNNING east, from the northern Afghan city of Mazar-e-Sharif, passes through some of the flattest, most barren landscape I have ever seen. There are no trees, no hills, no curves in the road; the Sakhi refugee camp is the only relief from the monotony of the plain. It is hard to imagine a worse place to put 11,000 people, who fled their homelands with only the proverbial clothes on their back. There is no reliable water-supply. A well-driller told me that he had managed to coax only a trickle from a tube well 500 feet deep. It is 15 miles to market in Mazar and, although the stalls there are well stocked with food, the Tadjiks have to rely on the generosity of the locals to vary their diet of rice fried in oil. But the worst thing is the wind. It screams down from the north-west, unhindered by hill or dale, and seems to focus on Sakhi camp with piercing intensity. The blue plastic tents, supplied by the United Nations, provide little shelter from the frequent gales and blizzards of the northern Afghan winter. So, each night, the people of Sakhi go underground—literally. The organizers of the camp have hit upon the idea of digging shelters six feet into the hard-packed earth and roofing them with boards and plastic. Between 15 and 20 people—three families—sleep huddled together for warmth. There is no privacy; but at least the wind isn't forcing the snow through the cracks.

It was in such a shelter that I met Behar Nessa. Like most of the Tadjik women in the camp, she had a jolly, handsome face and her clothes were a riot of colours and patterns. Her voice sounded happy too, as she spoke to our translator. But then the words came in English, and her despair was plain. Behar told us that the baby she clutched in her arms had been born on 1 January, the day she had arrived in Sakhi after a long, hard trip from her home in Tadjikistan. The infant girl's name was Delbara, which means 'beautiful possession', but Behar said she didn't care if her daughter lived or died. Why, we pressed her. She told us that her four-year-old son, her only other child, had disappeared the night that soldiers attacked and burnt their village. People scattered into the forests and many families were split up. But her boy wasn't there in the morning. They ran to the border, the *Amu Darya* or River Oxus, where they boarded flimsy boats made of firewood and inner tubes. Hundreds died in the mass crossings of the Amu in early December. Behar—nine months pregnant and deeply frightened and despairing—survived, even though she said she didn't want to. Now she lives in a hole in the ground, in the middle of a muddy plain in northern Afghanistan. Her husband, badly injured during their flight, was in hospital in Mazar-e-Sharif. And she wanted to die, along with her daughter.

Our translator, an Iranian United Nations worker named Paracheyr Sabety, said that Behar was getting better. She was caring for her baby and her sister's four-month-old son. Mother and daughter were physically healthy and they were getting extra food from the other people in the shelter. Her spirits were improving as well. Sahki camp is full of such contrasts of tragedy and survival. The people who work with the refugees say that they have rarely seen such cheerful, resilient people—this despite the fact many have lost family members and have seen their homes and lives shattered by war. That they have kept their spirits up amid such desolation is a source of constant wonder, even to the veterans of a dozen or more humanitarian crises who run the camp.

Walking between the tents with Paracheyr, we had to turn down dozens of invitations to tea and lunch. The people simply don't have enough to entertain guests but they insist. Paracheyr carries her own teabags and often slips them, surreptitiously, into the pot, or into a woman's pocket; guests must never be required to provide their own food or drink. Hospitality is a strict code in this part of the world; guests are sacred charges who must be cared for. And the refugees from Tadjikistan are the guests of the people from northern Afghanistan—welcome to share the slim bounty of the region. But with the return of the refugees to a peaceful, secure Tadjikistan still a long way off, it is increasingly becoming a question of which will run out first: traditional Afghan hospitality or the badly stretched resources of the United Nations and other international aid agencies.

AN ENGLISHMAN ABROAD

PAUL REYNOLDS   DELHI   30 JANUARY 1993

John Major visited India in January, stopping off in Oman and Saudi Arabia on his way home. He was the guest of honour at the celebrations to mark Republic Day, becoming the first British Prime Minister to be invited to do so. Mr Major was accompanied by a group of businessmen—an attempt to drum up trade.

THE T-72 TANKS rumbled slowly down Rajpath, the magnificent triumphal way laid out by Sir Edward Lutyens when Delhi was made capital of the British Raj in 1911. As they dipped their huge guns in salute towards the reviewing stand, they were reminders of India's close links with the old Soviet Union. Now those links are no more, of course, and Mr Major's presence on the stand was evidence of that. For India is going through a quiet economic revolution, discarding many of its old socialist and protectionist rules. It now needs the support of people like the Prime Minister, and the beleaguered British PM felt there were benefits for him, too. For he had come with one object in mind: to do business. He had brought with him a party of businessmen and they were his literal answer to those critics at home who said he had no business going abroad during a time of economic hardship. And so, for an hour and a half on a clear, bright morning, he joined the several million Indians along the route in Delhi to watch the patchwork parade.

It mixed memories of the Raj, in the precision of its marching and the tartans of its pipe bands, with folksy floats from the various Indian states.

The visit went without diplomatic incident because it was in the interests of both sides to make it a success. The British side certainly made few demands on Indian policy. Mr Major soft-pedalled—in public at least—on Kashmir and on India's nuclear capability, and he said all the right things about 'terrorism', by which India means Sikh extremism. The Indians, pleased to pocket the diplomatic points, gave way on the economics. They did not hark back to days of colonial oppression or complain about domination by the developed world. Instead, there was talk (not all of it entirely convincing) of free markets and even of privatization. That Britain needs all the export work it can get is well-known, and a couple of contracts were netted for the supply of natural gas and electricity transmission equipment; 'nice little earners', as one of the businessmen put it, though in fact the British government paid for nearly half of one of them through its aid budget.

That India needs a new direction is equally obvious. The visitor is struck by a country which is curiously caught in a bygone age. The English language, for example, is used in a delicate and charming but antique way, long discarded—some may think sadly so—in the country which gave it to India. Thus, the press is littered with what, to the British ear, are outdated words and phrases. Suspected terrorists are 'nabbed' by the police in the 'wee hours'. Riots are caused by 'scoundrels' and 'mischief makers'. Industrially, of course, India has long trodden its own path, and a slow one it has been. The locally manufactured Ambassador cars look like something Austin made in the 1950s; and I have not heard the growl of an Enfield motorcycle for years. To see one is to realize why the Japanese displaced the British motorcycle industry. Yet India clings to the old model.

Despite the proclaimed new policies, questions remain about the direction that India might take. One evening, while Mr Major was giving a rousing speech to Indian businessmen and the captains of British industry who had come with him, I spoke to an Indian diplomat. He wondered whether Mr Major was not being a little bit patronizing in giving out economic advice so liberally; he did not think the Germans or the French felt it necessary to give or withhold their approval. So some of the old resentment perhaps remains. The same diplomat also expressed some private sympathy for the Hindu nationalism which had its worst manifestation in the destruction of the mosque at Ayodhya in December. Of that he did not approve, of course; but there was, he said, an argument that the Hindus had been too passive historically, and that they should assert themselves more. They had often taken the easy way out, he remarked with a smile, telling themselves that they could always do better in their next life.

It was easy, in the comfort of big hotels in Delhi and Bombay, to listen to the experts talk of religion, secularism and nationalism. In the slums of the city of Indore, the intractability of poverty was the lasting impression. Mr Major came here to visit two slums (as they are officially called) which are being improved by British aid. 'Improved' is a relative word: although paths are paved, drains and sewerage are put in and health and family planning organized, no money is given for the actual huts that the poor people live in. They are supposed to improve their homes themselves. But these remain pathetic collections of sacking, bits of polythene, mud, brick and corrugated iron. I was not surprised that the people there were—as poor people all over the world often are—among the most polite we had met. They could not really have known who their visitor was, but he was showered with rose-petals and greeted with chants of 'Long live John Major'. A big black-and-white poster of him had been put up, prompting one of the British reporters to comment sardonically that it had brought a splash of grey into an otherwise colourful scene. Mr Major will be hoping that his visit to India will have a more lasting impact.

COSMETIC SURGERY

PHILIP SHORT   RANGOON   4 FEBRUARY 1993

In Burma, the military junta reiterated its unwillingness to relinquish power, or to release Aung San Suu Kyi, the opposition leader who had—by February 1993—spent more than four years under house arrest in the capital, Rangoon. But the regime was trying to make its rule more palatable—especially to potential aid donors.

THE SLOGANS IN bold English letters, white on red, relaying the junta's latest exhortations to its citizens, which once decorated the streets of Rangoon, were painted out late last year. Tourists are no longer told that 'only when there is discipline will there be progress'. And injunctions to 'Crush all Destructive Elements!' and 'Work Hard!' have given way to advertising hoardings for Goodyear and Nippon Paint, or even, in Mandalay, outside a building firm, the classic Buddhist entreaty, 'Be kind to animals by not eating them'.

Change of a kind, you may think, evidence that attitudes are shifting. Well, think again. Only the English text has been removed. The same Burmese-language slogans are as prominent as ever; but foreigners can't read them any more. And so it is with most, though not all, of the changes that have taken place in Burma since an ostensibly more moderate leadership emerged in the SLORC, the State Law and Order Restoration Council—as the junta calls itself—in April of last year. Market reforms are going ahead: the streets are full of shiny new Japanese saloons and Mercedes with gold-plated fittings. In Rangoon there is a new six-lane highway from the airport to impress visiting businessmen. The junta is trying, with some success, to persuade Japan, South Korea and Australia (as well as its South-East Asian neighbours) that help and encouragement, the so-called policy of 'constructive engagement', will pave the way for civilian rule and democratic institutions far more quickly than foreign pressure and grumbling about human rights and the brutality of military rule.

But the evidence to support such claims is, to say the least, inconclusive. It is true that 1,000 political prisoners have been released, but all the most important figures—student leaders, politicians and monks—are still firmly behind bars. And Aung San Suu Kyi, whose party won 80 per cent of the seats in an election which the SLORC ignored, remains under house arrest—guarded by steel-helmeted troops, precisely because most Burmese still believe she is the one person who can lead the country out of the morass into which the army has plunged it; the junta dare not risk freeing her. A national convention has started to draw up guidelines for a new 'democratic' constitution, but its primary objective is stated to be the preservation of the army's leading role. Military tribunals have been abolished but Burma is still under martial law. The universities have re-opened but professors and lecturers have been told that they will be held personally responsible—and punished accordingly—if their students engage in any form of political activity; and the same system has been introduced throughout the civil service. The window-dressing has changed, but the SLORC's stock-in-trade is the same: rule by fear, maintained by a network of informers, police and military intelligence, modelled on those used by the former regimes of Eastern Europe.

One small incident stands for many others. I happened to strike up a conversation with a tourist guide waiting at a travel agency. After about 30 seconds, she said nervously: 'Please stop talking to me, someone is watching us.' If even a tourist guide is afraid to be seen talking casually to a foreigner, what of ordinary Burmese? And indeed every shop assistant, every stallholder that you are seen with risks being questioned afterwards to find out what you discussed.

Of course the system isn't fool-proof. The government, mercifully, is inefficient and incompetent to a degree which should make the Japanese—and others eyeing Burma's immense natural resources—think twice before letting greed overcome humanistic scruples. It takes weeks to get an appointment to see a senior official. Even then, palms must be greased; and any major decision has to be referred up to the power-holders, because everybody lower down is too scared of making a mistake. So what hope, you may ask, for the future of this benighted land? Certainly no early release. Eventually, increased contact with the outside world will change attitudes, and some within the army itself believe that endless repression is not necessarily the best way to handle Burma's problems. But all that will take time. Meanwhile the people can only watch and wait because, as one student put it, 'They have the guns, and we don't.'

DESPERATELY SEEKING SPRATLY

TIM LUARD   KUALA LUMPUR   11 FEBRUARY 1993

The Spratly Islands in the South China Sea have been described as Asia's next flashpoint. Though tiny and practically uninhabited, they are the subject of a territorial dispute among six countries—five of which have stationed troops on those islands that they have been able to occupy. Trying to get to them, though, is no easy matter.

IT SEEMED A perfect destination for a reporting trip, warm and exotic and far away, unspoilt by tourists or journalists; at the same time a dramatic symbol, a veritable microcosm of post-Cold War tensions in East Asia. Maybe a lot of people hadn't heard of the Spratlys yet, but soon they would. After all, they lay at the heart of the most dynamic region in the world; the quarrel over ownership involved oil, strategic advantage and bitter historical rivalries between China, Vietnam, Taiwan, the Philippines, Malaysia and Brunei. I could see the headlines: SEEDS OF CONFLICT SCATTERED ACROSS THE SOUTH CHINA SEA. All that remained was to get there.

I knew that the scale of the islands was not impressive. None of them is more than a mile long, and many are submerged at high tide. Some have military bases on them, confronting each other across the water. Others are just big enough for a shack on stilts and a sovereignty marker giving the nationality of the current occupier. I started by asking at the London embassies of the various countries concerned whether their governments would be prepared to take me to their Spratly Islands. I thought they might be only too happy to lay on a little boat-trip or something, on the assumption that it could produce some favourable publicity for their particular claim. Then the rejections started coming in. Not only would no one take me to the Spratlys, they wouldn't even let me come to their countries to ask them about the Spratlys. Clearly, Spratly was a sensitive word in Asian capitals. So I set off anyway, to try to find out why.

Having been refused a journalist's visa, I entered China as a tourist. China was, after all, the most powerful and insistent of the six claimants, and I had already sent dozens of faxes to Spratly specialists at various Chinese institutes to line up interviews. Word had obviously got around, though, that I wasn't the sort of person with whom even the most third-rate Spratly specialist should be sharing information. One by one my would-be interviewees discovered they had other engagements. But I had to get something on tape for the half-hour radio programme I was making. If I couldn't talk to anyone else, I would just have to talk to myself. So I did a series of 'stand-ups', as they are known in the trade. I stood in the Forbidden City in Peking and spoke grandly into my microphone about China's imperial traditions until a large crowd gathered, under the impression that I was giving a guided tour of the palace. And on the southern island of Hainan I was reduced to standing under a palm tree and describing, for my unseen listeners, the nondescript government building across the road, from where China claims to administer the Spratlys. Once again I was engulfed in curious onlookers. At least that wouldn't happen, I told myself, when I reached my first uninhabited Spratly island and did a stand-up with just the waves and birds to keep me company.

The New China News Agency then announced that certain foreigners were stirring up the Spratly issue in an attempt to create trouble between China and her neighbours. As I made my way through South-East Asia, I found lots of officials prepared to swear that the Spratlys did indeed belong to their particular country, but that was about all they would say. Everyone wanted the islands mainly for their oil; but no one had proved that there *was* any oil. And when I asked ordinary people in the street about the Spratlys, I found they were almost as little-known in South-East Asia as they were in the West. Worst of all, no one knew how to get there. Plenty of Filipino generals were keen to show me how powerful they were, but when it came to authorizing a trip to the Spratlys, they vanished into thin air, just like the islands themselves. In Malaysia, I was told that I could charter a light plane (the Spratlys being inaccessible by sea in the monsoon) but only if I could prove that I was a scuba-diver rather than a journalist. I didn't have my diving gear with me, and I failed the test.

I never did get to any Spratlys, but I did see some—I think. As I gazed mournfully out of the window on a scheduled flight between Manila and Kuala Lumpur, the deep blue of the South China Sea was suddenly broken by a series of islets and sandbanks, each one surrounded by the translucent green of a coral reef. To the alarm of the person sitting next to me, I seized my tape recorder and launched into an excited announcement of the fact that we were flying over the Spratlys. Stand-ups can be just as embarrassing sitting down. I was just getting to the bit about microcosms of post-Cold War tensions when a stewardess leaned over to ask if I was all right. Rather than confirm her suspicions by asking for a parachute, I simply asked her to check the identity of the islands with the pilot. But even he was unable to help. It seems pilots aren't allowed to use the Spratlys as landmarks because no one can agree on which country's name for them should be used on the map. Whoever gets them in the end will, I hope, allow me to come and visit. My colleagues do, after all, refer to me these days—with just a trace of irony—as 'Spratly Luard'.

ALL ABOARD THE
PURI EXPRESS

JONATHAN AGNEW   BOMBAY   20 FEBRUARY 1993

*The England cricket team were coming to the end of a
somewhat unsatisfactory tour of India in February 1993.
Off the field, political turmoil and industrial action conspired
to add to their discomfort.*

IF YOU SIT on this particular hotel terrace and watch the early-morning
mist lifting over a deep blue sea, you could be virtually anywhere in the
world. Brightly coloured yachts bob up and down on the waves and it is
pleasantly warm. Slowly, the fog burns away to reveal the other side of
the bay. Columns of ugly, concrete, high-rise flats loom into view. Black
and yellow motorized rickshaws, complete with their kamikaze drivers
and squeaky horns, thread their way through the swarming traffic, and
young ladies in their saris break rocks with crude-looking sledgehammers
on the side of the road.

This is India: Bombay, to be precise. On the one hand, so bright,
colourful, vibrant and friendly; but dusty, desperately over-crowded and
disorganized on the other. At least that's the way it looks through Western
eyes and, no matter where in the world you have played cricket before,
nothing can prepare you for your first experience of the subcontinent.

Cricket in India is played and watched with a rare, if not unique,
passion. In a country where so little often means so much, a cricket match
is more than simply a game, it is a cause for rejoicing. Let's face it, having
wrapped up this Test series so conclusively, Indian cricket fans have
had plenty to celebrate recently. Thunderflashes, crackers and fireworks

explode as the Mexican wave sweeps around the terraces at an increasingly alarming rate. Police, with their brutal-looking batons, beat the living daylights out of the revellers who, through sheer excitement, dash on to the field of play. In the midst of this cacophony, it is perhaps not entirely surprising that England's cricketers looked just a little bemused and bewildered.

We all arrived, about 50 of us if you include the media, two months ago to an internal plane strike and, following the destruction of a mosque in Ayodhya, the greatest threat to India's domestic security since partition. Those early weeks were fraught with tension and for a while the tour seemed to be in jeopardy. More than 5000 troops threw a cordon round the centre of Lucknow, which is only 80 miles from Ayodhya, when the team arrived there to play their second match of the tour. From the top floor of our hotel we could see armed guards patrolling the roadblocks and sniffer dogs searching the stadium for explosives. Inside the hotel, security was just as tight. Soldiers with AK 47s accompanied us wherever we went, whether it was simply up a couple of floors in the lift, or around the 18-hole golf course. As we slept at night, our men would sit outside our bedroom doors. Funnily enough, we didn't feel threatened in any way, but just once in a while I found myself wondering why it was deemed necessary for 5000 soldiers to be on hand to protect a group of travelling cricketers. As it turned out, only one match was cancelled because of the political situation; we were told that our safety couldn't be guaranteed in Ahmadabad, for the first one-day international. And the fact that we are now in Bombay, where the unrest rumbled on for some time, is a sign that, at least for now, life has returned to normal here.

Cricket tours these days have largely lost the intrigue and romance of the early years, now that jet aircraft have replaced the ocean liner. Nowadays an international cricketer can expect to see a dozen or so airport lounges, his hotel rooms, the cricket grounds themselves—and that's about it. Thanks to the domestic air strike, about the only form of transport we haven't used on this tour has been a boat—and at one time even that was being considered. The highlight of the hastily rearranged travel-plan was undoubtedly the *Puri Express*, an overnight sleeper from Bhubaneshwar to Calcutta.

It was early evening and the platform was teeming with all manner of life. Porters scurried about between the various tradesmen selling tea, hot nuts and magazines. Beggars optimistically held out their hands, and those who were sleeping rough had already settled down for the night, lined up and huddled under blankets. Suddenly, from further down the platform, on marched the England players in their navy-blue-and-white tracksuits, followed by dozens of bearers carrying the entire team's baggage on their heads. There was no air-conditioned VIP lounge now, no official escort to give the players preferential treatment. They stood and waited on the platform just like everyone else. Safely aboard and, once again, there were no special arrangements for the eight-hour journey. There was not even any bedding. The bunks which lined the open carriage were simple, green, padded slabs, and that was it. A family of mice scuttled about, almost unnoticed, while the team drank beer and played cards, as the miles rattled slowly by. I am sure many of the cricketers wouldn't have appreciated it at the time, but that night they were closer in touch with the real India than would ever have been possible under normal circumstances. And while the results on the field have been bitterly disappointing to date, in time they should look back with fond memories on what has certainly been—in terms of modern international cricket—a tour with a difference.

DYING FOR SEX

PETER GODWIN   CHIANG RAI   27 FEBRUARY 1993

After many years of tolerating widespread prostitution, early in 1992 the Thai government—worried at the spread of Aids—ordered a crackdown on brothels. As many as two million Thai women and girls are thought to be involved in prostitution, and 95 per cent of Thai men will have used their services by the time they are 21. Unless something is done to try to prevent the spread of HIV, as many as four million people could be infected by the end of this decade.

WE SET OFF that day in a pick-up truck, the roof too low to sit upright. In front of us was a single loudspeaker, prominently marked 'stereo'. As we bounced along the road from Chiang Rai to Phan, blithely overtaking in the face of oncoming traffic, the demure sex educator and I got down to the gritty basics. Should there or shouldn't there be an air-bubble in the tip of a condom? It was number eight on the multiple-choice questionnaire that she presents to prostitutes. Answer: no. Number one had been: does Aids always lead to death? Answer: yes.

Phan, our destination, was a smallish market-town in northern Thailand, but according to the sex educator's meticulous sheet, it sported no fewer than 19 brothels, from a relatively big-time establishment with 15 girls to a more modest outfit with only two. We never did get to Phan's smallest brothel; in fact we never got past *Soi Sip*, Lane Ten, which passes for Phan's red-light district. About half of the town's brothels stand on this little back-street. They are little more than shanties made of wood and tin, not a right-angle in the place. A foul-smelling stream oozes along past their front doors. Between the brothels were great mounds of rubbish, shedding their top layer to the breeze.

On the corrugated-iron wall of our first stop was painted in red the words, 'this house sells girls'. Inside was the most unerotic atmosphere imaginable. The only concession to jollity was an ancient juke-box. On the wall was a framed 500-baht note: that just about summed up the philosophy. Before the condom lesson, the girls made up at a communal cosmetics tray. They were young, very young, 16, 15 or 14 even. The lesson itself was mostly about the medical details of Aids: how you get it, how you don't. But it was too late for six out of ten of these girls. They were already HIV positive.

Afterwards I conducted one of my least successful interviews: two girls together (they had insisted) who giggled at anything, especially eye contact with a foreigner. What did they think of the lesson? Much laughter behind backs of hands. I tried again. 'Do you always use condoms with customers?' 'Yes,' they giggled, glancing at the sex educator, lurking nearby. And so it went on: yes, they were afraid of Aids; yes, they had been tested for it. And finally, with the daunting insensitivity that journalism can demand, I asked what the results were. The giggling stopped abruptly and they hung their heads. The smaller of the two looked as though she was going to burst into tears. I resolved not to intrude on other people's grief, but it happened again, in another town, a few days later.

The town of Fang snuggles at the foot of the mountain range that runs along the Burmese border. It is a dishevelled sort of place to which town planning is an alien concept. But the local doctor runs a tight ship. His hospital is working at 140 per cent occupancy, with up to a third of the beds taken by Aids patients. Aids deaths are an almost daily ritual. Today's had happened at dawn; now three workers, donning masks, rubber gloves and butcher's aprons, were preparing to bag it. The body lay on a concrete slab in the little morgue, set back from the main hospital. The victim was a 36-year-old woman who had died of an Aids-induced wasting disease. She lay, emaciated and greyish, her eyes still half open. One skinny arm dangled over the side. They worked on the body gingerly, keeping contact to a minimum as they manoeuvred it into a giant plastic bag and sealed the end. If no one collected her within 12 hours she would be incinerated. Outside, workmen were busy widening the pathway to the morgue to allow for two-way traffic of stretchers. It was in anticipation of more business, the doctor said. Next to the morgue they had punched a new gate through the perimeter wall; 'death gate', he called it, like some medieval doorway. An hour later the victim's husband arrived to be told of her death. He was a jobbing labourer who had had to borrow a bicycle to get there. With him was their ten-year-old son, who wore a tattered baseball cap with its brim upturned. He was wide-eyed and bewildered.

Later, I saw them again; this time the husband was clutching a sheaf of bureaucracy—death certificate and the like—as though it might provide him with some security. He was being marched to the little counselling cubicle where there was more bad news in store for him, the results of his blood test. For half an hour the lady in the starched, white dress explained to him what Aids was all about. Then she asked him if he would like the results of his test. He nodded. 'Well, I'm afraid you're HIV positive,' she said. No disbelief; no histrionics. He simply blinked several times and murmured, 'Thank you.'

I thought of number one on the questionnaire. Does Aids always cause death?

AS SEEN ON TV

MARK TULLY   DELHI   11 MARCH 1993

*In India—as in many countries of the world—viewing habits
have been radically altered by the arrival of BBC World
Service Television. The success story does, though, have its
downside.*

IN JUST 17 months, BBC World Service Television has replaced the
Indian government's *Doordarshan* as the main source of television news
for the Indian élite. Although the news is transmitted to India by satellite
and can be received only via an expensive dish antenna, cable operators
carry the signal into the homes of the middle classes as well. I know from
my own experience what a difference this has made to Delhi viewing
habits. BBC World Service Television has also had a major impact on
my life and the lives of my colleagues in the Delhi office.

The most disastrous impact was in Ayodhya. A quarter of a million
Hindus had assembled in the town to take part in what they promised
would be a peaceful ceremony. But events got out of hand; the militant
Hindus pulled down the disputed mosque, standing on the site that they
claimed was the birthplace of their God, Ram. On the day before that
disaster, one of the Hindu leaders told a rally that BBC television had
reported that there had been a riot in the town. In fact, in a report written
in London, we had shown library pictures of an earlier riot to illustrate
the story of the Ayodhya dispute. That evening, I was surrounded by
angry young men shouting, 'Death to the BBC!' The next day, the press
corps was brutally attacked when covering the destruction of the mosque.
I was held in custody for two hours by militant Hindus. That rumour was
not the only reason for the attack; at least, I don't think it was. But I had

a great deal of explaining to do to those journalists who were beaten up in the name of the BBC.

I have, of course, lived through many rows sparked off by BBC World Service radio reporting. But with radio you can still be comparatively well-known and at the same time preserve a decent anonymity—if that's not a contradiction in terms. My appearances on BBC television mean that now I am recognized wherever I go, and that is not a happy experience. Perhaps there is some BBC training manual which teaches you to answer the question: 'You are Mark Tully, aren't you?' But I haven't come across it. I am always tempted to say, 'Yes. What of it?' In fact, I just mutter some inanity. But that does not shut up those viewers who want to let me know what I should have said on television.

Recently the capital, Delhi, was turned into a fortress to prevent the right-wing Hindu Bharatiya Janata Party, or BJP, holding a rally. The BJP had been much involved in Ayodhya and the Prime Minister was not going to run the risk of another disaster. World Service Television showed pictures of police beating and kicking BJP supporters, and knocking the BJP President over with a water-cannon. That weekend I was told by a customer in my bank that I had been very balanced; by a customer in the grocer's that I had been biased in favour of the BJP; and by a reader in a library that I had always favoured Rajiv Gandhi and the Congress. I suspect that means that the coverage was balanced. I certainly didn't succeed in persuading my critics that it was.

In all the many encounters I have had since that rally, I have been struck by the fact that viewers in India expect the BBC to take their side. The day after the abortive rally, a highly emotional fax landed in our office from a small group known as the People's Movement for Secularism. Among their grievances was the fact that we had shown the BJP supporters being attacked by the police. This, they claimed, made out the BJP supporters to be the victims of state repression. The secularists said that, instead, we should have portrayed the BJP as an organization 'whose belligerence and aggression had imperilled normal life'. Incidentally, almost all Indian newspapers showed similar pictures without the commentary required by the secularists. Among our many telephone callers was one who reprimanded one of my colleagues for not agreeing that we should call the BJP 'evil'.

Inevitably, we had complaints from the BJP, too. Some of its supporters were angered that we had described those who were attacked by the police as 'militant Hindus'. Others said that we had deliberately blacked out pictures of their leader recovering in an oxygen tent, after being knocked over by the water-cannon. There were also, of course, BJP supporters who said that we should have accepted their figures for the casualties they suffered at the hands of the police. I have discovered a good reply to most of our critics; it is: 'Well, at least we're not as biased as you are.' I have also learnt that there is such a thing as 'secular fundamentalism', which is just as biased and unreasonable as the religious variety. It is, I suppose, possible that the novelty of seeing, not just hearing, the BBC will wear off. Or, again, the government may wake up to the fact that it no longer has a monopoly over television and allow Indians to provide their own reliable and viewable news. But at present the audience for the BBC seems to grow every day, and the bureaucrats of the Information Ministry are still clinging tenaciously to the electronic media that they have controlled for so many years.

So it looks as though it will be some time before I can resume my weekly visit to the Gymkhana Club bar. I haven't been there since Ayodhya, for fear of being attacked by fundamentalist members of either or both schools. My father taught me that gentlemen did not discuss politics or talk shop in their clubs. Unfortunately, that rule no longer applies in the Delhi Gymkhana.

HUMAN RIGHTS

MAX EASTERMAN   SEMIPALATINSK   1 APRIL 1993

When the Cold War was at its height, the West found the consistent abuses of human rights a convenient political stick with which to beat the Soviets. Evidence was not hard to find, from the forced collectivization of agriculture to the harassment and incarceration of political dissidents. But at the start of 1992 details began emerging concerning human rights violations on a truly massive scale in the newly independent republic of Kazakhstan.

SEMIPALATINSK: THE FORTRESS of seven halls on the River Irtysh, founded by fur-trappers on the old caravan route from Mongolia to Russia. A romantic name, but an ugly city, even by the degraded civic standards of the post-war Soviet Union. Seen from the air, it squats like a huge black stain on the otherwise featureless, snow-bound steppe; once on the ground, my immediate impression was of filth, belching from chimneys, encrusting cars and buildings, blackening the melted snow that flooded the main streets. The drains were rarely able to cope, it seems, even in the better days of Soviet power. That was the heyday of Semipalatinsk, although no one quite realized it at the time. Under a regime given to proud lists of statistics, remarkably few were available for Semipalatinsk. Even today you will find no mention of its main activity in the encyclopedias and reference books, Russian or American. No mention of the Polygon, nor of the horrors it has wrought on the people who live around it. The horrors are not invisible, though their cause is. But it is everywhere: it is radiation.

For forty years, the Polygon, a few miles south of Semipalatinsk, was the main Soviet nuclear test-site. Over 700 bombs were exploded there, nearly a third of them above ground, before the atmospheric ban in 1963. The mushroom clouds could not be disguised; the earthquakes produced by underground tests damaged houses and roads; throughout it all, no official word was said: no warnings about radiation disease, short- or long-term; no advice on self-protection.

In 1952, Dr Saim Balmukhanov travelled up to the Semipalatinsk region. The Kazakh authorities in the capital, Alma-Ata, were concerned about reports of high levels of disease there. Men were losing their hair; their nails were falling out; they had cancerous, bleeding ulcers on their skin. Women were bleeding from the vulva, their periods were lasting weeks rather than days. The whole cardio-vascular system of both sexes was changing. Dr Balmukhanov concluded that the radiation from the nuclear tests was at fault. He went back again the following year and gathered yet more evidence, this time of massive growth-rates in stomach- and lung-cancer and other fatal diseases. He was sent back a third time; then Moscow intervened and put in its own team.

Remarkably (or perhaps predictably), these people decided that malnutrition was the real cause: that, and tuberculosis and brucellosis. The word 'cancer' was banned and Saim Balmukhanov was forbidden to publish his data. By 1958, Andrei Sakharov had been banished to Gorky for warning of radiation dangers, and he was a world-renowned physicist; there was no room for doubt as to what would happen to a mere Kazakh research doctor if he opened his mouth. But it was clear that the Russians (and they were only Russians) who ran the test-site were well aware of what was going on. They were, apparently, convinced that alcohol and a high-fat diet protected against radiation damage; they gave local people free vodka and *kolbasa* sausage, without ever saying that it was anything other than Party munificence. Later they sent Dr Boris Gusif to run a secret clinic, dispensing drugs to cancer victims of the Polygon tests.

Now he runs the newly formed Kazakh Institute of Radiation Studies, and he showed me the official maps and graphs on the spread of the mushroom clouds and the cancers that spread in their wake. 'They seem,' I remarked, 'to have crossed into China.' 'Of course,' he replied, but he didn't suppose that the Russians worried about that. Nor about the 70 or so villagers from Karaul who were deliberately left in the open to experience the full blast of radiation from one test. Two of them survived.

The hellish consequences of these atmospheric tests—cancer rates 20 times higher than at Hiroshima/Nagasaki—were still no preparation for what I saw the next day in the village of Znamenka. Unprepossessing, but prettier than Semipalatinsk, it gives the impression of having been strewn across the flat landscape by the random cast of a giant hand. Horse-drawn sleighs clop across the muddy snow, carrying bales of hay. This is sheep country, and the flocks range far across the steppe in summer, right up to and inside the test area. The people of Znamenka are literally bearing the poisoned fruit of the Polygon. Kairghali is 33; mentally, he is a five-year-old. He smiles and loves dancing with the local schoolchildren. His mother had watched the mushroom clouds exploding a few miles away, and she is now ailing. His father died a few days ago, vomiting liquid as blue as a cornflower from his cancerous stomach. His youngest sister was born so prematurely that she took a year to recover. But Kairghali smiles on. 'He's harmless,' his mother says, as if to reassure me.

A few doors away sits Birik. He is 13 and blind; blind because he has no eyes. Instead, two pustulous tumours disfigure his already oversize head. He knows he is different, knows he is a monster, and he resents my being there talking to his mother, Zeinil, about her grief and anger. But talk she will. It was all a secret for so long; now it is a relief, a catharsis, to tell the terrible truth.

These are the children who survived, 11 of them in a small village of 3,000 people. Back in Semipalatinsk, in the museum of the Medical Institute, I inspected row upon row of dead foetuses, incongruously preserved in Exide battery jars. A cyclops, the single eye in mid-forehead, the ears attached to the chin; a baby with two heads; another with its head at right-angles to the neck; a third with no skull, the brain perched above the sightless eyes. These are just some of thousands, and they are still being born. It will go on for generations. In some of the villages around the Polygon, life-expectancy is now as low as 27 years, and Kazakhs openly call it genocide.

In the main square of Semipalatinsk, opposite the old Party building, stands another monster, a huge statue of Lenin, arms flung wide to welcome the socialist millennium. 'Today,' I said, 'he would be saying "Look what a mess we made".' I was amused by the thought. My Kazakh companion remarked acidly, 'It's easy for men to make fools of ideas.' True enough; but equally true is that it is even easier for ideas to make fools of men.

MY COUNTRY RIGHT OR WRONG

HUMPHREY HAWKSLEY   HONG KONG   1 APRIL 1993

As the rift between Britain and China over the future of Hong Kong seemed to widen in April 1993, 49 prominent figures from the colony went to the Chinese capital to be appointed as advisers on the transfer of power in 1997. They were jostled and jeered as they were preparing to leave. Among the group was a very senior, former Hong Kong civil servant—a knight of the realm who was accused of being a defector.

THE DOOR BELL of David Akers-Jones's house hangs above the gate, and when we rang it with a rope, four dogs barked and scampered down the steps to hold us at bay until Sir David arrived and quietened them down. It was warm, but summer hadn't quite begun. Sir David wore slacks and a bright blue open-necked shirt. He greeted us with the ease of a man familiar with high office: 'I hope you found the house all right,' he said. 'Did the map I sent you work?' He ordered the dogs away into the garden, which stretches back up a hill with flowering shrubs and an out-house where Hong Kong's former acting Governor paints in his retirement. We could have been in Sussex. But we were in the New Territories of Hong Kong, on a winding coastal road which ends up near the Chinese border. We were shown up, past the swimming pool, to the paving-stoned patio, and inside to an extension off the sitting room, glassed all around to take advantage of the view: across the water is Lantao Island where a motorway is being built for the new airport . . . except the project is in trouble because of the row Britain is having with China over democracy.

Sir David has accepted the job of advising in the dispute not his own country, which is governed with parliamentary democracy, but a foreign power with a history of repression and autocratic rule. On a table are faxes sent from friends in England, newspaper cuttings about his decision to go to Peking. He is described as a defector, a Pekinese poodle. His appointment is a propaganda coup for the communists. He is accused of going native. Sir David has been here for 36 years. He speaks three Chinese languages and, in the shabby tenement buildings, they know him as *sok sok jung*, Uncle Jones. He has no plans to return to England. But he did serve the Crown throughout his career, rising briefly to become the acting Governor of Hong Kong, after Sir Edward Youde died of a heart attack in 1986. He would have shared many of the secrets of the negotiations going on with China at the time. He would have had substantial influence on policy.

What is significant about this twist of allegiance is that Sir David clearly believes Chris Patten has changed British policy unilaterally, and that he is not playing fair with agreements which had previously been made with China over Hong Kong's future. 'I am absolutely not a defector,' he says. 'There's no question of me giving secrets away. If I wanted to do that, I wouldn't have to be an adviser.' He speaks as a man, unused to public accountability, but keen to explain himself. 'I was a Hong Kong government servant, I think there's an important distinction. I didn't belong to the Diplomatic Service. I've made my home here. My friends are here, and I'm batting for Hong Kong.'

Most of the advisers are businessmen; there are a few academics, newspaper editors, a couple of artists and two other former civil servants. The common thread among them is that they are all opposed to British policy, and if Sir David's appointment is a propaganda coup for the Chinese, that is because he personifies the divisions that Chris Patten has forced on this community. They are not only among the people of Hong Kong but also in the corridors of power, within the colonial government and the British Foreign Office. Serving officials are, of course, tight-lipped, but they let indiscretions slip out at dinner and cocktail parties, that they don't think Chris Patten will win. But some who are retired, having held the reins of power on China policy for many years, like Sir Percy Craddock (an adviser to Mrs Thatcher), have spoken out publicly. He says that, if Britain is to look after Hong Kong properly, it is no good striking a heroic pose over democracy; it must co-operate with China. If it doesn't, Hong Kong will be hurt—that from a man who until recently was in the highest ranks of the Foreign Office. And in the colony itself there are men like Sir David Akers-Jones. He has taken the plunge, but so have Sir Jack Cater (formerly Chief Secretary), Sir Piers Jacobs (the former Financial Secretary) and David Gledhill, former chairman of the huge trading conglomerate, Swires. These men believe that a smooth transfer of power—with the same members sitting in the legislative council or parliament throughout the transition—is essential to maintain confidence here. Chris Patten, they say, is risking that in order to inject at least a form of democratic government before Britain makes what is hoped will be an honourable withdrawal. They believe that Peking will be so angry at the reforms that it will simply dismantle any democratic institutions as soon as it takes over. Britain might look good internationally, but Hong Kong would suffer.

Mr Patten has his supporters. John Walden, a former director of Home Affairs, lives, not in a lavish house in the New Territories, but in a tiny apartment in a noisy and polluted part of Hong Kong Island. The entrance is packed, floor to ceiling, with boxes on their way to Stanford University in California: archives about what he regards as the British betrayal of Hong Kong; secret deals with China made when men like Sir David Akers-Jones and Sir Percy Craddock were running the show. Mr Walden believes that Sir David should at least pitch in his knighthood.

This is a suggestion that the new adviser to China says is insulting. Sir David is very much the topic of debate this week. He has widened the rift between Patten supporters and opponents even more. He has raised questions about honour, loyalty, allegiance to the Crown. As he saw us out, with the dogs running backwards and forwards around us, he said: 'It's lovely to have visitors all the way out here. Come again. Come for lunch when you're not working. You can. I'm not Anthony Blunt, you know.'

SRI LANKA'S BLOOD FEUDS

HUMPHREY HAWKSLEY   COLOMBO   6 MAY 1993

President Ranasinghe Premadasa of Sri Lanka was assassinated by a suicide bomber on Saturday, 1 May. This was the second political murder in a fortnight—Mr Premadasa's main rival, Lalith Athulathmudali, was shot at a political rally a week before. People on the island were shocked by the killings, even though political violence is fairly commonplace.

IN A QUIET Colombo suburb, leafy and lush with tropical plants, lives a maternity doctor. She is in late middle-age, attractive, lively, intelligent. When we went to see her this week, she shouted through the shuttered window: 'Can you wait a minute? I'm still washing.' Then she came out, drying her long, grey hair in a towel, and ushered us, with the grace of an accomplished dinner party hostess, into her tiny bed-sit: kitchen, basin, bed, all in one room. Two dogs, Porgy and Bess, named from the Gershwin opera, fussed at our feet; a copy of James Herriot's *All Creatures Great and Small* lay on the bed; there were some aspirins, a box of vitamin E tablets, a packet of cigarettes on a small table; a bottle of red wine stood next to a pencil sketch of a young and brilliant man, a Shakespearean actor and a campaigning journalist, Richard de Zoysa, who had earned a living, until February 1990, by working with United Press International in Colombo. Dr Manorani Sarabanamuttu is his mother.

We sat on the bed (there weren't enough chairs) and she told about a night, the type of night that had become all too common a characteristic of political life here. It was 3.30 am when the doorbell rang. She went down to answer it because sometimes they send people from the hospital to get her if there is an emergency. On the other side of the door grille she saw a group of armed men; one was in police uniform, another one in a black T-shirt and black trousers. He had what she called 'a sophisticated weapon'. At first she refused to let them in. Then the weapon was cocked. She opened the door, they came in and dragged off her son and bundled him into a car. Richard's body was found two days later on a beach.

Richard de Zoysa was murdered when President Premadasa was at the height of a campaign to crush a rebellion of disaffected, left-wing youths. Human-rights groups say up to 60,000 people may have died in similar circumstances over the two-year uprising. Premadasa won and underlined his reputation as an uncompromising, authoritarian leader.

Over the past few days, Sri Lanka has mourned his death with flags at half-mast and lines of people stretched along Colombo's beautiful seafront to see the coffin lying in state before the cremation. Sri Lanka is also taking stock of itself. Premadasa was a tough man of the people who built houses for the poor, purified water in the villages, shut down casinos and banned his ministers from going to diplomatic functions. He tolerated no dissent within or outside his ruling party, and even expelled the former British High Commissioner, accusing him of interfering in domestic politics. He died with his country effectively partitioned. The south is prosperous with foreign investment, a growth rate of more than 4 per cent, liberal economic policies, together with planeloads of European tourists who fly in to lie on the beaches. The north is in the hands of Tamil guerrillas, who are blamed for the assassination. They are ruthless, fanatical and uncompromising about wanting a separate state. The east is a no-man's-land of spying, collaboration and more dirty killings between the Tamil guerrillas and a fairly inefficient and brutal army.

I asked Dr Sarabanamuttu, who in her campaign to get justice for Richard has become something of a cult figure, how she thought Sri Lanka could emerge from its cycles of violence. 'People should come out and say enough is enough,' she said, 'enough killing.'

I put the same question to a representative from the Tamil community, Meelan Triuchelvan, who is afraid of a backlash by the majority Sinhalese. 'This could be an opportunity,' he said, 'for the international community to intervene—like it has done in Cambodia and the former Yugoslavia.'

We started to pursue that idea, but both of us trailed off because we knew it simply wasn't going to happen.

The next stop was a cabinet minister, Ranil Wickremasinghe, who could emerge as one of the most powerful men in the country. How could Sri Lanka get rid of this culture of violence and death squads? 'So far, no political party has come to power with goons and death squads,' he said.

'Are you saying there's no intimidation and harassment here?'

'Well, if there is, the election law does make provision for you to go to the courts. Certainly there's nothing like private armies,' he finished.

Dr Sarabanamuttu identified the leader of the death squad which abducted Richard, and took the number of his car. She reported the details to the police. Shortly after that, she received a letter saying that if she continued with her venture of vengeance, she would meet her death in an unexpected way. When a suicide bomber rode a bicycle into President Premadasa's May Day entourage on Saturday, 24 people were killed. Many were bystanders, but most of Premadasa's personal bodyguards were among the victims, including the man Dr Sarabanamuttu says forced his way into her house that night in February 1990. What did she think now? 'It's senseless,' she said. 'It solves no problems; the security forces must be tired of losing their loved ones; the people in the north must have had enough. It must now be possible to have an enormous campaign to end the violence.'

INTO THE VALLEY OF DEATH

CHRIS BOWERS   KABUL   20 MAY 1993

An Afghan who worked for the BBC in the capital, Kabul—first as a translator then as a freelance journalist—Mohammed Massoum became yet another casualty of the country's gruelling civil war. Our Central Asia Correspondent, Chris Bowers, who spent some time reporting events from Afghanistan, went back to the country for the funeral to see how it had changed since he was last there, a year ago.

THE FORMER SOVIET Union and Afghanistan are joined by Friendship Bridge; a hugely inappropriate name for a bridge that bore Soviet tanks into Afghanistan and carried them back again a decade later. The gap in terms of development looks, at times, like centuries. The railway line from Central Asia stops abruptly on the former Soviet side. The border guards there are faceless, formal and unsmiling, awash in paperwork; it still feels like the Soviet Union. Cross the bridge and you pass from concrete and grass to mud and dust, from a land where much is wasted to one where nothing is, from where popular culture and history have been wiped away by Soviet rule to one where the weight of centuries hits you in the face. I felt myself sliding back noiselessly into a gentle world of open friendliness, charm and languid politeness, in a land where the Cold War happened to have deposited—for a reason now forgotten—thousands upon thousands of Kalashnikovs, tanks and mines. Its seems that only the military hardware disrupts the ageless patterns of Afghanistan, standing out horribly and cruelly from the dust and wind that has moved gracefully over this land, changing little.

The Afghan border official (the only one in sight) let down the piece of wire strung across the road, beamed and invited us to fill in a form, in the same breath and in the same manner as he asked us to drink some tea with him. We drove on. A man stopped and looked, his shoeless foot poised on his shovel, prodding at the stony ground. Adjusting his turban, he dipped and pushed down again. Just off the road a ten-foot circle of empty shells served as a gravestone. Bundles of dried grass provided a living for a wizened old man crouching over a stick. Another man tried to pull a piece of metal from the burnt-out chassis of a lorry that had already been stripped of everything of value. As he tugged, the rest of the twisted metal rocked gently, like a bridge in the wind that linked one patch of desert to another. My driver, a Russian, gripped the steering wheel tighter each time we passed a clump of armed men squatting by the road. Afghanistan is still a dangerous land. Ahead of us still, the snow-capped Hindu Kush mountains.

I was back, but my business was death. More than a million dead in Afghanistan over the last 14 years, but the death of Massoum, my colleague and companion for a year, had hit me like a punch in the stomach. They say that death is always as unexpected as a plane falling out of the sky. That was just how it was for Massoum. We left the northern Afghan plain, drove off the road and then walked up the mountain into which the over-burdened, badly maintained transport plane had smashed. Fifteen men came with us. They picked up the remains—one small cloth bag each—of more than 70 people. What was left fitted into a wooden trunk the size of the table I am now writing on. By chance, perhaps by providence, I found Massoum's BBC diary and bloodstained notebook. More of his paper had survived the crash than of his body.

I went on down to Kabul over the Hindu Kush, by bus this time. The responsibilities of power have done little to mend the divisions and rivalries that bedevilled the mujaheddin while fighting the Red Army. One year after mujaheddin fighters swept into the capital, Kabul Radio can—without a hint of irony—announce proudly that some of the forces loyal to the prime minister designate have agreed not to fight the president's men.

The state in Afghanistan remains untended: that means that the schools in Kabul have been closed for a year; there is no power for half of the time; and planes do not get maintained but still fly—until they crash. That accounted for Massoum. Of the rest of the people who worked with me in Kabul, the cook—a kind, gentle man—dons a rifle when he finishes work and, for two hours a night, patrols his district on the look-out for marauders. I didn't dare ask him how often he has to fire his gun. The gardener was kidnapped on the grounds of his ethnic background: he is from a minority group. He says he was beaten up. All I know is that he didn't have grey hair before. The washerwoman has sent her children abroad. The driver left his house because of the shelling. Who knows what has happened to it?

The innocent, medieval charm of Afghanistan wears off when you look inside one of its hospitals or hear the dull thud of artillery exchanges, day and night—as pointless as birds twittering in the morning. Shells, fired with little concern for accuracy, have knocked down trees that, in turn, have fallen on and broken some headstones in the small European cemetery. It marks the graves of 1970s hippies, 1930s philanthropists and 1870s British would-be conquerors.

Afghanistan—one of the most beautiful, proud and heart-wrenching of countries—is still tearing itself apart. A land that for Afghans is sacred—if only, perhaps, because so many dead lie around.

HONOURABLE
MR WALKAROUND

GORDON BREWER   TOKYO   22 MAY 1993

While many countries in the West seem to be suffering from ever-increasing crime rates, it's not a problem that plays on the minds of many Japanese. The country's success in tackling crime seems to stem largely from a certain state of mind.

I HAD MY first contact with *omawari-san* a few weeks after I arrived in Japan. Returning home one evening, I found a card that he had left in the mail box. He'd called, he said, just to check that I was OK. Perhaps I could give him a ring to arrange a proper visit? From that time on, he's been a constant background presence. When I cross a street without waiting for a green light—considered unacceptable and dangerous behaviour in Japan—*omawari-san* is usually nearby to give a warning frown or occasionally bark an order not to do it again. He's always good for directions in this city of few street-names. If I lost a bag or a wallet, I could be fairly confident that it would turn up in his little box, a couple of blocks away.

With his drab, grey uniform and his drab, grey routine—in which fending off boredom is his biggest challenge—*omawari-san* is an unlikely hero. His very name sounds faintly ridiculous. We have the 'Old Bill', the 'fuzz', the 'filth'; the Americans have the 'cops', the 'pigs'; *omawari-san* means 'Honourable Mr Walkaround'. It is derived from his habit of constantly patrolling the few streets under the jurisdiction of his *koban*, the tiny police substations which dot Tokyo with the frequency of fish and chip shops in London. But Mr Walkaround is something of a hero: delegations from foreign police forces are forever flying over to examine his activities; academics spend solemn pages wondering if his methods could be the latest Japanese export to the West. The reason is simple: if it's difficult to find *omawari-san* actually fighting crime, that is because there is little crime to fight. Japan's Justice Ministry basks in the glow of Mr Walkaround's international street credibility. On a recent visit, a committee of men in grey suits was ready with a deluge of impressive statistics: murders and attempted murders are running at under a third of the number in England and Wales, even though Japan has more than twice the population; Japan has 5 per cent of the robberies and a quarter the number of rapes. As for the Americas—well the statistics there are so embarrassing that it's best not to mention them.

The explanation for all this seems pretty obvious. Japan has done what the rest of the world just talks about: it has policemen out on the streets—their little boxes an inextricable part of the local community. There is training in the martial arts for children at the local schools. And the population responds. The 'honourable' attached to Mr Walkaround's name isn't just a strange quirk of oriental languages—if only it were so simple!

The first doubts come when you take a closer look at *omawari-san* in operation. At a police training college near Tokyo I watched new recruits practising for the annual visit to every house in their neighbourhood—the visit which led to my calling-card from the local officer. 'Anything happening?' asks recruit. 'Well,' replies trainee-policewoman-dressed-up-as-housewife, 'in that building over there, on the room on the left, three or four people often gather and play music quite loudly. Can you check it out?' And that was just a training exercise. Now would you—never mind the population of Detroit or Chicago—welcome the police taking such an intrusive interest in your affairs and those of your neighbours? Well, perhaps you would. But if one of those neighbours was arrested, would you automatically assume that they were guilty and then shun them, even if they were never charged? In Japan they would. Japan is a policeman's dream, a sort of police state of the mind.

In a small room above a community hall, Chisako Tezuga fought back the tears as she told me what had happened to her when she was arrested on suspicion of fraud. At the local police station she was strip-searched and forced to adopt humiliating postures while she was looked over. At police headquarters it was the same, only worse. Ms Tezuga was trying to arrange funding for a centre for mentally and physically handicapped children at the time of her arrest. She was completely innocent and was not charged; she suspects that local opposition to the presence of handicapped people in the neighbourhood was behind the whole affair. But more upsetting than her treatment at the hands of the police were the reactions afterwards. Far from sympathizing, her friends and even her family refused to speak to her. They simply couldn't believe that someone could be arrested by the all-powerful state without having done something wrong. And that's not an isolated incident. I met one man who had spent four years in jail before he was acquitted of a charge of conspiracy to commit murder. After his release, his friends and neighbours were so hostile that he has been obliged to change his name and build a new life in a different area.

Such social attitudes to crime may go a long way to explaining *omawari-san*'s apparently stunning success. But they are not the only factor. At the National Police Agency's research department, Yutaka Harada pours scorn on explanations which rely on what most officials here refer to as 'our unique Japanese culture'. He points out that, before 1960, Japanese crime rates were much the same as anywhere else. What happened after 1960, of course, was that the economy took off and employment was guaranteed. It still is, even though the country is presently struggling through recession.

Whichever explanation you choose, it hardly supports the view that the techniques of policing play a decisive role in fighting crime. *Omawari-san* may be bored, not because he has successfully headed off the villains, but because there weren't any villains in the first place. The next time you are in Tokyo, cheer him up by crossing the street to ask him directions. But make sure you wait for the green light.

IN THE LAP OF THE GODS

PHILIP SHORT   TOKYO   10 JUNE 1993

The wedding in June 1993 of Crown Prince Naruhito fuelled speculation that his bride, a former career diplomat, might breathe new life into Japan's archaic monarchy. The world's oldest reigning dynasty was indeed changing—but not quite in the way outsiders might have supposed.

THE JAPANESE VALUE stability and consensus above all else: change comes imperceptibly, like the shifting of sand-dunes in a desert. That doesn't make headlines in the newspapers, and even on those rare occasions when there is a headline event its full import often becomes apparent only years afterwards. So it was with the coronation of Emperor Akihito in November 1990. At the time it was reported as an occasion of medieval splendour; the Emperor and his consort, in silk robes of russet and gold, accepted the inheritance of the imperial ancestors in ceremonies that resembled a scene from an ancient scroll, choreographed with exquisite stateliness, like a sacred dance. And when, two weeks later, he underwent the *daijosai*—a mystical rite in which he is said to commune with the sun goddess, as Japanese emperors are supposed to have done since the dawn of time—comment ranged from the lubricious (with the tabloids wanting to know what really happened in the ritual bed where the goddess spent the night with him), via the utilitarian (Japanese leftists were furious that the government had agreed to foot the bill), to scholarly articles on aspects of the ritual symbolism whose meaning was lost centuries ago.

Almost no one asked why such a ceremony was taking place at all: it was as though no one had noticed that the last time the *daijosai* was conducted, by the Emperor's father, Hirohito, in 1928, he was regarded as a living god, a status which Hirohito renounced, at the behest of the Americans, after the Second World War. For the first coronation of an emperor under the post-war constitution, there should have been no place for the *daijosai*. The Emperor was no longer a god to commune with other deities; he was a mortal man. It would have been so easy for the Japanese government to advise the court that, in view of the Emperor's changed status, the ritual was inappropriate. Quite deliberately, it didn't do so.

Why not? You may well ask. Ancient ritual in any faith, Christianity included, often seems bizarre to modern eyes; why shouldn't Japan cleave to its past? The problem is that this *isn't* Japan's past. Much of it is simple invention, concocted at the end of the last century, at a time of intense nationalism provoked by westernization. The argument then was that, if Japan were not to lose its soul to imported Western culture, it was essential for it to reaffirm its spiritual identity through the exaltation of the national symbol, the Emperor. The result was a catastrophic mixture of Prussian Kaiser and Son of Heaven, which led inexorably to the fascism of the 1930s. The *daijosai*, the coronation, the wedding ritual, all emerged as part of this process—based on earlier rites, but endowed with a new significance for nationalistic ends. Even the ancestral tombs, which the Crown Prince and the Princess will visit to report their marriage to their forebears, aren't what they seem. The first emperor, Jimmu, didn't actually exist, so there couldn't be a tomb; but because the imperial myth demanded it, 100 years ago they went out and built one.

To maintain the fiction, all such areas are, to this day, closed to archaeologists by government decree. Falsification of the past isn't unique to Japan, but here it is carried out systematically: school textbooks are vetted by Education Ministry inspectors to ensure that they follow orthodoxy about what are known as the 'unfortunate events' (Japan's conduct during the war). And it is in this perspective—of the conscious manipulation of history for political purposes—that the decision to hold the *daijosai* three years ago must be viewed. That, it is now clear, was a watershed in redefining the Emperor's role. Some Japanese intellectuals go further and today speak of a deliberate policy of re-deification—re-investing the throne with a divinity that it was supposed to have abandoned half a century ago.

Hence the contradiction: on the one hand, Crown Prince Naruhito, educated at Oxford, and his bride, a diplomat's daughter who grew up in Washington and Moscow and then became a diplomat herself, are outgoing, intelligent people who breathe modernity. But they are puppets in a gilded cage, without power of their own: and the imperial straitjacket which confines them is growing slowly tighter, as the Japanese establishment struggles to protect the mystique of the throne from twentieth-century encroachments, and to preserve the ambiguous symbolism of the small, still space that forms the empty heart of Japan's imperial system.

TUVA—LAND OF THROAT-SINGING AND MILK VODKA

TIM WHEWELL   KYZYL   26 SEPTEMBER 1992

Tibet's spiritual leader, the Dalai Lama, toured the Buddhist regions of Russia in September 1992. The Buddhist religion was suppressed under communism, probably more severely than any other faith: nearly all the monasteries were destroyed and several monks were killed. Tim Whewell travelled with the Dalai Lama to Tuva—an isolated region on the border with Mongolia where people still live a nomadic way of life.

IT IS HARD to decide how to approach the Dalai Lama, particularly at six o'clock in the morning in the waiting room of a Siberian airport. He is fairly unmistakable as he sits in his flimsy red robes and incongruously sensible black shoes. So anything like 'I'm Tim Whewell; you must be the Dalai Lama' would clearly sound absurd. How forward can you be with a living god? But on the other hand, how long can you hover silently in front of someone who's already looking quizzically at you? In the end I went for the direct approach and was greeted not only with a disarming grin but also with a firm squeeze on the arm. His Holiness remembers faces and over the next few days, as he sat enthroned at interminable ceremonies, we exchanged several grins over the heads of the intervening monks and officials.

It was the Dalai Lama's first trip to Tuva, a wild tract of mountains and steppe on the northern fringes of Mongolia. For the Tuvans it was the first visit by a foreign statesman since Genghis Khan passed by in 1207. Stalin, Brezhnev and Gorbachev all avoided Tuva. Yeltsin has never been there either. And yet, until the Second World War, the country was an independent state. In the tiny capital, Kyzyl, you can see the white-columned house that served as the Soviet legation and the former parliament where Tuva's communist deputies voted, in 1944, to request admission into the USSR. But apart from the commemorative plaques on those buildings, virtually the only other traces of the country's lost independence are the triangular Tuvan stamps, preserved in schoolboys' albums all over the world.

The memory of those stamps, with the exotic name and pictures of camel- and yak-herders, inspired the Nobel prize-winning American physicist, Richard Feynman, to embark on a ten-year struggle with Soviet bureaucracy in a bid to reach Tuva—then a region closed to foreigners. Feynman died of cancer just before an invitation finally arrived from the Soviet Academy of Sciences, but his friend, Ralph Leighton, did get to Kyzyl and wrote a moving and funny book, *Tuva or Bust*, about their joint quest to rediscover the mysterious, forgotten country. It is a measure of Tuva's isolation that, even now, few people there have heard of Feynman or Leighton. And of those who have, some get the story a bit mixed up. One told me that the American physicist had been unable to reach Tuva because he wasn't allowed out of his own country. Another said that Feynman's chief aim had been to stick a pole through the geographic centre of every continent, and he was frustrated because he had already done them all except for the centre of Asia, which is in Kyzyl.

Tuvans seem to regard their location at the centre of Asia as their chief claim to fame. One local businessman told me of his plans to set up an association uniting the centres of each continent, which could become an important international trade network. When I suggested that the centres of some continents, such as Africa and South America, were mainly jungle, he pulled out Tuva's other joker, its peculiar tradition of throat-singing. The art, developed by shepherds on lonely hillsides, involves a single singer producing two notes simultaneously; one can been a low, prolonged rattle and another, a piercing whistle.

Tuvan officials hope that throat-singing concerts in the West can become a major source of hard currency for their country. Already several groups have made successful foreign tours and, when local people talked about Britain, the place they seemed to know most about was Langoleen. Langoleen? It took me a while to work out that they meant Llangollen, the Welsh town which, every year, hosts an international musical eisteddfod. Not surprisingly, it is famous in Tuva, and when I visited people's homes they proudly brought out battered copies of the local newspaper, the *Shropshire Star*, and its special Eisteddfod supplement—'not to be sold separately'—with pictures of throat-singers on the front. Showing a degree of self-confidence that would have been unthinkable in most Soviet citizens a few years ago, the Tuvan group that visited Llangollen this year deliberately missed their return flight to Moscow and went busking on the streets of Manchester. They caused a minor sensation in Chorlton-cum-Hardy shopping centre, and were soon being interviewed by Granada TV. It is all a long way from the high pastures around Kyzyl, where the singers' parents or grandparents moved their round, felt tents, or *yurts*, from season to season.

In fact a surprising number of Tuvans still lead nomadic lives. One evening, just outside the capital, I was welcomed into a *yurt* by an old woman and her son, who immediately began apologizing that, since they had no torch or electric light, it was already too dark to kill a sheep for me. They did, however, offer traditional Tuvan tea—brewed with salt—and a strong spirit distilled, while I waited, from a boiling cauldron of sour milk.

Down on the main square of Kyzyl, the Dalai Lama had been sitting through hours of prayers and speeches. As a Buddhist monk, he avoids alcohol, even milk vodka. But his smile at the end of a gruelling day was as boyish and mischievous as ever.

PLAYING THE TUVA GAME

TIM WHEWELL   LOS ANGELES   8 JULY 1993

Tim Whewell's despatch from Tuva (see previous article) elicited an invitation to America to meet a man who has devoted his life to popularizing Tuvan culture. At the end of his posting in Moscow, he took up the invitation and discovered the thread linking yak-herding, physics, the rock legend, Frank Zappa and the pubs of northern Shropshire.

THE GRAVE WAS a tiny brass plaque set into the grass, and in front of it was a small pile of half-eroded cigarette-ends. I have seen that form of tribute many times in the Soviet Union, on the graves of pop stars and even in a museum beneath photographs of soldiers killed in the Afghan war. But this was California, a cemetery in a prosperous suburb of Los Angeles, where the manicured lawns seemed as un-Russian as it is possible to be. The grave belonged to Richard Feynman, the Nobel Prize-winning physicist who died in 1988; the cigarettes, to a group of visiting Tuvan throat-singers.

The man who brought them to America and encouraged the unusual act of homage, was Ralph Leighton. He was a friend of Feynman who shared his fascination with Tuva—that mysterious state marked in pre-war atlases and which later vanished, leaving only a series of strange, triangular stamps. Leighton, now in his early 40s, has given up his job as a high-school teacher and devotes himself full time to putting Tuva back on the map. When he heard my report on the *World Service*, he instantly faxed our Moscow bureau, inviting me to come and stay; and so it was that I was thrust into the bizarre world of the Friends of Tuva. Ralph ends his letters with the words 'Big-with-full-am-I', a literal translation of the Tuvan phrase for 'yours gratefully'. When conversation at the dinner-table flags, and especially when it doesn't, his four-year-old son, Ian, emits long, low, gargling noises, a form of throat-singing which Tuvan herdsmen may have invented while talking to their camels.

The Friends of Tuva newsletter (worldwide circulation 3,000 and rising fast) raises funds for future activities through a mail-order section which will supply you with Tuvan hunting maps, throat-singing cassettes, piggy bank globes showing Tuva as an independent state, and—to my initial disbelief—recordings of my radio reports from the country. The advert makes particular play of 'Whewell's northern accent', which is said to be highly entertaining.

If I was taken aback at this sudden fame, I wondered what the Tuvans who had left the fag-ends had made of it. Their concerts were a sell-out; the rock legend, Frank Zappa, invited them round for an improvisation session; and when they rode on horseback through Pasadena as part of the town's annual parade, the crowds, who had been primed by an article in the *Los Angeles Times*, yelled '*Ekii!*'—Tuvan for 'Hi there!' The visitors must have concluded that, despite its isolation, their country had already become known for its beauty and the richness of its culture. Certainly that was what the people I met in Tuva believed. They were, at first, baffled at the title of Leighton's book, *Tuva or Bust*, and eventually assumed it must be translated as Tuva—incomparable jewel. Of course that is wrong, but somehow I didn't have the heart to tell them, and I don't think they would have understood anyway. *Tuva or Bust* isn't about a country, it's about a quest. Ralph Leighton sums up his attitude to life with the motto, 'Invent your own game and then play it.' And he admits that some people think the Tuva game was more fun when the country was just a dream. Now communism is finished, anyone can get there, and when you do there is not that much to see except bare steppe. Meanwhile, Tuvans themselves are beginning to travel and, as with other ex-Soviet citizens, one of their main interests in meeting Westerners is often to propose far-fetched business schemes.

But Ralph is still playing his game. He has done a lot to help Tuva, and he has found that he can make a living out of it for himself. He is now thinking of proposing 'invent-your-own-game' courses at the Esalen Institute—a New Age study centre on the Californian coast. On my way to

Los Angeles, I also dropped in at Esalen; the prospectus offers workshops in 'Advanced Holotropic Breathwork', 'Cross-cultural Shamanic Practices', and one entitled 'Cliff-dwelling: the Adventure of Spontaneity'. A five-day course costs $675, including the use of the hot springs where students go after supper to wallow, naked, in the open-air pools, gazing up at the stars and listening to the Pacific Ocean crashing against the cliffs below. Luxuriating there at one o'clock in the morning, it wasn't hard to dream up all manner of Tuva-related courses. How about 'Yurts: Living and Thinking in the Round'? Or 'Throat-Singing: Empowering the Inner Spirit'? But I wondered also whether Tuvans, having already lost their remoteness, might not also lose the spontaneity and ancient culture that places like Esalen seek to re-create and eventually become—God forbid—games-players themselves.

Happily, there is not much sign of that happening yet. By all accounts, Ralph's throat-singing friends found California as weird as the average American might find Tuva, and while they admired many of the consumer durables, they were not sorry to go home. Moreover, just as Westerners have re-invented Tuva, Tuvans may have re-invented us. Knowing little about Richard Feynman, they instinctively felt that he was the kind of semi-mythical hero who deserved an offering of cigarette-ends.

Meanwhile, I've got another invitation to take up: the Richard Feynman Memorial Bicycling Society (motto *Floreat Tuva*) has asked me to join one of their excursions along the Cheshire–Shropshire border, which, I'm told, invariably end with refreshments in a rustic hostelry. I suspect that their rituals may be equally baffling to Tuvans and Californians alike.

THE AMERICAS

COSTA RICA— WHERE WORK IS A FOUR-LETTER WORD

ISABEL WOLFF   SAN JOSÉ   3 SEPTEMBER 1992

The tiny Central American republic of Costa Rica has acquired the reputation of being one of the most peaceful countries in an otherwise troubled region. Because of this, and the purchasing power of the dollar, the country acts as a magnet for a growing number of American expatriates. But for them, work is something of a four-letter word.

THE TRICKLE OF Americans to Costa Rica, which began in the early 1970s, has now become a flood. As unemployment and recession have gripped the United States, these *pensionados* have fled south to a country where the dollar is still the object of worship. It may be called the 'Rich Coast', but in Costa Rica $600 a month, which is all foreigners are obliged to invest, is very serious money. Most *Ticos*, as the Costa Ricans call themselves, are lucky to earn a third of that.

From Pittsburgh they come and from Kentucky, from Dayton, Ohio, and from Maine; there are now about 50,000 Americans in a population of only three million Costa Ricans. Blue-collar workers for the most part, and ex-servicemen, they say they came to Costa Rica because it is so peaceful. The army was abolished in 1949 and, because of its solid liberal and democratic traditions, it has earned the soubriquet, 'the Switzerland of Central America'.

Costa Rica lies snugly between Panama and Nicaragua, yet it has been untainted by the violence which has beset the rest of the region. 'This is the most civilized of all Latin countries,' said one *pensionado* from Philadelphia. We were sitting on the verandah of the Key Largo Bar one evening, in downtown San José, the capital. 'The people are lovely,' he told me, 'the climate is perfect and the food is great.' He offered me a large, pink prawn. 'You can eat wonderful seafood here which would cost you *mucho mucho* dollars in New York.' He gave a little sigh of contentment, and then his face lit up with inspiration. 'This place is fantastic; it's a new frontier—like Alaska—it's wide open.'

I ventured inside where the atmosphere throbbed with the rhythms of salsa, and lambada-twisted bodies moved languorously across the parquet. The red-illuminated interior was full of young Costa Rican women and middle-aged American men. I sat at the bar, beneath a swirling fan, next to a handsome-looking *pensionado* of about 40. He bought me a Margarita, then downed his own in two abrupt gulps. I enquired, by way of conversation, what had brought him to Costa Rica.

'The Latino women,' he replied unhesitatingly, slipping his arm round his companion, who looked as though she ought to have been in school. 'They're lovely, they're free, they're gregarious, and they like American men.' I asked him what he missed about the States. 'Absolutely nothing.' Why had he left? 'Too many lawsuits.' What was he going to do here, was he going to work? After all, as I pointed out, he was still young. The word 'work' seemed to have an electrifying effect. He flung himself off the barstool like a crocodile leaping off the riverbank and stared at me accusingly. 'You've been sent by the *Ticos,*' he hissed through orthodontically perfect white teeth. 'You're a spy, you're a goddamn government spy.'

'No honestly,' I replied, 'I'm a journalist.' But by then he was already halfway across the dance-floor and was soon lost in the writhing mass of bodies.

The next day, Peter Brennan, a reporter with the *Tico Times*, cast some light on this rather odd piece of behaviour. He said that the Americans were allowed to invest in Costa Rican companies, but they were not allowed to do any work themselves. Some of them did, though; and then there are others who enter the country illegally, or without the necessary funds. As Brennan explained, they tended to get rather jumpy if you asked them too many questions. Costa Rica is not a wealthy country, and the government needs the dollars that the Americans bring in. But, at the same time, they are worried about negative influences from abroad, particularly with regard to drugs; so far, Costa Rica has been a relatively dope-free zone. They check out the background of every foreigner who applies to live there and investigate their past with the help of Interpol. A criminal record in any part of the world is an automatic disqualifier. Nevertheless conmen and criminals do get in; the problem is identifying them as big-time crooks.

But most Costa Ricans, when quizzed about the *pensionados*, display a pragmatic tolerance (after all, Costa Rica is one of the few countries in the region not to have been invaded by the United States or to have had its government overthrown in a coup staged by the United States), although you do hear them grumble, from time to time, about the fact that the Americans have relatively easy lives. Only the estate agents are unequivocally happy to have them there, because they all buy up houses and plots of land. 'Let's face it, we need their greenbacks,' said one hotel manager to me with a shrug. 'They've become an important part of our economy. But I think we ought to stop letting them in now. Otherwise Costa Rica will soon become just an appendage of the United States—you know, like a little, tropical Alaska.'

BULLDOZING HISTORY

TOM GIBB   SAN SALVADOR   8 OCTOBER 1992

October 1992 marked the 500th anniversary of the arrival of Europeans in the Americas. The voyage of Christopher Columbus was the focus of much festivity on both sides of the Atlantic, but his reputation for brutality towards the indigenous peoples meant that the anniversary was not the cause for universal celebration. And the settlers' penchant for destroying ancient civilizations goes on to this day.

IT WAS IN the early sixteenth century that Pedro de Alvarado, one of the cruellest of the Spanish captains, first arrived in what is now El Salvador, at the head of a small army. He found a rich land, well populated, with large towns. But he met fierce resistance from the Pipil Indians who, in true Salvadoran style, disappeared into the hills to fight a prolonged guerrilla war. In one battle, Alvarado had his thigh bone shattered by a Pipil arrow, leaving him with one leg that was four fingers shorter than the other. He wrote plaintiff letters back to Hernán Cortés in Mexico to explain why he had been unable to subject the stubborn Indians of Cuscatlan to the rule of the king of Spain. But eventually the Pipiles paid a high price for their resistance. After being subdued, many were executed as traitors or became enslaved. Their capital, Cuscatlan, was deserted and lost in the depths of time—lost, that is, until the archaeologists and the bulldozers turned up.

The story starts in 1976 when Paul Ameroli, an archaeologist from the United States, did a survey of the coffee plantations to the south-west of the modern city of San Salvador. In a report for the National Museum, he concluded that the ancient capital of Cuscatlan was buried there. He recommended that the site be preserved for further investigation. His findings were confirmed earlier this year when bulldozers, working on a big housing project, discovered a group of four pyramid structures. The archaeologists started to excavate. Sure enough, they began to uncover the finely laid stone walls of the temples and palaces of the Pipiles. They found beautifully decorated ceramics and finely carved statues and figurines. Digging deeper, it appeared that the Pipil city had been built on the ruins of an older Mayan site.

The modern housing project is owned by one of the wealthiest families in the country, the Mathias Regalado family, who most definitely trace their ancestry from Pedro de Alvarado rather than from the Pipil warriors. Their reaction to the discovery was to ban the archaeologists, put guards armed with machetes around the site, and continue the bulldozing. They flattened one of the temples which had survived the 500 years since the conquest.

The land developers, however, are not the only culprits. Just next door, the massive, new US embassy has just been completed. The United States bought the land a year after Paul Ameroli's initial report which recommended preservation. Covering eight acres, at a cost of $80 million, the embassy was designed as a fortress against El Salvador's modern-day left-wing guerrillas, whom the United States spent billions of dollars and more than a decade trying to destroy. But this year, with the civil war over, rebel leaders have become frequent dinner guests of the ambassador. US involvement is diminishing and the embassy is much bigger than it needs to be. The designers say that it was modelled on a Mayan village; in fact, it is probably built on one. During construction there were reports of ceramics and other artefacts being found and sold off. The archaeologists say that it will be impossible to tell now how much was destroyed. 'It's amazing what a bulldozer will do,' said Paul Ameroli.

The partial destruction of Cuscatlan is only the final act in a long saga. Much of the indigenous culture in El Salvador actually survived until the end of the last century, when Indian lands were confiscated by a small, European oligarchy to make coffee plantations. Native dress and language were then abolished. In 1932 the Indians rebelled, but the uprising was put down and some 30,000 peasants were killed in just over a week. Today, practically no one speaks the native Nahaut. The few villages that still use indigenous dress have to import the material from Guatemala.

But for Cuscatlan, at least there is still a possibility of a happy outcome. The news that the ancient city was being bulldozed by one of the country's richest families caused a national outcry. Most Salvadorans, after all, still call themselves 'Cuscatlecos'. The president was forced to intervene; and there is now a possibility that part of the site may be expropriated from the landowners at well below market value. That, at least, might discourage other developers from using bulldozers on their national heritage.

RAIN STOPS PLAY

SIMON CALDER   GEORGETOWN   10 OCTOBER 1992

Guyana is the only Commonwealth country in South America; it was once described by Evelyn Waugh as a 'little gob of Empire'. In October 1992 a new government came to power following elections, and the voters chose a Marxist as their president. So the country seemed to be swimming against the tide in Latin America—both in terms of its ideology and in its choice of sport.

TEST CRICKET FANS have had a raw deal in South America recently. Not a ball has been bowled in any of the last three Test matches that England were due to play in Guyana, which for cricket purposes is regarded as part of the West Indies. Two games were rained off (a perennial hazard in this saturated tropical enclave) and the third failed to start because of a political disagreement over the South African connections of an England player. But while international cricket has waned in Guyana, this week the country has presented the world with a psephological phenomenon widely believed to have vanished. In elections which everyone, from European Community observers to former US President Jimmy Carter regarded as free and fair, a Marxist has been elected president. And this wasn't some young, ideological upstart: Dr Cheddi Jagan is 74 years old and was first elected leader of Guyana 39 years ago.

The Co-operative Republic of Guyana is a geopolitical eccentricity. The country occupies a dim and dismal corner of South America, a belt of jungle and swamp with few resources and fewer prospects. The Atlantic coastline has none of the spectacular beaches found in neighbouring Brazil and Venezuela. Broad rivers run like veins through the whole country, depositing muddy sludge liberally along the seashore. When you fly out of the capital, Georgetown, streaks of beige smudge the coast as far as the eye can see, as if some catastrophe had befallen an artist's palette. But Guyana has some great attractions. The back of the $100 note carries a picture of the Kaiteur Falls, a spectacular flume of water exploding over the brink of a granite monolith. At least that's what it looks like on the banknote: all flights to the interior were cancelled until further notice, so I had no chance to see for myself.

The national airline, like much of the country's infrastructure, is in a sorry state. Guyana is the poorest nation in South America. Known as British Guiana from the time when it was prised from the Dutch until independence in 1966, it has never enjoyed economic success and, were it to acquiesce to the claims on its land, it would almost cease to exist. Venezuelan maps show two-thirds of Guyana as Venezuelan territory; and neighbouring Surinam (formerly Dutch Guiana) also claims a slice of the country. This is largely based on linguistic ambiguity, for half the towns in Guyana have Dutch names. But leaving aside place-names like Vryheid's Lust and Nieuw Amsterdam, to all intents and purposes Guyana is part of the anglophone Caribbean. The ethnic mix is vastly different from the rest of South America: descendants of Asian immigrants, especially Indians, are in the majority. This week's election brought the mainly Indian People's Progressive Party to power, much to the relief of Dr Jagan.

In the colony's first election in 1953, the PPP won a clear victory against the mainly black People's National Congress. The British were alarmed at Dr Jagan's left-wing views, so sent in troops to topple his government and impose Forbes Burnham as president. In 1964 power was again wrested from the PPP by an unlikely alliance of the PNC and a right-wing party, again aided by the West. But Forbes Burnham showed little gratitude to those who had helped him to power and set about establishing a system modelled on the Soviet Union, a kind of 'Eastern Europe on Sea'. He created a personality cult which Stalin would have envied and even had a Lenin-style mausoleum built for his remains—though when he died in 1985 it proved impractical to preserve them in Guyana's hot and humid climate.

Desmond Hoyte inherited the presidency; Comrade Desmond Hoyte, that is, since he adopted the Soviet form of address. He introduced totalitarian touches, such as draconian currency controls and a rule that public buildings should not be photographed. Tourists taking pictures of the pretty post office in Bartica are still being picked up for that offence. It is hard work becoming a tourist in the first place: the process for obtaining a Guyanese visa is fraught, including a protracted interview and demands for proof of your financial resources. But it is worth persevering to get a glimpse of a charming, if crumbling country.

The mile-wide Demerara River washes languidly against the dirty old quayside in Georgetown, a capital straight from a Graham Greene novel: peeling paintwork, clapperboard wreathed in vegetation, permeated with the musty smell of gentle decay. This impression of urban senility is rather soothing, until you discover that Georgetown is the most dangerous city in South America. Visitors are warned not to leave the hotel except in a taxi; even if your destination is just the bar across the road, you summon a cab. A couple of hundred Guyanese dollars change hands for a ride of a couple of hundred yards. You don't gamble on your life in Guyana.

You can, though, gamble your life-savings on the 2.30 at Ascot this afternoon. Horse racing is immensely popular in Guyana, and British racing commentaries are transmitted by satellite. The busiest place in the country is the bookmakers' quarter in the capital. The favourite won the election by a mile. But Dr Jagan's new government will need help to unravel the strings of corruption which bind Guyana. Everything seems heavy and slow-moving: the sky, the rivers, and the leaden hand of a bureaucracy borrowed from Whitehall and the Kremlin, but barely adapted to the terrain. To change Guyana's image as a wayward former colony unprepared for the harsh realities of life in the free world, the new leader has to stop the poison of impoverishment from spreading. Guyana's people deserve better. They also deserve a decent game of cricket—weather and politics permitting.

ROCKIN' ALL THE WAY TO THE TOP

ANDY KERSHAW   LITTLE ROCK   5 NOVEMBER 1992

The election of Bill Clinton in November 1992 marked not just a shift from Republican to Democrat but also a generational change. George Bush is a veteran of the Second World War; Bill Clinton was heavily criticized during the election campaign for avoiding the draft for Vietnam.

I HAD TO give them a double-take before I realized who they were. Strolling across Markham Street in downtown Little Rock, dressed in T-shirts, jeans and sneakers, you could have mistaken them for just another bunch of young friends on their way to a leisurely Sunday breakfast at the local diner; I nearly did. Yet here was the core of Bill Clinton's campaign team, en route for their eggs over easy. They were just two days away from the promotion of the Governor of Arkansas to 'most powerful man on the planet'. Now these masterminds behind the world's first rock'n'roll president looked, for all the world, like a college entertainments committee.

It was the dreamy eyes of George Stephanopoulos that I recognized first. I've thrilled many times to his towering intellect, ripping into Republican feebleness on television. So it was a shock to discover that Clinton's communications director is a midget. TV distorts age as well as stature. On screen, Stephanopoulos looks much older than his 31 years; on the street, he looks about 19. Tipped for high office in the Clinton administration, by journalists much closer to this campaign than me, Stephanopoulos, like Governor Bill, is an Oxford University Rhodes

Scholar. He has an MA in theology. Not only is he bright, he makes female reporters go wobbly at the knees as well.

Lolloping around little George was the semi-skinhead, string-bean chief strategist, James Carville. Although there was no formal hierarchy, insiders at Democratic National Headquarters—an elegant old newspaper building on 3rd Street—regarded Carville as the brains and energy of the campaign. 'He's the Clint Eastwood figure around here; a wild and crazy man,' said Phillip Gould, an English political consultant to Clinton—and rather raffish himself. Gould was drafted by the Democrats from among the British Labour Party's general election strategists. After the double-breasted conventions of British politics, Gould couldn't believe what he had walked into in Little Rock. 'I arrived here with a selection of suits,' he said. 'And they laughed at me. After two days, I had to go out and buy some casual American clothes.' Carville, he was to discover, embodied the new Democrat disrespect for convention—dominating what they called the 'Clinton War Room'. Its occupants were known as 'the strike force'. 'He lives for this,' said Gould. 'A real political animal. No other life. You should see his flat in Washington; a complete dump.'

Carville's tactical strength was to go on the offensive against every one of George Bush's character assaults on Clinton. Carville is six foot three inches of aggression. Ordinary mortals like myself couldn't get an official audience with him; we did speak briefly a couple of times, in the bar of the splendidly restored Capital Hotel where he has been billeted over the long months of the campaign. He would jog through in the early evening, swill down a Coca-Cola and disappear through the revolving door into the night, even before heads had time to turn. One time, he was wearing a T-shirt with the slogan 'Ragin' Cajuns'—Carville is from Louisiana. Our exchanges in the Capital bar never touched on the presidential election; we discussed only music. Carville is an expert on New Orleans rhythm-and-blues. In the War Room it was said that he was fond of drinking fiery Louisiana hot sauce straight from the bottle. The Thursday before voting—when polls put Bush and Clinton almost neck and neck—he must have been knocking it back like a Californian on mineral water. Apparently he was in a rage. Curiously, the following day, the spectre of Iran–Contra came back to haunt old George.

At 48—though you would put him a decade below that—Carville was one of the more senior strategists behind the President-elect: the average age of the activists in Clinton's headquarters was 26. What they lacked in long-term political experience they made up for with youthful exuberance, the imagination of garden-shed eccentrics, and a sense of fun. The campaign was stylish, witty and oddly innocent. Bill Clinton's victory was as good as in the bag by 9.15 last Tuesday night. I was standing in the foyer of Democrat headquarters. Carville came rushing through, diving out into the rain to meet his old boss, and future president, at the State House. His face was thunderous, and fixed on the floor. For a moment I thought George Bush had just got another four years. Onlookers in the hallway were—believe it or not—pressed against the wall by the Carville charisma as it roared by. He was attired, for this historic rendezvous, in a sloppy old jumper, scruffy jeans and loafers. And for reasons known only to himself, in the centre of his forehead he had slapped an enormous gold star.

Later I spotted him—not on the platform before the eyes of the world, accepting presidential gratitude and the public embraces of the guy he had just put into the White House, but in the thick of the crowd, punching the air and barking along with the rock music, indistinguishable from the other 50,000 people around him. The favoured anthems: Fleetwood Mac's *Don't Stop (Thinking about Tomorrow)*, and Steely Dan's *Reeling in the Years*. Phillip Gould, the former adviser to Walworth Road, didn't really need to state the obvious after I'd spent a week in Little Rock. 'I'd much rather work with these people than the Labour Party,' he said.

Bill Clinton's natural inclinations, and the animal instincts of Carville, needed no 'phone and marketing strategies: this is a president-elect who had his own high school rock band; appeared as a vision-in-denim in *Rolling Stone*; jogged for the world's press in the magazine's T-shirt; is considered a 'home-boy' by Little Rock's teenage blacks; has blown his saxophone at election rallies and on late-night TV talk shows; and kept the crowds entertained before his victory speech by hiring a sensational black gospel choir. If Bush had won, the crowd in Houston would probably have been served with the limp country dilutions of the Oakridge Boys. It made me think of England: imagine the awkwardness of John Smith in a denim shirt, sleeves rolled up, on the cover of *Q* magazine. (And remember when Kinnock wore jeans?—they never seemed to fit him.) Then picture, if you will, Robin Cook playing guitar on *The Late Show*—I can't. Tony Blair possibly, but he's about the only one.

It sounds flippant, I know, but we are close, here, to the soul—if not the substance—of the Clinton landslide. On Tuesday night I only hoped that the gonzo journalist guru, Hunter S. Thompson, for once left his bar-stool at the Capital Hotel, where he had been drinking and growling for three days—and that was when he was in one of his sociable moods. If he did leave the bar, he saw his vision realized from the distant campaign trails of Eugene McCarthy, George McGovern and Jimmy Carter: a rock-and-roll president of the United States of America—and an anti-Vietnam, dope-smoking, fun-loving president at that.

George Bush made a serious miscalculation in his Clinton character attacks. Steve, a former air force technician from San Antonio, Texas—dancing in front of the State House—was, I guess, one of millions of Americans (already alienated economically) that President Bush wouldn't have recognized: 'Hell,' he said, ' I was in the armed forces. But if I'd pulled myself up from nothin', gone to Oxford, and then they'd hit me with the draft to a stupid war in Vietnam—I wouldn't have gone either. Sure I've smoke pot and cheated on girls. I looked at Bill Clinton and thought, this guy here is just like I am.'

Steve would have loved the victory party in the University Convention Centre. George Bush would have loathed it. The disco first blasted us with rap and house music; then Bill and Al's excellent adventure came to its climax: an appearance on stage, in a blizzard of confetti, to the deafening accompaniment of John Lennon and the Plastic Ono Band's *Instant Karma* and *Power to the People*. Carville, of course, was right in the middle of the crowd. 'I feel so young!' a woman gushed, writhing in front of me. She couldn't have been more than 35. John Lennon—if he was still with us—would be 52; President-elect Bill Clinton is 46.

THE LANGUAGE BARRIER

JONATHAN FREEDLAND   WASHINGTON
24 DECEMBER 1992

It was George Bernard Shaw who once said that Britain and America were two nations divided by a common language. Jonathan Freedland discovered that, 50 years on, the message was still true. At the end of 1992, he had completed a four-month fellowship on the staff of the Washington Post, *where he learned to write American.*

ENID, OKLAHOMA, IS not the kind of place you would make a point of visiting. It is a small, not particularly picturesque, farming town—home to no more than 40,000 people. But that didn't matter: in fact, it was its very averageness that had brought me here, one September morning. I had come to Enid, along with the entire White House press corps, to hear George Bush make a campaign speech. The President wanted an all-American backdrop for his address which would, once again, question Bill Clinton's patriotism.

So, along with Air Force One and the presidential entourage, I touched down in Enid, except—unlike them—I was expecting something bigger. It was the sign saying 'Welcome to the City of Enid' that misled me. To me, a city should be big, and this was anything but. It's not that Enid is an arrogant place with delusions of grandeur. Instead, the town was merely displaying a trait shared by all Americans, and one which affects the language they speak. The characteristic is a collective aversion to smallness.

They can't bring themselves to call even a portion of chips 'small'. It has to be 'regular'. They go to the ocean, when we would go to the sea. When we have pain they have agony. Just as the cars and milk cartons are bigger here than anywhere else in the world, so the language likes to pump things up. It is as if everything in this vast country has been stretched to fit. Perhaps this need to expand—to call little Enid a city—is the product of fear. After all, the founders of the United States were so daunted by the emptiness of their huge, new land that they launched a great move west to fill it. Maybe some of the impulse of those pioneers remains in today's Americans. Their affection for flat, sprawling cities—like their preference for big words—is perhaps evidence of a desire to fill the void.

Then there is the word 'Americans'. Here it is used as a synonym for human beings. Covering the presidential candidates, I was struck by the way Messrs Perot, Bush or Clinton would refer to 'The American People', when their British counterparts would simply speak about the 'public'. Stump speeches would declare that 'every American has the right to a college education', or that 'no American should go without health care'. In Britain we would say that 'everyone' deserves X, and that no 'person' should go without Y. To say that 'every Briton' has the right to this or that would be taken to mean that people of other nationalities do not. At best, it would sound parochial; at worst, jingoistic or even racist.

I was puzzled by this until an evening in front of the television put me straight. I watched ABC's *World News Tonight*, which turned out to be nothing of the sort. In a 22-minute show, only three minutes were dedicated to events outside America. Over on CBS, a round-up of stories 'from around the world' featured these datelines: Portland, Oregon; Dallas, Texas; Miami, Florida and the San Fernando Valley in California. Later, viewers could soak up the World Series—a tournament confined to North America and dominated by teams from the United States. In each case, America and The World amounted to the same thing. Small wonder then that 'Americans' and 'people' seem like interchangeable terms here.

A similar habit governs America's invocation of its own name. Still with television as my guide, in a two-minute commercial break I counted that 'America' was mentioned no fewer than 11 times—often in the most trivial contexts. 'They fought for America', began a trailer for a TV movie, while a Chrysler advert trumpeted 'the renaissance of the American car'. It reminded me of the three-year-old child who delights in running around saying his own name. Unsure of his identity, he must state it out loud to convince himself that he really exists. Maybe it is because Britain is older, and is not a nation of immigrants, that we don't feel quite this same need to beat our national breast.

Of course there are plenty of other differences. Even the most educated Americans tend to dislike polysyllabic, Latinate diction, just as they shun elaborate, rococo sentences, embellished with subordinate clauses, of which this is an example. They like their sentences simple. Like that. The American style is more democratic. Professors here talk in a language that plumbers and postmen can understand. It's telling that it took a left-winger like George Orwell to call for a similar approach to British English. For this difference in language is a reflection of a social difference: America is not nearly as class-based a society as Britain; that is why equality and classlessness are always built into the US dialect.

Still, I wouldn't swap my 'British' for their 'American'; my hosts seem to like it, too. I have noticed that when I say 'fortnight' instead of 'two weeks' or 'engaged' instead of 'busy', they feel they have heard a museum piece come to life. People laugh, as they hear what they believe is the voice of their own ancestral past. They chortle, delighting in the sound of a distant, national memory. Either that—or maybe they just think I talk funny.

BOYS FROM THE BLACK STUFF

HUGH O'SHAUGHNESSY CERREJÓN 9 JANUARY 1993

Colombia's economy is heavily reliant upon exports of energy—mainly coal and oil. The coal reserves in one region alone, Cerrejón, are almost as great as all the reserves in Britain put together. But the wide variation in safety standards from one pit to another is something of an embarrassment to the government.

THIS IS THE tale of two coal mines, both of them in Colombia.

As I sat over scrambled eggs in the scrupulously clean, air-conditioned canteen at the Cerrejón mine, not far from the airstrip, the swimming pool, the tennis courts and the branch office of the local bank, I pondered that I'd never visited such a strange, modernistic place. Across the road was the earth satellite station. Around the corner were the maintenance bays, capable of handling some of the most complicated pieces of electrical and mechanical equipment on earth. I reminded myself that, until a few years ago, no coalmine as modern as this one had ever existed.

El Cerrejón, whose coal arrives weekly in the Thames Estuary to feed British power-stations, is sited in the Guajira, a barren area in the north of Colombia; it is a part of the former Spanish empire of which the Spanish king once thought so little that he pawned it to his German bankers. The local oysters in the Caribbean Sea yielded some good pearls, but that was about all there was. In 1976 Exxon, the US oil company, in partnership with the Colombian state coal company, won a contract to develop the vast deposits of coal that had subsequently been found just below the surface in the Guajira. Exxon transformed the place. Today more than a million tons of coal a month are scraped out of a vast, open pit by huge excavators. The coal is taken by massive lorries, each with a capacity of 154 tonnes, to the special trains which haul it on the company's private railway for 150 kilometres, to a purpose-built port. From there, it is sent in bulk-container ships far and wide, to consumers in the US, Europe and Israel.

The creative capacity of a modern multinational massively to develop the natural resources of a Third World country could hardly be better illustrated. The only fly in the ointment (apart from the present low international price of coal) appears to be the complaints of the local Indians that their traditional lands are being spoilt by the coal dust which rises from the mine and which flies off the railway wagons as they whiz down to the port.

Hundreds of miles away, near the city of Medellín, in the centre of Colombia, I visited a coalmine where the conditions of work were so unutterably bad that they would certainly have alarmed Charles Dickens or Emile Zola. La Carolina is little more than a hole roughly cut into the side of a hill, one of hundreds of such mines around the little town of Angelópolis. Worked by a few men who lease the mine from a local landlord, La Carolina has no safety precautions at all; the miners, who work stripped to the waist in almost total darkness, don't even have helmets to wear. Slipping and sliding down the muddy tunnel, I eventually got close to the coalface. There, young boys, aged ten and eleven, were hauling bags of coal out of narrow crevices to the porters whose job it is to carry the coal to the surface. In the absence of electricity, the only light they had was a candle mounted in a tin can which they held in their teeth. We were all kept alive in the bowels of the mountain by a wheezy air-pump, which sent air down to us through a fragile, leaky plastic tube. Some of the young workers, who put in a 12-hour day for the equivalent of £2–3 a week, start in the pits at the age of five or six. Not strong enough to pull a load or wield a pick, they are employed carrying food and water, or running errands in the foetid darkness.

The leaders of the Colombian coal industry, and the Exxon company, are clearly highly embarrassed by the conditions of semi-slavery in which young boys work in places like Angelópolis. Given the controversy that coal imports are causing in Britain at a time when many modern British pits are being closed, they know that reports of child labour do not help their business at all. Though there are laws against child labour in Colombia, the government of President Cesar Gaviria doesn't enforce them. For its part, the industry claims that none of the coal won by child labour is exported, though the coal exporters also realize that in a free market it's impossible to give a guarantee.

Perhaps, for their own good, the large companies which import Colombian coal into Britain and the rest of Europe, and the directors of Exxon, should have a quiet word with President Gaviria about the plight of the boy miners of Angelópolis.

THE COMEDIANS REVISITED

HUGH SCHOFIELD   PORT-AU-PRINCE
13 FEBRUARY 1993

One of the most enduring works of the late Graham Greene is his novel, The Comedians. *The book was written in 1965, during the worst excesses of the dictator, François Duvalier. Nearly 30 years later, some things have changed, but the book remains a useful text for anyone visiting Haiti today.*

'We were the only boat, and yet the shed was full: porters, taxi-drivers . . . police, the occasional Tonton Macoute in his black glasses and his soft hat, and beggars, beggars everywhere. They seeped through every chink like water in the rainy season.'

IN GRAHAM GREENE'S day, you came to Haiti by boat. You prayed that you would get in before dark because of the power-cuts. Today it is the airport, but the confusion is identical and, as you drive along the rutted alleys into town, the street-hawkers loom like ghosts in the candle-light. Thirty years on, the lamps still go out in Port-au-Prince.

The Comedians is about a man, Brown, who returns to Haiti to his hotel, the Trianon, and to a doomed affair with the wife of a South American diplomat. In the background the ghastly terror of Papa Doc unravels. The book is a classic. I decided to see how much of it is still here.

The starting point is Brown's hotel: it is, in fact, the Oloffson, where Graham Greene himself stayed when he came. They still remember him:

how he asked the staff to lay a cross on his pillow every day, and his voyeuristic fascination with the local Creole girls. The Oloffson is one of the greats, a tropical pile half-way between a cricket pavilion and a French château, with a view through mango and palm trees to the mountains of the northern peninsula. Nothing significant has changed there since *The Comedians*: the massive bed where Brown's mother dies—*in flagrante*—is still in place, and from the balcony you can see the swimming-pool and the spot where Dr Philipot, the secretary for social welfare, lay in the shadows with his throat cut. But the greatest surprise is on the terrace: a tiny figure with a white cane, and still giggling, in Green's words, like 'a monkey, and he seemed to swing from wall to wall on ropes of laughter'. This is Aubelin Jolicoeur—the model for Petit Pierre in the book: journalist, social flitter and self-styled Monsieur Haiti. He is still all three.

Across Port-au-Prince, other landmarks. The brothel—Madame Catherine's, where Brown has a run-in with the Tontons Macoute—is still there; so is the spot by the port where he and Martha met for love-making. Sadly, the statue of Columbus has gone (it was torn down in 1986) and so have the illuminated globes proclaiming Papa Doc's ubiquitous message, 'I am the Haitian flag'. But otherwise it is the same. North of the capital is Duvalierville, today called something else, but with the massive cock-fighting pit now built. This is where Brown goes with the ever-trusting American presidential candidate, Smith, who wants to set up a vegetarian centre. It was, incidentally, with a surreal jolt, a few days ago, that my eyes fell on a newspaper headline, 'Presidential Candidate Arrives in Haiti'. Fact and fiction were becoming strangely mixed until I remembered that Jesse Jackson had just been in town.

But then, the surreal is endemic to Haiti. The next port of call was the police-station, a low building in lurid yellow beside the palace. It is here that Brown visits his co-traveller, Jones. I went on similar business, accompanying a young journalist who had disappeared a week before, then had been dumped, badly beaten but alive, in the middle of Port-au-Prince. This was to be where he made his statement, though the absurdity of the police—the anti-gang service, as they are officially known—pretending to be concerned, lent the occasion an almost theatrical air. The captain was pleasant enough; he had a set of mug-shots in a frame by his desk which reminded me of the picture of the dead rebel described by Greene. But the interview couldn't proceed because he wanted it taped. The only recording device he had was his answering machine, so in the end the absurdity was completed, torture-victim and police-chief addressing each other in polite Creole across the desk—both speaking into ancient Bakelite 'phones.

That is one thing, of course, that hasn't changed either: torture, beatings, disappearances. It is hard to say how this compares with the days of Papa Doc. It seems to me that some of the more blatant excesses have gone: the desperation, for example, that drives a minister to cut his own throat. But many Haitians disagree.

The last stop was to see the character in the book called Hamit. He is the Syrian who lends Brown and Martha a bed and who later is taken off and killed. In real life, Issa was indeed taken off while Greene was here, and the reason that he had him killed in the book was because he assumed that was what would happen. In fact he was set free and is now a prosperous art dealer. I asked him how life had changed. Maybe he was exaggerating, but he said that it was worse, much worse. Thirty years had gone by, and Haiti was still—in Graham Greene's ringing phrase—'a shabby land of terror'.

FAMILY VALUES

GAVIN ESLER   WASHINGTON   20 FEBRUARY 1993

In February 1993, President Clinton revealed details of his package to bring America's enormous budget deficit under control. The President invited the people to join him on what he called 'a great national journey'. One area of expenditure, health care, was central to the President's plans, since it accounted for about half of the growth in the deficit. But squaring the circle with regard to the health service would be no mean feat.

PRESIDENT BUSH ALWAYS used to say that the United States of America had the finest health care system in the world. But how would he know? If, like Mr Bush, you happen to be an oil millionaire from a family so rich that you were driven to school by a chauffeur during the Great Depression, then health care in America is indeed wonderful. For someone who can afford triple by-pass heart surgery, or a baboon-liver transplant, then high-tech, high-cost, high-intervention America is the place for you. On the other hand, if you are an ordinary middle-class or working-class family, the fear of losing a job (and the health care that goes with it), the fear of bankruptcy because you cannot afford the treatment, the fear of being unable to pay thousands of dollars in prescription charges—these are now facts of life.

Last year my wife had a baby. The cost of two days in hospital, and a few check-ups afterwards, was more than £8,000. Aspirin-like painkillers were billed at £4 a time. That must have been what President Bush had in mind when he talked of 'family values'; mine is valued at £8,000 a head, apparently. Of course, insurance picks up most of the bill. But to meet spiralling health costs like these, the premiums are so high that 37 million Americans are without insurance, while 20 million more have inadequate cover. Since businesses insure their workers, health costs have become the single biggest cause of bankruptcy and the chief cause of strikes, as employers tell their workers that they just cannot afford to pay any more. And the costs to the government, especially for the poor and elderly, are so great that health costs now account for one dollar in seven spent in America, the largest single factor in the ballooning budget deficit.

A few months ago, a friend pulled something in his foot while running. He limped to the doctor and was ushered in to a wonderful office building, replete with gadgets to poke and prod and analyse. There was a lot more paraphernalia than in a British doctor's surgery. But while waiting for the doctor, who rapidly shuttled between patients in different rooms, my friend decided to set his stopwatch to record what he called 'face time' with the doctor. It came to seven minutes—two of which were spent in chit-chat. For those five minutes of high-powered care, the bill was £80—and the doctor told him to rest and it would get better. His foot did; but his wallet is in agony.

The doctors, who are every bit as caring as their British counterparts, recognize the absurdity of their situation. Frightened of being sued by disgruntled patients, doctors have admitted to me that they insist on extra (and costly) tests. No one was ever sued for doing too much; and in any case some doctors have a financial interest in high-technology equipment and refer patients for unnecessary tests to make money. But that is hardly surprising. Delivering babies is so legally risky that an American obstetrician might pay £35,000 a year in malpractice insurance; he has spent £35,000 before seeing a single patient. Almost three times as many babies are delivered by Caesarean section in America as in Britain. By whipping the babies out of the womb, American physicians may avoid lawsuits, and they certainly stand to profit from a more costly procedure, but is that the best care? And the death rate for children around the time of birth in the United States is actually worse than that of many other industrialized countries.

The result in an otherwise highly efficient America is that health care is often a Kafka-esque bureaucracy, delivering to millions of Americans Third World standards at superpower prices with all the compassion of the KGB. A recent comparison between the United States (the only industrialized country without a basic, universal health system) and

Canada (which has) was most revealing. As in Britain, the Canadian system has problems, such as waiting-lists for non-urgent care. But a 300-bed Canadian hospital needed just one bureaucrat to send out the bills. The same-size hospital in America had 42.

And as for preventative health—as Huckleberry Finn once observed—there ain't no profit in it. President Clinton pointed out that the United States has an immunization record for children worse than all of the countries of the Americas, except for Haiti and Bolivia. Measles has made a comeback; so has tuberculosis. But the health system, which is capable of spending tens of thousands of dollars on high-tech, emergency, life-saving equipment for a child with polio, can't always find the few dollars necessary to immunize that child in the first place.

West Virginia is a poor, rural state which might yet provide a model for some of the Clinton health reforms. The Lincoln County Clinic is truly a community venture. It started in the front room of a grocery store, in an area notorious for having one of the worst health-care records anywhere in the United States. Now doctors and medical students from all over the country come to West Virginia, to provide basic care inexpensively and to prescribe free drugs donated by the big pharmaceutical companies. You can't get a baboon-liver transplant, but they will help pregnant women with nutrition, and have seen fewer perinatal deaths than ever before.

But Mr Clinton's goals may be incompatible. He wants to extend basic health care to all, while cutting the crippling costs and not blunting America's reputation for high-tech excellence. He risks offending everyone: doctors, nurses, hospitals, insurance companies and any patient who has to wait for treatment. There is no perfect health-care system, but ordinary Americans are paying more and getting less, while all the time some repeat, in incantatory fashion with Mr Bush, that this is the best health care in the world. Maybe, but just don't get sick here; you probably can't afford it.

BAPTISM OF FIRE

GARY DUFFY   WACO   4 MARCH 1993

In the United States, the leader of a religious cult, along with more than 100 followers, barricaded himself inside his fortified farm in Waco, Texas. The Branch Davidians' leader, David Koresh, claimed to be Jesus Christ. The siege lasted 51 days and came to a bloody end: 78 people were killed when federal agents forced their way in. It began when a raid by agents of the Bureau of Alcohol, Tobacco and Firearms went badly wrong. Four of the bureau's agents were killed in the ensuing gun-battle, as well as two cult members. Gary Duffy—who normally reports events from Belfast—found this, together with the bomb-blast at the World Trade Center in New York, a somewhat unnerving start to his spell in the United States.

IT HAS BEEN a strange seven days since I left behind the troubles of Belfast, to take up a temporary attachment in the BBC office in New York. I had hardly arrived and started to become accustomed to the frenetic pace of life here, when the first reports came in of a bomb explosion at the World Trade Center. It was a familiar scene for any journalist who has covered the problems in Northern Ireland for the last eight years: smoke billowing through a building full of people, the sense of fear and the many acts of courage. For a city well used to drugs-related crime, rape or individual murders, this was indiscriminate violence of a different sort. Americans have long felt immune to the kind of terror that can suddenly invade a busy street in many of the cities of Europe. But New Yorkers can, with a great deal of justification, feel proud of their reaction. Although more than 40,000 people work in the twin towers which dominate the Manhattan skyline, there was not the wide-scale panic that could have been expected.

As so often in Northern Ireland, while others searched for a motive and began the task of finding which group or individual had placed the bomb, it was ordinary families who were left to face the tragedy of burying their dead. Here, too, their grief came under the media spotlight for a few days. But the months and years of sorrow that lie ahead will be theirs alone. As for New York, it has all the appearance of a city prepared to overcome any adversity. Before the week was out, traders were on the streets selling T-shirts which proudly proclaimed, 'I survived the terror in the towers'.

The impact from this event had not even begun to subside when news of a different kind came in from an isolated, rural community near the small city of Waco in Texas. Federal officers had tried to serve a warrant on a small religious cult in order to search their compound for arms, and to arrest the leader of this little-known sect, the Branch Davidians. The group's leader, known either as Vernon Howell or as David Koresh, had proclaimed himself Jesus Christ. He was described, bizarrely, as a charismatic guitar-player who had as many as 15 wives. When the federal agents arrived to serve the warrant, cult members responded with a devastating display of firepower: bullets pounded through the walls of the complex in a fierce and bloody gun-battle. The dead included a number of sect members and four agents from the Bureau of Alcohol, Tobacco and Firearms, one of the worst losses suffered in its long history. Although it often carries out its work with a low profile, its most celebrated agent was Elliot Ness, who led the effort to convict Al Capone and whose exploits were made famous in the film, *The Untouchables*.

The cult, which the Bureau was called upon to face last Sunday, was a small remnant of a group that had broken away from the Seventh Day Adventist Church; it included just over 100 men, women and children. They lived self-contained lives in their headquarters, waiting anxiously and defensively for Armageddon. Koresh himself had envisaged a bloody conflict which would represent his crucifixion. Compared with the complex layers of sectarianism in Northern Ireland, this was a straightforward tragedy of a demented individual who had used his charisma to warp the lives of others, weaker than himself. In the years ahead, more people around the world will remember the name of David

Koresh and the city of Waco, and will recall how many died and who they were.

As you fly into Waco, the surrounding countryside seems to have few distinctive features. Flat land stretches out, apparently for miles and miles, interspersed here and there with some urban sprawl or an isolated community. The people are kind and welcoming, and they seem as genuinely surprised as the rest of the world at the events which have unfolded ten miles to the east of their city.

The Branch Davidians have, for many years, been an unobtrusive part of life here. Vegetarians and pacifists, they did not wish their neighbours any ill. When David Koresh took over their leadership in the mid–1980s, all that changed. Feuds and violence soon followed, and it was not long before this once peaceful community began to attract the attention of the authorities. Allegations about possible child abuse, and concerns over illegally held weapons, finally prompted federal agents to act last Sunday in an operation that had been planned for months. But, apparently alerted by a tip-off, some members of the Branch Davidians were armed and ready. They were, it seems, willing to kill and be killed at the request of their leader. The cult was said to possess assault rifles and explosives, and the compound had the protection of a look-out tower and underground passages. Koresh would, in all probability, have remained a failed rock singer and leader of an obscure American sect but for those 45 minutes of violence which claimed so many lives. Instead, within hours, his words were to be brought to millions of people by satellite TV, radio and newspapers. As the siege continued, the world waited for David Koresh's next move; he said he was waiting for God to tell him what to do.

As I said, it has been a strange seven days.

TELLY ADDICTS

HUGH O'SHAUGHNESSY   RIO DE JANEIRO
11 MARCH 1993

*In Brazil in the spring of 1993, concern was being expressed
about the power of the privately run Globo television network.
The head of Globo, Roberto Marinho, had even been described
as 'the owner of Brazil', and moves were afoot to limit his, and
his company's, influence.*

DO NOT, REPEAT not, ring a Brazilian between the hours of eight and
nine o'clock at night. He or she won't thank you for it, and indeed might
become short with you or even abusive. After all, you will have broken
in on a ritual which, dare I say it, is stronger even than Macumba and
the other forms of African religion so favoured by Brazilians. You will
have interrupted the *Novela das Oito*, the eight o'clock soap opera
on the Globo network, which nightly holds 80 million Brazilians in its
thrall. You will have broken into private grief or heartfelt celebration,
depending on what the evening's episode will have brought. The soap
opera, in fact, doesn't hit the screen until gone half-past eight, just after
the *Jornal Nacional*, or TV news, but the two programmes are pretty
much as inseparable as Gilbert and Sullivan or Laurel and Hardy—and
a good deal more venerable.

The principal producer of *Novelas* is Rede Globo, the Globo television
network which dominates the airwaves in the second most populous
country in the western hemisphere. Globo attracts anything between two-
thirds and three-quarters of the audience. The business, which includes
radio stations and a powerful newspaper empire, is privately owned; it
is the property of the Marinho family whose patriarch, Roberto Marinho,

rules it with a rod of iron. Though they are not published, the profits must make the 88-year-old Marinho one of the richest and most influential men on the face of this earth.

After the national and world news, the people of Brazil settle down to the soap opera of the day, to follow the fate of strong men, beautiful women, scoundrels and simpletons. Invariably, the Globo offerings are superbly well produced, with a strong and interesting story-line, told in a masterly way by talented actors and actresses. Cleverly, Globo takes soundings through public-opinion surveys once a soap opera has been launched and is established, and can vary the plot in accordance with how the punters would like it to go.

Globo does not impinge merely on the dreams of Brazilians; it has some impact on their political attitudes as well. It did much to promote the presidential candidacy of Fernando Collor de Melo. It presented him as the fresh, crusading and clean figure who would sweep away the existing political class which Globo constantly presented as old, tired and irredeemably corrupt. Fernando Collor did indeed achieve the highest office, but at the end of last year he was forced into resignation when the full extent of his corrupt deals was revealed by his brother, Pedro.

Now there are murmurings against Globo in Brazil—a development that had hitherto been undreamt of, given Globo's power in the land. In January, Cardinal Lucas Moreira Neves, Archbishop of Salvador and Catholic Primate of Brazil, without ever mentioning Globo by name launched a fierce attack on Brazilian television which, he said, was reducing Brazilians to a nation of imbeciles. He added that it was breaking the law into the bargain by acting against the constitution which prescribes an educative role for television. Dom Lucas's strictures have now been echoed by Marinho's many opponents. They include Leonel Brizola, the governor of Globo's home state of Rio de Janeiro, and Luis Inacio da Silva, 'Lula', the trade union leader; both men were beaten by Fernando Collor in the race for the presidency. Questions are being asked in Congress. Marinho, sometimes rather extravagantly termed 'the owner of Brazil', is certainly under attack, an attack against which he is defending himself and his network vigorously. But there is no sign yet that viewers are switching off.

So my initial warning stands. Do not call a Brazilian between eight and nine in the evening.

BEL SHOT!

HUGH SCHOFIELD   CASTRIES   11 MARCH 1993

*On the Caribbean island of St Lucia people speak French—
or French-based patois—but the national sport is cricket. It is
a legacy of the island's former colonial masters, first France,
then Britain.*

ACTUALLY, IT'S A slight distortion to say the language of St Lucia is
French: the official language is, of course, English. This was a Crown
Colony until 1979—now it is a full member of the Commonwealth. Even
as I write, the royal yacht *Britannia* lies moored in the harbour below.
But that is only half the story; the real language—the one in which the
150,000 St Lucians actually talk to each other—is Creole: the simplified
form of French that developed here, and in other French colonies around
the world, among the enslaved African population. For St Lucia was
French long before it was British. A pirate with the glorious name of
'Jambe de Bois'—Peg-Leg, I suppose—claimed the island back in the
1550s, and it wasn't until nearly three centuries later, after the Napoleonic
Wars, that it was finally ceded to Britain. Since then, of course, Britain
has left its ineradicable mark, and the upshot today is this curious hybrid,
a French-speaking, Roman Catholic nation that is utterly obsessed with
playing cricket.

Just how obsessed is apparent to the visitor as soon as he arrives.
Especially on a Sunday, every patch of level ground has been turned into
an impromptu wicket, often—for this is a mountainous country, with
supreme ingenuity. Some of the teams are in full whites; some are
barefoot boys in shorts, with stumps made out of twigs. But everywhere
the same code of rules, the same air of decorum that mark out real lovers

of the game: the batting side sitting together on a low wall and watching in silence as the bowler comes in, and the fielders stalk the wicket; the next man in taking a few practice balls up against a tree; and, floating through the dusty air—past the shebeens with their signs for bottled Guinness and Mount Gay rum, past the banana groves and on into the forest—these strange cries: *Bon Shot!*, *Voyes Bol-la!* (Quick, throw me the ball!) and *Bel Pawe!* (Good catch!).

The temple of Creole cricket—St Lucia's answer to Lord's—is the ground known in colonial times as Victoria Park, now renamed the Mindoo Phillip Park. If you are not from St Lucia and are not one of those people who memorize batting figures from *Wisden*, then you won't have heard of Mindoo Phillip. Even at the height of his powers, in the 1950s, he never played for the West Indies, so his fame didn't spread far. But in St Lucia, they have named their national ground after him, and in the bookshops one of the few local books you can buy is his biography—perhaps panegyric would be more accurate. As the author puts it, there are two St Lucians who have been endowed in their sphere of endeavour with that rare quality which is genius. One is Derek Walcott, the Nobel Prize-winning writer; the other is Mindoo Phillip, batsman. He would easily qualify for the office of St Lucian cricketing legend, were it not for the fact that he is still very much alive, and is supervising the ground that bears his name. With a little prompting he will reminisce, in his accented, deliberate English, about the early days. In the 1930s and '40s, it was only the better-off, English-speaking St Lucians who could afford to play club cricket. The only way that he and his Creole friends could join in was by laying bets on the stumps that they could bowl the batsmen out. Later, when he was a recognized player, he and his friends devised a shot they called the *coupay jambe*—or leg amputator—where the ball is slammed back angrily at the bowler's feet. It was, as his biographer puts it, a kind of social revenge. These days there is none of that antagonism, and all the St Lucian team speak Creole. Indeed, it is a useful advantage in their matches against other West Indian islands: they can shout instructions to one another without the other team understanding.

And so to the high point of the trip: a one-day match at the Mindoo Phillip Park between the Windward Islands, of which St Lucia is one, and the Leewards. It's part of the Geddes Grant Cup, between the six West Indian regional sides. In the pavilion stand, a Rastafarian is fast asleep on the back wall. An old woman is frying patties on a paraffin stove and selling them to the schoolboys. Across the pitch, beneath a spreading saman tree, is the scoreboard, one of the old-fashioned, manual variety, with the heads and limbs of the seven or eight young scorers poking around the sides. We are all listening to our FM radios and the ball-by-ball commentary from the press-box. With a radio, you are part of an élite company; there is no better feeling than to be tapped on the shoulder and asked who the bowler is, and then be able to reply. The commentary is immaculate, rich, serene, eminently civilized. All very English, but when the cry goes up, it's still *Bel Shot!*

PC COMPATIBLE?

GAVIN ESLER   WASHINGTON   3 JUNE 1993

One of the most curious phenomena of recent years in the United States has been the fashion for so-called 'political correctness'. The Politically Correct—usually abbreviated to PC—have devised a whole new vocabulary in which black Americans become African-Americans and Indians are native-Americans. But there are other pretenders to the title of PC, the arch-rivals of the Politically Correct—the Patriotically Correct.

IN HIS BOOK, *Culture of Complaint*, the art critic, Robert Hughes, rages against two types of whining that have deeply infected American life. On the left there is 'Political Correctness', which may begin with worthy motives of what is called gender and racial sensitivity, yet which quickly degenerates into a cultural war against the tyranny of those—like Shakespeare, Tolstoy, Columbus and Aristotle—who are DWEMs: Dead White European Males who, it is claimed, unfairly dominate American culture. On the right, Mr Hughes identifies a different type of PC, the 'Patriotically Correct', such as the ultra-conservative Pat Buchanan, whose speech at last year's Republican Convention declared another kind of cultural war against homosexuals, abortion rights and single parents. Buchanan's speech would not have been out of place in the Nazi Reichstag, according to Mr Hughes.

An American friend, who agrees that this deadening cultural war between the Politically Correct and the Patriotically Correct has reduced much social debate to a series of incomprehensible shrieks, asked if I would point out that most Americans are not like that, that this remains a largely tolerant, magnificently diverse country where most people still believe in the right to be different. But even my friend admitted that megaphone ranting of the Politically Correct and the Patriotically Correct often drowns out more reasonable voices.

To take a minor example: while David Koresh and his followers were holed up in Waco, journalists were tipped off that relatives of British families inside were travelling to Texas. One middle-aged Briton, who happened to be black, was said to be on a commuter flight. At the airport, as we waited an American television journalist asked British reporters who they were waiting for.

'How will you recognize him?'

'Well, he is British and he is black,' one British reporter replied.

'Oh,' the American said. 'He's African-American.'

'No!' the British journalist protested. 'The man is not African-American. He is British.'

'But,' the American persisted, 'you *said* he was African-American.'

There was an embarrassed silence before the American reporter finally asked: 'Well, could I say he is African-British?'

'Maybe you should try African-West-Indian-British,' was the sarcastic reply.

I re-told this story to one African-American friend who, by the way, says that he prefers to be referred to as 'black' and is proud both of his skin-colour and of his African heritage. 'Do people not realize,' he laughed, quoting a phrase often used by black preachers, 'that it's not the name that we're called, but the name that we answer to that's important?'

In his book, Robert Hughes dismisses much politically correct talk ('challenged' for handicapped, 'waitperson' for waiter or waitress) as partly harmless, partly politeness, but often a dangerous 'linguistic Lourdes', in which all pain is supposed to be healed by changing a few words in order to lose or soften the meaning. The result is Alice in Wonderlandspeak, where words can mean anything you say they mean, where there is no 'right' or 'wrong' behaviour, merely 'appropriate' or 'inappropriate', where you are not fired but you have been 'let go' because the company has been 'downsized', never 'cut'.

The most serious or most publicized, yet essentially trivial, of these incidents led Hillary Clinton herself to call on American universities not to stifle free speech. In the University of Pennsylvania, a white male student was studying late at night when a group of other students was celebrating so loudly that he was disturbed. He admits that he yelled:

'Shut up, you water buffalo!' It just so happened that the rowdy students were female and black, and they took this to be a racial epithet; so began a series of events somewhere between Buster Keaton and Franz Kafka.

At most British universities, you might expect people who disturb others' study to be disciplined. But the University of Pennsylvania agonized between the right to yell 'water buffalo' and the right to take offence. Finally it decided that it was not the rowdy students but the studying student who should face disciplinary proceedings. But after the story received national coverage—and considerable ridicule—the female students finally withdrew the charge. No one emerges with much credit: the women were rowdy; the male student was plain rude.

But the real trouble, as Mr Hughes vigorously asserts, is that, while noisy battles are fought on whether 'water buffalo' is racial abuse, or whether the word 'chairman' demeans women, black people and women are still underpaid compared with white males, and the really serious spectres of racially motivated crimes, rapes, violence against women, can be pushed to the side by all the PC blah from centre stage.

On the right, meanwhile, the Patriotically Correct have been in retreat since the Clinton election victory. But Mr Hughes points to the vigour with which their foot-soldiers walk around abortion clinics carrying human foetuses, or try to have the National Endowment for the Arts disbanded because it subsidizes feminist and homosexual artists. A Patriotically Correct television talk-show host, Rush Limbaugh, has even become a cult figure with his attacks on feminists as 'feminazis', and his ridicule of the other PC.

In fact both PCs—right and left—have many things in common. They are often humourless and incapable of anything other than absolute certainty: 'A Vote for Bill Clinton is a Vote Against God', was one Patriotically Correct slogan, though one wonders how they know. But the most significant common feature of both PCs is their determination to silence everybody else, especially the majority who stand, deafened and bewildered, in the cultural war's no-man's-land. The good news is that even before Mr Hughes' eloquent statement of militant moderation, there is something called the First Amendment to the United States Constitution, which forbids any law 'abridging the freedom of speech or of the press'. It turns out that those Dead White European Males, referred to by most Americans as the 'Founding Fathers' of the Constitution, are more alive to modern stupidities than their critics had thought.

OWN GOAL

TOM GIBB   GUATEMALA CITY   5 JUNE 1993

*President Jorge Serrano's suspension of the constitution in
Guatemala in May 1993 was being referred to as a 'self-coup'.
Ironically for Mr Serrano, that was exactly how it turned out:
a week after he had dissolved the Congress and Supreme Court,
it was Mr Serrano who found himself with a military escort,
speeding towards the airport and away from power. President
Serrano left behind him a scene of political confusion, with rival
factions fighting for the country's institutions and the allegiance
of the all-powerful military.*

IT WAS, PERHAPS, the visit to the topless bar in New York in January
that started the rot. Normally, being caught in such a place after a hard
day's meetings wouldn't create a public scandal for a Latin American
politician. Guatemala's last president, the Christian Democrat, Vinicio
Cerezo, had given his party's name a new meaning through his sexual
exploits: Guatemalans joked that he was Christian from the waist up, and
Democrat from the waist down. But for President Serrano, a born-again
Christian who likes to talk about God and family values, it did little to
help his credibility. And in his bid to take over all the powers of the state
ten days ago he needed all the credibility he could get.

Essentially, President Serrano tried to copy Peru's Alberto Fujimori, by
appealing over the heads of the politicians to the population. Complaining
that the country was ungovernable, he suspended the Congress and the
Supreme Court, both of which (everyone seems to agree) are corrupt,
and promised law and order and strong government. This appealed to the
military, for decades the real power behind the throne, and they initially

supported him, as long as he did all the talking. But unlike what happened in Peru, it failed to spark mass popular appeal. Among the political classes he stirred up a hornet's nest: almost everyone accused him of taking the country back to the dark, bloody decades of military rule. All week there were extraordinary scenes for Guatemala as conservative businessmen, left-wing union leaders and politicians—normally bitter enemies—huddled together in groups in hotel lobbies, conspiring to overthrow the President. President Serrano also underestimated the international response. The United States, worried that 'self-coups' could become a fashion for presidents facing popularity problems, withdrew $70 million in aid and threatened economic sanctions.

Last weekend the army, perhaps by now realizing that it was on to a loser, withdrew its previously unqualified support. The press started openly to defy government censorship; everyone clamoured for President Serrano to resign. On Tuesday morning, throwing insults at reporters and swearing that history would vindicate him, he was escorted from the National Palace by army officers. When the Defence Minister appeared on television that afternoon to announce the deal reached between political, business and military leaders, everyone hoped that the crisis was over. He said President Serrano had been removed and the Vice-President had resigned. To save constitutional form, however, he said the resignation would not be accepted until Congress could meet to elect a new head of state. Finally, he announced that Congress would purge itself of corrupt members. The plan lasted for less than a day. First, Congress refused to purge itself, then Vice-President Gustavo Espina, who was supposed to be a figurehead for the transition back to constitutional rule, gave a press conference denying that he had ever resigned. 'According to the constitution,' he said, 'I'm the real president.' And he demanded that Congress swear him in. Almost immediately the Defence Minister did another about-face and publicly supported Vice-President Espina. Everyone else in the country was furious at finding the man who, the week before, had appeared on television with President Serrano to announce the suspension of the constitution, now appealing to the same document to take power with military support. 'Serrano and Espina, they're both pigs!' shouted left-wing protesters outside Congress.

The Attorney General, backed by opposition parties, filed a suit against the Vice-President, accusing him, among other things, of violating the constitution, rebellion, corruption and abuse of power. The climax to the whole farce came when Mr Espina arrived at Congress in the middle of the night, supposedly to be sworn in. Most of the deputies stayed away, although, obligingly, the Vice-President's brother, nephews and some other friends filled the gaps. Claiming he had a majority, which he did not, Mr Espina then dramatically turned down the presidential sash, saying that, in the interests of the nation, he would look for greater consensus. One deputy who supports him burst into tears with the emotion of it all.

For outsiders it is easy to laugh at the comic antics of Guatemala's politicians, but it is also easy to forget the reality behind the farce. In the past decade, tens of thousands of civilians have been killed in what is perhaps the most brutal counter-insurgency campaign and dirty war against left-wing rebels in Latin America. Abuses, while fewer than before, are still endemic. Drug-trafficking has boomed, the justice system hardly works, there are huge differences between rich and poor, and the majority Indian population is almost totally cut out of the system. And now there is a power-vacuum, with no one in control and with fears of a new military coup. There are those in the business community, human-rights groups and the political parties trying to improve Guatemala's lot and find a solution. They fear that, if the present crisis continues, what until now has been a comedy could quickly turn to tragedy.

MAKING CONNECTIONS

MARTIN DOWLE   RIO   17 JUNE 1993

Setting up as a foreign correspondent in the developing world poses numerous problems, both bureaucratic and logistical, for the hapless journalist. As Martin Dowle discovered when he began his posting as the BBC's Rio Correspondent, dealing with the telephone company was no mean feat.

WHEN I MENTIONED to a visiting acquaintance that I was about to buy a telephone, he rather innocently replied that, had he known, he would have brought one in for me from the United States. I explained that, unfortunately, it wasn't that simple: I wasn't so much trying to buy the instruments as the lines which go with them. Rio's 'phone company, Telerj, had a waiting-list of 18 months, and I explained that I simply couldn't wait that long to be connected.

Instead, I had looked in the classified column of the newspapers where, side by side with ads offering massage services and occultism, there was a small section where various agencies offered the buying and selling of telephone lines. It was a complicated business, with the intermediary trying to co-ordinate seller and buyer at a price acceptable to all: not an easy task with inflation running at 30 per cent a month. It reminded me of that sketch in *Dad's Army* where the platoon try to synchronize their watches. By the time they have agreed on the second at which the watches are to be set, the time has, of course, already moved on. And so it was with us: the price of 59 million cruzeiros would rise to 61 million the next day, then 63 million the following day, and so on. Eventually, however, a price was set, and a rendezvous agreed outside the 'phone company's offices.

Since this was, technically, an illegal transaction, our intermediary, Senhor Martins, explained that payment by cheque, credit card or in dollars was out of the question. We would have to bring cash. So a colleague and I arrived in a nervous state—our pockets bulging with the 130 million cruzeiros needed to buy two lines. It was the one day that I would have given anything not to be a multi-millionaire. The exchange of the lines was a pleasant affair. Indeed, by the time it had been completed, the vendor, a chic lady in her 40s, had already invited me to spend the weekend at her holiday home at Buzios, a trendy resort outside Rio. But then came the tricky part, handing over the wads of money. Telerj, who up to now had willingly participated in the deal, suddenly behaved like the client at an up-market bordello who insists on leaving the money behind the clock. They unceremoniously informed us that the cash couldn't be exchanged on their premises; and we were then horrified by Senhor Martins' suggestion that we conclude the transaction on the street. Instead, we adjourned to a small bar where, rather shiftily, we bundled the wads of 500,000-cruzeiro notes, all 280 of them, into our chic friend's ample handbag.

Occasionally the Brazilian government promises to simplify these matters, simply by providing more lines. But everyone knows that, if it did, there would be an outcry, for 'phone lines are a valuable asset. Unlike the cruzeiro, they, at least, keep their value; indeed, families even pass them on in their wills. Only the affluent can by-pass this problem, by buying Rio's latest status symbol, the mobile 'phone. The city's yuppies can be spotted nowadays barking loudly into these instruments while sunbathing on Ipanema Beach, or posing ostentatiously with them on their new mountain bikes, which rarely go more than ten feet above sea level.

But there is another category of *Carioca* that covet their mobile 'phones: they are the city's mafia, who control the illegal gambling in Rio. Now, a feisty judge, Denise Frossard, has declared war on these *bicheiros*, as they are known, giving 14 of them hefty prison sentences. And she has caused a major sensation by removing their privileges inside jail, taking away their well-stocked fridges, TVs and videos. But, more importantly, for the first time she has ordered that their mobile 'phones be confiscated, on the not unreasonable grounds that they might be co-ordinating their illegal activities from inside jail. With growing evidence of a link between the Medellín drugs cartel in Colombia and these gangsters in Rio, with their sinister nicknames such as 'O Turcao' and the 'Big Turk', Judge Frossard's campaign is of huge importance to Rio. Now the net may really be closing in on the *bicheiros*, with the arrest in Switzerland of a senior Brazilian ex-policeman, considered to be the intermediary between the *bicheiros* and the cartel. The drugs connection makes the judge's clampdown all the more courageous. Dismissing any possibility that she might give up her dangerous work, it was perhaps no accident that she should comment: 'In the judiciary, you only leave though death or expulsion.'

BOLIVIA'S HEADY BREW

DAVID ADAMS   HUATAJATA   1 JULY 1993

In July 1993, the government of Bolivia was trying to restore the somewhat tarnished image of the coca plant. It is used, of course, in the manufacture of the drug, cocaine; but the Bolivians say that the plant has a multitude of healthier uses, and they are now making a range of coca-based products, from toothpaste to wine.

WHEN I ARRIVED in Bolivia's capital, La Paz, friends promised to meet me at the airport with an oxygen tank and an invigorating cup of *mate de coca*—tea made from coca leaves. At 12,000 feet, visitors to La Paz find the thin air difficult to adjust to; it can cause severe headaches and nausea, as I was soon to discover. The best remedy for altitude sickness is coca tea which, with its mild herbal flavour, helps to settle the stomach. It is easy to prepare, and is available in tea bags everywhere in Bolivia. Outside Bolivia, of course, the authorities take a less favourable view of the tea bags; after all, the drug barons use the same leaves to make cocaine.

Drinking coca tea may be illegal in some countries, but I'm told that the Pope did it on a visit to Bolivia; so did Queen Sofia of Spain. Even the former American Vice-President, Dan Quayle, did it. I did, too: five or six cups a day for ten days. I can honestly say that it works. Last year, President Jaime Paz Zamora began a campaign to decriminalize the coca plant. Bolivia hopes that, by restoring the good name of coca, it can create jobs and increase the national income from exports of coca products. At an international summit of Latin American leaders in Madrid, he wore a coca pin in his lapel and made a speech saying that the leaves are healthy when not processed into cocaine.

But, not surprisingly, Bolivia is having a hard time trying to promote
the virtues of the coca plant. When the Bolivian government sent 18
pounds of coca leaves to Spain last year for the World Fair in Seville, the
plants were impounded. The leaves were to be featured in an agricultural
exhibit at Bolivia's pavilion.

The merits of coca have been known for centuries. The plant had
mystical values for the ancient Indians. Pre-Columbian artefacts show
men with bulging cheeks chewing coca leaves. In the sixteenth century
the Spaniards administered coca leaves to workers in the silver mines in
order to prevent hunger pains. And Bolivian Indians still habitually chew
the leaves as a mild stimulant. Although Indian peasants in Bolivia sell
coca to drug traffickers, they themselves have never been consumers of
cocaine, which is chemically processed from the paste of coca leaves.

To find out more about the other uses of coca, I travelled just over an
hour from La Paz to Huatajata on the shores of Lake Titicaca. There, in
the breath-taking surroundings of snow-capped Andean mountains and the
deep-blue water of the lake, an enterprising Bolivian tourist operator has
built an unusual five-star health spa. The owner, Darius Morgan, is the son
of a half-Romanian, half-French mathematician and poet who emigrated to
Bolivia 40 years ago. He has sought to capitalize on the government's coca
diplomacy by attracting tourists with coca-leaf health tonics and coca cream
massages. With good cause—and good fortune for Mr Morgan—Bolivia
has been honoured with the title of Latin America's cradle of natural
medicine. It's hard to imagine anywhere that better demonstrates how
that title was earned than on the shores of Lake Titicaca. The spa serves,
of course, coca tea. For the more adventurous, it also offers a sweet-tasting
coca wine. There is a potion called *jarabe de coca* which is promoted as
an anti-depressant and aphrodisiac. You can brush your teeth with coca
toothpaste, which Mr Morgan says has been proved to be highly effective
in preventing cavities. You can also chew coca gum. In the gym, there
are baths with coca soap. The spa has attracted many overweight tourists
with its weight-watchers' programme which guarantees a loss of one pound
a day. The treatment includes Turkish baths, saunas, walks by the lake
and a diet of natural foods, including a nutritious coca soup and a coca
diet syrup.

Lately, Bolivia's tourist industry has been in decline because of its
dependence on visitors who come on package holidays from Peru. The
threat of terrorist attacks by Peru's guerrilla group, Sendero Luminoso,

coupled with an outbreak of cholera, has stifled Andean tourism. But Mr Morgan has won back some clients to Bolivia—which has been spared the violence of its neighbour—by offering the unique blend of natural-health treatments with tours of the lake. From the hotel a fleet of hydrofoils make short trips out to islands in the lake. The Island of the Sun is where, legend has it, the Inca empire was founded, and the Island of the Moon is where the Incas kept a bevy of beautiful virgins. One small 28-foot hydrofoil, named *Glasnost Arrow*, was originally sent as a gift to the American President, Richard Nixon, by the Soviet leader, Leonid Brezhnev.

Mr Morgan's latest innovation is a seven-day tour advertized as 'The Ultimate Esoteric Experience'. Visitors are afforded the opportunity to immerse themselves in the mysticism of the local Andean culture, including fortune-telling with—what else?—coca leaves, natural medicine using local herbs and spices, and spiritual healing—all of them still a vital part of daily life among the local Aymara Indians. On the hotel pier, Mr Morgan is now building an observatory to study the Andean constellations, in preparation for the biggest eclipse of the sun this century, due to take place on 3 November 1994.

Mr Morgan is hoping that the Bolivian government will press ahead with its efforts to legitimize the coca plant. American anti-drug officials are not happy, and Bolivia could stand to lose the millions of dollars it receives in foreign aid if it persists with challenging the prevailing anti-coca wisdom. But there is one good sign. When I flew out of Bolivia to the USA, I thought that I had better declare the boxes of coca tea bags in my luggage. An American customs agent warned me that, officially, the tea bags are prohibited, but he smiled and waved me through with my precious cargo intact.

CONTRIBUTORS

David Adams	Reports from Central America
Jonathan Agnew	BBC Cricket Correspondent
Martin Bell	BBC Berlin Correspondent
Colin Blane	Former BBC East Africa Correspondent, now BBC Scotland Correspondent
Julian Borger	BBC Warsaw Correspondent
Chris Bowers	Reported for the BBC from Central Asia
Malcolm Brabant	BBC Athens Correspondent, often reports from the former Yugoslavia
Gordon Brewer	Former BBC Tokyo Correspondent
Alex Brodie	BBC Jerusalem Correspondent
Simon Calder	Travel writer
Tom Carver	Reports for the BBC from Southern Africa
Kevin Connolly	BBC Moscow Correspondent
Kieran Cooke	Reports for the BBC from Malaysia
Martin Dowle	BBC Rio Correspondent
Gary Duffy	BBC Irish Affairs Correspondent, spent some time reporting from USA
Max Easterman	BBC reporter for *The World Tonight*
Leo Enright	BBC Dublin Correspondent
Gavin Esler	Chief BBC North America Correspondent
Jonathan Freedland	BBC reporter
Matt Frei	BBC Southern Europe Correspondent
Tom Gibb	Reports for the BBC from El Salvador
Misha Glenny	Former BBC Central Europe Correspondent
Peter Godwin	BBC Reporter for *Assignment* and *Panorama*
Humphrey Hawksley	BBC Hong Kong Correspondent
William Horsley	BBC Bonn Correspondent
Stephen Jessel	BBC Paris Correspondent

Fergal Keane	BBC Southern Africa Correspondent
Bridget Kendall	BBC Moscow Correspondent
Andy Kershaw	Writer, broadcaster and music specialist
Daniel Lak	Reports for the BBC from Pakistan
Graham Leach	BBC Europe Correspondent
Allan Little	Reports for the BBC from the Balkans
Tim Llewellyn	Former BBC Middle East Correspondent
Simon Long	BBC Hong Kong Business Reporter
Tim Luard	Reports for the BBC Far Eastern Service
James Miles	BBC Peking Correspondent
Hugh O'Shaughnessy	Correspondent with *The Observer*
Paul Reynolds	BBC Diplomatic Correspondent
Stephen Sackur	BBC Middle East Correspondent
Hugh Schofield	BBC Foreign Affairs Correspondent
Philip Short	BBC Tokyo and Far East Correspondent
Bob Simpson	BBC Foreign Affairs Correspondent
Mark Tully	BBC Delhi Correspondent
Carole Walker	BBC Foreign Affairs Correspondent
Tim Whewell	Former BBC Moscow Correspondent
David Willey	BBC Rome Correspondent
Isabel Wolff	Freelance writer and broadcaster
Penny Young	Freelance journalist, spent some time in Istanbul